Ultimate Web Automation Testing with Cypress

Master End-to-End Web Application Testing Automation to Accelerate Your QA Process with Cypress

Vitaly Skadorva

www.orangeava.com

First published: December 2023

Published by: Orange Education Pvt Ltd, AVA™

Address: 9, Daryaganj, Delhi, 110002

ISBN: 978-81-96782-69-6

www.orangeava.com

Dedicated To

My beloved wife

Tatyana Shkoda

and

My Daughter Maria and My Son David

About the Author

Vitaly Skadorva holds a Master's degree in Civil Engineering and a Bachelor's degree in Computer Science, blending a unique perspective of structured engineering principles with cutting-edge technological expertise. With over fifteen years of experience in the software testing industry, he has carved a niche as a seasoned professional, deeply passionate about web automation testing and dedicated to pursuing quality assurance excellence.

His journey in the tech world has involved collaboration with a broad spectrum of clients and work on various technologies, contributing to the delivery of superior web applications globally. Renowned for his expertise in Cypress and other contemporary testing tools, the author has, in recent years, focused on honing his skills in web automation testing using Cypress. This specialization has enabled him to lead and mentor teams, integrating Cypress into their testing workflows and enhancing efficiency and accuracy.

Beyond his professional accomplishments, the author is an avid contributor to the software testing community. He frequently shares valuable insights on best practices in testing, drawn from his extensive experience and testing practices, and keeps abreast of the evolving trends in web automation. His commitment to sharing knowledge and fostering learning has earned him respect in web application testing.

About the Technical Reviewer

Veerkumar Patil is a highly experienced Software Testing Professional with a remarkable track record spanning over a decade in the field of Information Technology. He has made significant contributions across diverse sectors such as e-commerce, travel, banking, and telecommunications. Veerkumar's expertise extends to testing complex applications across various technology domains. He is well-versed in Test Automation, utilizing a range of testing frameworks including Selenium, Cypress, and Playwright. His proficiency extends to Continuous Integration and Continuous Deployment (CI/CD) practices, where he has worked with tools such as Azure DevOps, Gitlab, and GitHub Actions.

Veerkumar has a solid foundation in API Testing and has excelled in building automation frameworks for API testing using tools like Rest-Assured and Karate. He is also recognized as an open-source contributor for various NPM packages designed to facilitate parallelization of Cypress Testing. Veerkumar's extensive experience includes crafting automation frameworks for testing intricate business applications and processes.

Currently, he serves as the QE lead at Red Hat, where he plays a pivotal role in testing customer-facing applications for Red Hat's products. Beyond his professional responsibilities, Veerkumar is passionate about sharing his knowledge with the community through his YouTube channel and actively participates in various testing communities, where he presents valuable insights and experiences.

Acknowledgements

Writing this book has been a journey of exploration, learning, and immense satisfaction. Reflecting on the process, I see several individuals and a particular tool without which this journey would have been incomplete.

First and foremost, I extend my deepest gratitude to my wife, Tatyana Shkoda. Tatyana, your unwavering support, encouragement, and patience have been the bedrock of my strength and perseverance. Your belief in my abilities and endless love has fueled my dedication to this project. I am eternally grateful for your companionship and understanding throughout this endeavor.

To my children, Maria and David, you have been my source of joy and inspiration. Your youthful curiosity and boundless energy have a way of simplifying the complexities of life and work. In many ways, this book is a testament to the bright future I envision for you both, filled with the wonders of learning and the power of knowledge. Thank you for your patience and bearing with the many hours I spent away from you while pursuing this project. You are the light of my life, and I hope to instill in you the same passion for learning and growth that has driven me.

A special acknowledgment goes to Gleb Bahmutov, whose expertise and insights into Cypress have been invaluable. Gleb, your contributions to the field of web testing and your pioneering work with Cypress have inspired this book, greatly enhancing its content with your profound knowledge and experience.

Lastly, I must express my appreciation for Cypress as a tool. Cypress has revolutionized the world of web testing, providing a powerful and user-friendly platform. It has been an integral part of my professional life and the writing of this book. The capabilities and ease of use offered by Cypress have significantly contributed to the success of many projects, and for that, I am immensely thankful.

To everyone who has been a part of this journey, directly or indirectly, I extend my heartfelt thanks. Your support and influence have shaped this book and my professional journey in countless ways.

Preface

In the rapidly evolving landscape of web application development, the need for robust and efficient testing methodologies is more pronounced than ever. As developers and testers grapple with increasingly complex web applications, the role of automation testing has become crucial. Recognizing this need, "Ultimate Web Automation Testing with Cypress" emerges as a comprehensive guide meticulously designed to navigate the intricacies of Cypress - a modern web automation testing tool.

As an experienced software testing professional and an ardent advocate of Cypress, I have witnessed firsthand the transformative impact of this tool in web testing. With its intuitive syntax and powerful features, Cypress has redefined the testing standards, making it accessible, efficient, and, most importantly, aligned with the real-world demands of web application development.

This book is a culmination of my experiences and lessons learned over the years, distilled into a format that is both educational and practical. Whether you are a software tester, a manual QA engineer transitioning to automation, or a developer keen on mastering testing skills, this book is tailored to enhance your understanding and application of Cypress.

Structured in a clear and logical format, the book covers many topics, from setting up Cypress and writing your first test to developing advanced techniques like custom commands, API testing, and CI/CD integration. Each chapter is crafted to build upon the previous one, ensuring a seamless learning curve for readers of all levels.

Real-world examples and exercises throughout the book provide hands-on experience, bridging the gap between theory and practice. This approach ensures that readers understand the concepts and apply them effectively in their projects.

Writing this book has been an enriching experience, and I hope it serves as a valuable resource for professionals seeking to excel in the dynamic field of web automation testing. With Cypress as your tool, you are well-equipped to deliver flawless web applications and accelerate your professional growth in the competitive software testing landscape.

Chapter 1 introduces the reader to Cypress, which is a well-known test automation tool for web applications. The advantages of utilizing Cypress for automated testing will be highlighted and compared to other testing frameworks, including Selenium. Additionally, this chapter will offer an overview of the latest Cypress 12 release's key features and enhancements.

Chapter 2 will guide readers on how to prepare their development environment to start using Cypress. This will involve the installation of Node.js, the installation and customization of Cypress, and the initiation of a new Cypress project. The chapter will supply a sequence of clear instructions and address different configurations to guarantee an uninterrupted setup process.

Chapter 3 will guide readers through the process of composing their initial test utilizing the Cypress Test Runner. It will offer an explanation of the application of Cypress commands, hooks, and aliases and how to implement these principles while devising test scenarios. By the conclusion of this chapter, readers will have a strong base for generating and executing Cypress tests.

Chapter 4 will concentrate on Cypress-based end-to-end testing. It will teach the audience how to perform tests on user interactions, manage various types of elements, and handle timeouts and retries in their tests. The chapter will present sample cases and recommend optimal approaches to enable the audience to craft efficient and dependable E2E tests.

Chapter 5 delves into component testing using Cypress. The chapter explains how to test individual web components and distinguishes between component testing and end-to-end testing. It provides step-by-step guidance to configure tools and libraries for component testing with Cypress.

Chapter 6 explains how to perform API testing using Cypress. The chapter will include instructions on testing both RESTful and GraphQL APIs, as well as validating API responses. Practical examples and helpful tips will be provided throughout the chapter to assist readers in creating complete API tests with Cypress.

Chapter 7 will introduce readers to the concept of data-driven testing with Cypress. The chapter will cover the use of JSON files, reading data from databases, and implementing data-driven test cases. Upon completion of this chapter, readers will be able to develop adaptable and reusable test cases by utilizing a variety of data sources.

Chapter 8 delves into advanced techniques with Cypress, including creating customized commands, utilizing videos and screenshots for debugging, and working with plugins. These techniques will enable readers to enhance their test automation process, resulting in more efficient and maintainable tests.

Chapter 9 offers information on Cypress Cloud and its features, such as Smart Orchestration and Flaky Test Management. Additionally, readers will be introduced to Cypress Analytics, a tool that provides valuable insights into the performance and reliability of their test suite. This chapter will provide readers with the knowledge necessary to optimize their test automation process by utilizing these advanced features.

Chapter 10 covers the integration of Cypress with popular version control systems like GitHub and GitLab, as well as the implementation of Behavior-Driven Development (BDD) using Cucumber with Cypress. This chapter will enable readers to adopt a more collaborative approach to test automation while utilizing Git hooks for automated testing.

Chapter 11 provides readers with insights on CI/CD principles and the process of integrating Cypress into their CI/CD pipelines by using tools such as Docker and Jenkins. The chapter also discusses other CI/CD tools that are compatible with Cypress, thus giving readers a range of options to choose from based on their project requirements.

Chapter 12 delves into different reporting techniques and tools that Cypress offers. It covers built-in Cypress reporting, third-party reporting tools and plugins, and generating custom reports. After reading this chapter, readers will have a clear understanding of how to effectively present and analyze their test results.

Chapter 13 offers a summary of the key concepts covered in the book, shares best practices for using Cypress, and gives guidance for further research. By the end of this chapter, readers will have a solid understanding of Cypress and its capabilities, and they will feel confident in applying these skills to their projects. Additionally, it concludes with a list of resources and communities to help readers continue their journey with Cypress and stay up-to-date with the latest developments in web automation testing.

Get a Free eBook

We hope you are enjoying your recently purchased book! Your feedback is incredibly valuable to us, and to all other readers looking for great books.

If you found this book helpful or enjoyable, we would truly appreciate it, if you could take a moment to leave a short review with a 5 star rating on Amazon. It helps us grow, and lets other readers discover our books.

As a thank you, we would love to send you a free digital copy of this book, and a **30%** discount code on your next cart value on our official websites:

www.orangeava.com

www.orangeava.in (For Indian Subcontinent)

☑ **Here's how:**

Leave a review for the book on Amazon.

Take a screenshot of your review, and send an email to **info@orangeava.com** (it can be just the confirmation screen).

Once, we receive your screenshot, we will send you the digital file, within 24 hours.

Thank you so much for your support – it means a lot to us!

Downloading the code bundles and colored images

Please follow the link to download the
Code Bundles of the book:

https://github.com/ava-orange-education/Ultimate-Web-Automation-Testing-with-Cypress

The code bundles and images of the book are also hosted on
https://rebrand.ly/bbdaa7

In case there's an update to the code, it will be updated on the existing GitHub repository.

Errata

We take immense pride in our work at **Orange Education Pvt Ltd,** and follow best practices to ensure the accuracy of our content to provide an indulging reading experience to our subscribers. Our readers are our mirrors, and we use their inputs to reflect and improve upon human errors, if any, that may have occurred during the publishing processes involved. To let us maintain the quality and help us reach out to any readers who might be having difficulties due to any unforeseen errors, please write to us at :

errata@orangeava.com

Your support, suggestions, and feedback are highly appreciated.

DID YOU KNOW

Did you know that Orange Education Pvt Ltd offers eBook versions of every book published, with PDF and ePub files available? You can upgrade to the eBook version at **www.orangeava.com** and as a print book customer, you are entitled to a discount on the eBook copy. Get in touch with us at: **info@orangeava.com** for more details.

At **www.orangeava.com**, you can also read a collection of free technical articles, sign up for a range of free newsletters, and receive exclusive discounts and offers on AVA™ Books and eBooks.

PIRACY

If you come across any illegal copies of our works in any form on the internet, we would be grateful if you would provide us with the location address or website name. Please contact us at **info@orangeava.com** with a link to the material.

ARE YOU INTERESTED IN AUTHORING WITH US?

If there is a topic that you have expertise in, and you are interested in either writing or contributing to a book, please write to us at **business@orangeava.com**. We are on a journey to help developers and tech professionals to gain insights on the present technological advancements and innovations happening across the globe and build a community that believes Knowledge is best acquired by sharing and learning with others. Please reach out to us to learn what our audience demands and how you can be part of this educational reform. We also welcome ideas from tech experts and help them build learning and development content for their domains.

REVIEWS

Please leave a review. Once you have read and used this book, why not leave a review on the site that you purchased it from? Potential readers can then see and use your unbiased opinion to make purchase decisions. We at Orange Education would love to know what you think about our products, and our authors can learn from your feedback. Thank you!

For more information about Orange Education, please visit **www.orangeava.com**.

Table of Contents

CHAPTER 1

Getting Started with Cypress Testing

Introduction

This chapter introduces the reader to Cypress, a famous test automation tool for web applications. It will describe the benefits of using Cypress for automated testing and compare it to other testing frameworks, such as Selenium. This chapter also provides an overview of the most important features and improvements in the latest Cypress 12 release.

Structure

In this chapter, we will discuss the following topics:

- Introduction to Cypress
- Benefits of using Cypress for automation testing
- Difference between Cypress and Selenium
- Key features of Cypress 12

Introduction to Cypress

The history and development of the Cypress automation tool can be traced back to 2014, when it was initially released by Brian Mann, the founder and creator of Cypress.io. The tool aimed to provide a better alternative to existing automation tools, such as Selenium. Cypress was designed to be easy to use and give the developers a more robust and reliable testing experience. Over the years, Cypress has undergone numerous updates and improvements, with the latest version, 12.10, at the time of writing this book.

One of the most significant advantages of Cypress over other test automation tools is the unique architecture that allows it to run directly in the browser. This approach enables faster execution times and gives developers more control over the testing environment.

Moreover, Cypress offers a comprehensive set of features for end-to-end testing, including automatic waiting, real-time reloading, and an easy-to-use API. Its integration with popular frontend frameworks such as React, Angular, and Vue.js also makes it a preferred choice for many developers across the globe.

Overall, Cypress has come a long way since its first release and has positioned itself as a powerful automation tool that continues to evolve to meet the ever-changing needs of the software development industry.

Overview of Cypress

Cypress is a robust JavaScript-based end-to-end testing framework designed to simplify and streamline web application testing. It was built specifically for modern web development. Cypress enables developers and testers to create and run tests directly within the browser, allowing real-time interaction with the application under test. With its intuitive API, automatic waiting and retries, and seamless integrations with popular web technologies and frameworks, Cypress has become a popular choice for teams seeking to improve the efficiency and reliability of their testing processes. As an end-to-end testing framework, Cypress covers the entire spectrum of the user experience, from UI interactions to API calls, ensuring that applications function correctly and meet user expectations.

Cypress is an open-source testing framework that strives to simplify and streamline the testing process. Here are its key features:

- A user-friendly interface that provides visual feedback during test execution.
- Automatic waiting and real-time reloading help eliminate the need for manual timeouts and reloading.
- The ability to easily stub and mock network requests allows greater control over test scenarios.
- A rich set of APIs simplifies creating and managing test suites and cases.

- The ability to preserve cookies, local storage, and session storage between tests to maintain a consistent browser context.

According to experienced Cypress experts, one of the best practices for using Cypress is to write small test cases that focus on specific features or functionalities of the application instead of writing large test suites that test everything simultaneously. This approach can help identify and isolate issues, making troubleshooting and fixing them easier.

Advantages of Cypress

Under the advantages of Cypress, we usually understand the features that are beneficially different from the Selenium-based testing frameworks. There are several key advantages of using Cypress including:

- **Ease of setup**: Cypress requires minimal configuration and can be easily integrated into existing projects.
- **Speed**: Cypress executes tests directly in the browser, which results in faster test runs and more accurate results.
- **Debugging capabilities**: The Cypress Test Runner offers an interactive interface that allows developers to debug tests in real-time.
- **Improved reliability**: Cypress automatically waits for elements to become available and actions to complete, reducing the likelihood of flaky tests.
- **Cross-browser testing**: Cypress can run tests across multiple browsers. It supports Chrome-family browsers (Chrome, Electron, and Microsoft Edge), Firefox, and WebKit (Safari's browser engine) - experimental support based on Playwright WebKit.
- **Test Retries**: Cypress can retry failed tests to help reduce test flakiness and continues integration build failures.

One of the most significant advantages of Cypress is its ability to run tests in real time, with automatic reloading of code and tests.

Integration with Modern Web Technologies and Frameworks

Cypress is designed to work seamlessly with popular web frameworks and technologies, making it an ideal choice for testing modern web applications. Some examples of its compatibility include:

- **JavaScript-centric**: Focusing on JavaScript as its primary language, Cypress is a natural fit for modern web development. JavaScript is the dominant language for both front-end and back-end development. This allows developers to work with a single language throughout the entire development and testing process.

- **Framework agnostic**: Cypress is not tied to any specific front-end framework, which means it can be used for testing applications built with popular frameworks like React, Angular, Vue, and more. This flexibility allows teams to adopt Cypress regardless of their chosen front-end technology.
- **Integration with modern tools**: Cypress can be easily integrated with popular development tools and platforms, such as Webpack, Babel, and TypeScript. This allows developers to leverage existing tooling and configurations to streamline the testing process further.
- **Support for Single Page Applications (SPAs)**: Cypress is well-suited for testing SPAs, which have become a typical architecture in modern web development. It can handle dynamic content loading, routing, and asynchronous operations, ensuring that tests accurately represent real-world user interactions.
- **Extensibility through plugins**: Cypress has a thriving plugin ecosystem, allowing developers to extend its functionality and integrate it with other tools and services. Plugins are available for tasks such as visual regression testing, code coverage, and accessibility testing, making incorporating Cypress into a comprehensive testing strategy easy.
- **Built-in CI/CD compatibility**: Cypress can be easily integrated with Continuous Integration and Continuous Deployment (CI/CD) pipelines, enabling automated testing as part of the development and deployment process. It supports popular CI/CD platforms such as Jenkins, Travis CI, CircleCI, and GitLab CI, among others.

In conclusion, Cypress is a powerful and versatile end-to-end testing framework that offers numerous advantages over traditional Selenium-based testing solutions. In addition, its compatibility with modern web technologies and frameworks makes it an excellent choice for developers to streamline and improve their testing processes. As we delve deeper into Cypress, you will discover how its unique features and capabilities can significantly enhance the quality and reliability of your web applications.

Benefits of using Cypress for automation testing

Diving deeper into Cypress, we must recognize the benefits that made Cypress famous as a test automation tool.

Easy to use and set up is one of the most significant advantages of Cypress. It is straightforward to install, and the documentation is comprehensive, making it easy for beginners to get started with Cypress quickly. In addition, with Cypress, you can write tests in JavaScript, a widely used language, further adding to its accessibility.

Cypress has excellent documentation, making it easy for developers to learn and start with the framework. Moreover, it has a robust community support system, with numerous forums and resources for users to help each other. The community is continually growing, and Cypress is evolving, making it a reliable and future-proof choice for automation testing.

Also, we will learn a few more key benefits of using Cypress as a test automation tool including:

- Real-time reloading and time-travel debugging.
- Automatic waiting and retries.
- Simple and easy-to-understand API.
- Built-in parallelization and dashboard features.
- Integration with CI/CD tools.
- Wide range of plugins and community support.

Real-time reloading and time-travel debugging

Cypress is designed with a focus on providing a better developer experience. One significant feature differentiating it from other testing tools is its real-time reloading and time-travel debugging capabilities.

Real-time reloading means that whenever you make a change to your test code, Cypress will automatically reload the test in the browser, allowing you to see the effects of your changes instantly. This feature significantly speeds up the development and debugging process.

Time-travel debugging refers to the ability to move back and forth through your test's execution, enabling you to see the exact state of your application at any given step. This powerful feature makes it much easier to identify and fix issues in your tests.

Example:

```
// cypress/e2e/spec.cy.js
```

```
describe('My first test', () => {
  it('Visits the home page', () => {
    cy.visit('http://example.com') // Your application URL
    cy.get('h1').contains('Welcome')
  })
})
```

As you modify the preceding test code, Cypress will automatically reload the test, and you can see each step in action using the time-travel debugging feature.

Automatic waiting and retries

Cypress eliminates the need for manual waiting or hard-coded timeouts by automatically waiting for elements to be available and visible before interacting with them. It also retries commands until they pass or time out, ensuring tests are stable and less flaky.

Example:

```
 // cypress/e2e/automatic-waiting.cy.js
describe('Automatic waiting and retries', () => {
  it('Waits for an element to be visible before interacting', () => {
    cy.visit('http://example.com')
    cy.get('#my-element').should('be.visible')
  })
})
```

In the preceding example, Cypress will wait for the element with the ID `my-element` to be visible before proceeding. The test will fail if the element is not visible within the default timeout (4 seconds).

Simple and easy-to-understand API

Cypress offers a straightforward API that is easy to learn and understand. This makes it accessible for both beginners and experienced developers alike. In addition, the API's intuitive design enables developers to write clean, readable, and maintainable test code.

Example:

```
 // cypress/e2e/simple-api.cy.js
describe('Simple API test', () => {
  it('Logs in a user and checks for a welcome message', () => {
    cy.visit('http://example.com')
    cy.get('#username').type('username)
    cy.get('#password').type('password)
    cy.get('#login-button').click()
    cy.url().should('include', '/dashboard')
    cy.contains('Welcome, username')
  })
})
```

The preceding example demonstrates how easy it is to understand and write a Cypress test. The code is clear, concise, and easy to read, making it straightforward for developers of all experience levels.

Built-in parallelization and dashboard features

Cypress has built-in support for parallel test execution, allowing you to scale your tests across multiple machines and browsers. This feature helps reduce test execution time and provides more efficient feedback.

The Cypress Dashboard Service offers additional features like test analytics, video recording of test runs, and team collaboration tools. These features can be invaluable for managing large-scale test suites and improving overall testing workflows.

Such features are available only by purchasing a paid plan in Cypress Cloud. But by using free plugins like cypress-parallel or cypress-split, you can run tests in Parallel.

Integration with CI/CD tools

Cypress can easily integrate with widespread continuous integration (CI) and continuous delivery (CD) tools such as Jenkins, GitLab, and CircleCI. This seamless integration helps ensure that your tests are always up-to-date and that your application remains reliable throughout the development lifecycle.

Example:

To integrate Cypress with GitHub Actions, create a `.github/workflows/main.yml` file with the following content:

```
name: Cypress Tests
on: push
jobs:
  cypress-run:
    runs-on: ubuntu-latest
    steps:
    - name: Checkout code
      uses: actions/checkout@v3
    - name: Run Cypress tests
      uses: cypress-io/github-action@v5
      with:
        build: npm run build
        start: npm start
```

The preceding example is a basic CI setup and job using the Cypress GitHub Action to run Cypress tests within the Electron browser.

Wide range of plugins and community support

Cypress has a growing ecosystem of plugins that extends its core functionality, allowing you to tailor the framework to your specific needs. These plugins cater to various use cases, including visual testing, accessibility testing, and integration with popular JavaScript frameworks. Additionally, the Cypress community is active and supportive, providing valuable resources and assistance to help you succeed with your testing efforts.

Example:

The `cypress-axe` plugin is famous for integrating a11y (accessibility) testing with Cypress. The plugin adds the axe-core library to your Cypress tests, allowing you to run accessibility audits on your web application.

To install and use the cypress-axe plugin, follow these steps:

```
npm install --save-dev cypress-axe
```

Import the plugin:

```
// cypress/support/e2e.js
import 'cypress-axe'
```

Use the plugin in your test:

```
// cypress/e2e/accessibility.cy.js
describe('Accessibility testing', () => {
  beforeEach(() => {
    cy.visit('http://example.com')
    cy.injectAxe()
  })
  it('Checks for accessibility violations', () => {
    cy.checkA11y()
  })
})
```

In this example, we installed and used the cypress-axe plugin to check for accessibility violations in our web application.

In conclusion, Cypress offers many benefits for web automation testing, including real-time reloading, time-travel debugging, automatic waiting, a simple API, built-in parallelization, CI/CD integration, and a wide range of plugins with solid community support. As a result, you can create more robust and reliable web applications by incorporating Cypress into your development workflow.

Difference between Cypress and Selenium

As Selenium is a primarily known library for test automation, it will be beneficial to compare it with Cypress. Here, we will explore the key differences between Cypress and Selenium. The comparison will include the following aspects:

- Architecture: Cypress's direct browser access versus Selenium's WebDriver-based approach
- Language support: JavaScript in Cypress versus multiple languages in Selenium

- Automatic waiting and command retries in Cypress
- Speed and performance comparison
- Ease of setup and learning curve

Architecture: Cypress's direct browser access versus Selenium's WebDriver-based approach

Cypress and Selenium have different architectures, resulting in differences in capabilities and performance.

Cypress operates directly within the browser, executing commands as soon as they are issued. This allows Cypress to provide real-time feedback, time-travel debugging, and automatic waiting. Additionally, since it runs in the same run-loop as your application, it can access and manipulate the DOM directly, offering better control and reliability.

Selenium, on the other hand, relies on the WebDriver protocol to communicate with the browser. This means that commands need to be sent from the test script to the WebDriver server, which then forwards them to the browser. This extra communication layer introduces latency and can result in slower test execution.

It can be summarized as follows:

Feature	Cypress	Selenium
Architecture	Direct browser access	WebDriver-based
Real-time feedback	Yes	No
Time-travel debugging	Yes	No
Automatic wait	Yes	No (requires explicit waits)

***Table 1.1**: Comparison of architecture*

Language Support: JavaScript in Cypress versus multiple languages in Selenium

Cypress is built exclusively for JavaScript, meaning you can only write your tests in JavaScript. This can be an advantage for teams that are well-versed in JavaScript and want a consistent language across their development and testing stack. Therefore, Cypress tests anything that runs in the context of a browser, no matter which language has been used to write an application.

Selenium supports multiple programming languages, including Java, C#, Ruby, Python, and JavaScript. This flexibility allows developers to choose a language that best suits their skillset or the requirements of their project.

Automatic waiting and command retries in Cypress

One of the critical differences between Cypress and Selenium is how they handle waiting and retries (refer *Table* 1.2).

Cypress automatically waits for elements to become available and actions to complete before proceeding, eliminating the need for manual timeouts and retries. This intelligent waiting mechanism significantly reduces flakiness and improves test reliability.

Selenium, by contrast, often requires explicit waiting strategies and timeouts to handle asynchronous operations, which can make tests more complex and prone to flakiness.

Feature	Cypress	Selenium
Automatic waits	Yes	No (requires explicit waits)
Command retries	Yes	No (must be implemented manually)

Table 1.2: *Comparison of waiting and retries*

Speed and performance comparison

Regarding speed and performance, Cypress has some advantages over Selenium (refer *Table* 1.3).

Cypress's direct browser access architecture and automatic waiting capabilities lead to faster test execution, as there is less latency and no need for manual waits. Additionally, Cypress has built-in parallelization support, which can significantly reduce the overall test execution time when running multiple test suites.

Selenium's WebDriver-based approach can result in slower test execution due to the additional layer of communication between the test script, WebDriver server, and browser. Parallelization is possible in Selenium but requires additional setup and configuration, such as third-party tools like Selenium Grid or TestNG.

Moreover, Cypress's real-time feedback and time-travel debugging capabilities allow developers to quickly identify and fix issues in their tests, further improving the overall testing process's efficiency.

Feature	Cypress	Selenium
Test execution speed	Faster due to direct browser access	Slower due to the WebDriver-based approach
Parallelization	Built-in	Requires additional setup (for example, Selenium Grid, TestNG)
Real-time feedback and debugging	Yes	No
Browser support	Chrome-family browsers (Chrome, Electron, and Microsoft Edge), WebKit (Safari's browser engine), and Firefox.	Chrome, Firefox, Safari, Edge

Table 1.3: *Comparison of speed and performance*

Ease of setup and learning curve

Cypress is known for its ease of setup, with minimal configuration required to start writing and running tests. In addition, its user-friendly API and extensive documentation make it relatively easy for developers to learn and adopt.

Selenium, while powerful, can be more challenging to set up and configure, particularly when integrating with different browsers and testing environments. The learning curve for Selenium can be steeper, particularly for those who are new to WebDriver API and its associated concepts.

Feature	Cypress	Selenium
Easy of Setup	Easier	More complex
Learning Curve	Lower	Higher

Table 1.4: *Comparison of easiness of setup and learning curve*

In conclusion, both Cypress and Selenium offer valuable features for web application testing. Still, their differences in architecture, language support, waiting mechanisms, speed, performance, and ease of setup can make one more suitable, depending on your specific needs and preferences.

Cypress may be better for teams primarily working with JavaScript or TypeScript and seeking a faster, more user-friendly testing framework. However, it might be more practical to use Selenium for teams that require support for multiple programming languages or have existing test suites written in Selenium.

It is also worth noting that the choice between Cypress and Selenium doesn't have to be mutually exclusive. In some cases, teams may choose to use both frameworks, leveraging the unique strengths of each to create a comprehensive testing strategy. For example, Cypress could be used for end-to-end and component testing for JavaScript-heavy applications. At the same time, Selenium could be employed for cross-browser testing or tests written in other languages.

Ultimately, the best choice depends on your specific requirements, team skillset, and project goals. However, by understanding the key differences between Cypress and Selenium, you can make an informed decision that best supports your testing needs and helps ensure the quality and reliability of your web applications.

Key features of Cypress 12

Initially released in 2014, Cypress has been continuously evolving and improving over the years to become a leading choice for web automation testing. Its strong focus on delivering a superior developer experience has attracted a significant user base and a thriving community. Over the years, the Cypress team has been dedicated to incorporating user feedback and addressing the ever-changing landscape of web development, resulting in a robust and feature-rich testing tool.

At version 12.10, Cypress has come a long way since its inception. It boasts numerous advanced features, such as real-time feedback, time-travel debugging, automatic waiting, a simple JavaScript API, a built-in parallelization, supporting multiple browsers, supporting not only end-to-end testing but also component testing, multiple origins, caching sessions when logging, and switching users in tests.

Cypress persistently rolls out new features, enhancements, and bug fixes to ensure an up-to-date and reliable testing experience. Accompanying these updates is extensive technical documentation thoroughly covering all alterations associated with each release. This thorough documentation enables users to stay informed about the latest improvements and adapt their testing strategies accordingly, ensuring optimal utilization of the Cypress testing tool.

Consequently, it is essential to examine the crucial features introduced in Cypress version 12, as these enhancements significantly contribute to the tool's overall capabilities and user experience. Furthermore, by understanding the latest updates and advancements, we can better appreciate Cypress's value to the web automation testing landscape.

Multiple origins testing with 'cy.origin()'

One of the most significant new features in Cypress 12 is the ability to test multiple origins in a single test using the new `cy.origin()` command. This command allows you to change the origin of the current page and test interactions between different domains.

Example:

```
// cypress/e2e/cross-origin.cy.js
describe('Cross-origin test', () => {
  it('User should be able to login', () => {
    cy.visit('http://example.com');

    //clicking log in button redirects to another domain
    cy.get('#login-button').click();

    cy.origin('auth.yourAuthDomain.com', () => {
      cy.get('#username').type('username);
      cy.get('#password').type('password);
      //clicking on submit does auth and redirects back to example.com
      cy.get('#submit-button').click();
    });
    cy.contains('Welcome, username')
  })
})
```

In the preceding example, we visit `'http://example.com'`, then click the Login button that redirects us to another domain, `'auth.yourAuthDomain.com'`, where we authenticate using the username and password and click the Submit button.

The last action redirects us back to the original domain, '`http://example.com`' already logged in.

Browser context preservation with `cy.session()`

Cypress 12 `cy.session()` command became generally available for end-to-end testing, allowing you to preserve cookies, local storage, and session storage between tests to maintain a consistent browser context. This is particularly useful when testing complex applications that rely on cookies or other persistent data.

Example:

```
// Caching session when logging in via page visit
cy.session(name, () => {
  cy.visit('/login')
  cy.get('#username').type('username);
  cy.get('#password').type('password);
  cy.get('#login-button').click();
  cy.contains('Welcome, username')
})
```

In the preceding example, we create a session with a specific name, and after successful login, we cache the session by caching and restoring cookies, local storage, and session storage. Our login code's steps to create the session will only be performed once when it's called the first time in any given spec file. After that, subsequent calls will restore the session from the cache.

Test isolation

One of the significant updates in version 12.0 is test isolation. While Cypress has always recommended writing tests in a clean context, this feature now enforces running tests in a clean browser context through test isolation. This means that each test runs in its clean browser context, with cookies, local storage, and session storage cleared between tests. This ensures that each test has a consistent starting point and is not affected by any previous tests. This option is configurable but is enabled by default.

```
// Example configuration in cypress.config.js with testIsolation disabled
const { defineConfig } = require('cypress')

module.exports = defineConfig({
  e2e: {
    testIsolation: false,
    // other configuration options
  },
})
```

It is important to note that any tests that relied on the browser to be at a particular state will not work with the new test isolation behavior.

This feature is only available for e2e testing configuration. Cypress does not support the test isolation feature configuration in component testing. By running the component tests, Cypress always resets the browser context before each test.

Fix for dreaded detached DOM errors

Cypress v12 has introduced a fix for one of Cypress's oldest and most annoying issues, the "Detached DOM" error. Cypress throws an error when an element is queried from a parent element and becomes detached from the DOM. The new fix involves enhancing the DOM resolution logic to re-query new elements that might have replaced the older elements due to DOM updates. This will lead to tests being more reliable and stable.

The current behavior throws an error when Cypress tries to interact with a detached element, with a suggestion to re-query for the element or add 'guards,' which delay Cypress from running new commands. However, the desired behavior is for Cypress to re-query the previously found element and continue the command with any newfound elements. The proposal is to make this an option passed to the command to allow this or not.

Here's an example of the issue:

```
it('this will fail but should not', () => {
```

```
    cy.visit('index.html')
    cy.get("select").select("First")
    // adding any wait time will make it pass
    // cy.wait(0)
    cy.get("input").type("Hello")
})
```

In the preceding example, when the `cy.get("input").type("Hello")` command is run, if the select element has been detached from the DOM due to a framework re-render or code reacting to an event, Cypress throws an error.

The fix for this issue will make tests more reliable and eliminate the need for 'guards' or re-querying elements.

In summary, keeping yourself updated with Cypress's changelog is crucial for making the most of this impressive testing tool. By attentively monitoring the changelog, you can be confident that you're utilizing the most recent features, enhancements, and bug resolutions the Cypress team constantly delivers. Not only does this empower you to maintain a state-of-the-art testing approach, but it also assists you in adjusting your tests to accommodate any potential breaking changes or deprecated features. Additionally, being well-informed about Cypress's ongoing progress enables you to offer valuable input to the community, nurturing a robust ecosystem that supports the tool's growth and improvement. In the end, staying vigilant about the Cypress changelog is a vital practice for tapping into the full capabilities of this versatile web automation testing tool and achieving consistent and effective testing results.

Conclusion

This chapter is all about introducing Cypress, a tool that is widely used for checking web applications automatically. In this chapter, we delved into why Cypress is a great tool for this job and how it is different from other similar tools, especially Selenium. We also took a close look at Cypress 12, the latest version of the tool, on the day of writing this book, discussing its new features and how it has been improved. By the end of the chapter, readers had a solid understanding of what Cypress is, its advantages, how it stands against its competitors, and what makes the new version of Cypress 12 special.

As we move forward to *Chapter 2: Setting Up the Development Environment*, we are going to explore the initial steps to start using Cypress. This includes setting up the necessary software on the reader's computers, such as Node.js and Cypress, and learning how to start your very first Cypress project. Instructions will be provided in a step-by-step manner to ensure a smooth process.

Further Reading

Certainly, it's always beneficial to delve deeper into the topic to gain a more comprehensive understanding. Here are some resources that would supplement the material covered in the book:

1. **Cypress official documentation**: The official Cypress documentation (https://docs.cypress.io/) is an invaluable resource. It provides a detailed overview of all aspects of Cypress, from installation to advanced concepts.

2. **Cypress GitHub repository**: The Cypress GitHub repo (https://github.com/cypress-io/cypress) is a great place to check for updates, report issues, and even contribute to the project. This can help you stay up-to-date with the latest developments and understand common issues users face.

Remember, the key to mastering any tool is a mix of theoretical understanding and practical application.

Chapter 2

Setting Up the Development Environment

Introduction

In this chapter, readers will learn how to set up their development environment to start using Cypress. We will go through the processes like installing Node.js, installing and configuring Cypress, and creating a new Cypress project. The chapter will provide step-by-step instructions and cover various configurations to ensure a smooth setup process.

Structure

In this chapter, we will discuss the following topics:

- Installing Node.js
- Installing Cypress
- Configuring Cypress
- Creating your first Cypress project

Installing Node.js

Node.js is an open-source, cross-platform JavaScript runtime environment built on Chrome's V8 JavaScript engine. It was created by Ryan Dahl in 2009 to address the limitations of traditional web servers that needed help to handle numerous concurrent connections efficiently.

Node.js enables developers to use JavaScript to write server-side code, allowing them to build scalable, high-performance web applications. Before Node.js, JavaScript was used primarily for client-side programming in web browsers. By expanding JavaScript to the server side, Node.js has revolutionized web development and allowed developers to use a single language for both front-end and back-end development.

There are several reasons why Node.js has become so popular, including:

- **JavaScript everywhere:** As mentioned earlier, Node.js allows developers to write server-side code using JavaScript. This means that developers proficient in JavaScript can now work on both the front-end and back-end without learning a new programming language, leading to more efficient and streamlined development processes.
- **Event-driven, non-blocking architecture:** Node.js is built on an event-driven architecture that uses a non-blocking I/O model. This makes it particularly well-suited for handling concurrent connections and building scalable, high-performance web applications. For example, in traditional server-side environments, each connection request creates a new thread, which can lead to performance issues as the number of connections increases. Node.js, on the other hand, uses a single-threaded event loop to handle multiple connections, making it more efficient in managing resources.
- **NPM (Node Package Manager):** Node.js has a built-in package manager called npm, a vast repository of open-source libraries and modules. Npm makes it easy for developers to find, share, and reuse code, resulting in faster development cycles and a vibrant community of contributors.
- **Wide adoption:** Many prominent companies and organizations, including Netflix, LinkedIn, Walmart, and NASA, have embraced Node.js for their web applications. This widespread adoption has led to a thriving ecosystem, a wealth of resources, and an active community that continually contributes to the platform's growth and development.
- **Easy to learn:** JavaScript is one of the most popular programming languages widely taught in computer science programs and coding boot camps. This makes it relatively easy for new developers to learn Node.js and quickly become productive.

Node.js has gained popularity due to its ability to enable JavaScript on the server side, its event-driven and non-blocking architecture, the extensive npm ecosystem, widespread adoption, and ease of learning. This combination of features has made Node.js a powerful tool for web development and an attractive choice for developers and organizations.

In this chapter, it is essential to mention about package managers. We've already mentioned NPM (Node Package Manager). The alternative choice can be Yarn - a package manager that Facebook designed.

NPM and Yarn are two popular package managers in the JavaScript ecosystem. They help developers manage dependencies and install, update, and remove libraries or packages required for the projects. Both package managers aim to make it easier to work with JavaScript libraries, but they differ in their approach and features.

NPM (Node Package Manager)

NPM is the default package manager for Node.js and was introduced in 2010. It provides a command-line interface for developers to interact with a vast repository of open-source libraries and modules. NPM has become popular due to the following reasons:

- **Extensive library:** NPM hosts a massive collection of open-source packages, making it easy for developers to find and use the libraries they need for their projects. This comprehensive library promotes code reuse and speeds up the development process.
- **Ease of use:** NPM makes it simple for developers to manage dependencies. With a few commands, they can install, update, or remove packages, making dependency management more accessible and efficient.
- **Built-in with Node.js:** As the default package manager for Node.js, NPM is readily available to developers working with Node.js projects, contributing to its popularity.
- **Semantic versioning:** NPM follows semantic versioning, which helps developers manage package updates by providing a standardized versioning system.

Yarn

Yarn is another package manager for JavaScript, developed by Facebook and released in 2016. It was created to address some of the issues and shortcomings of NPM, such as performance and security. Yarn has gained popularity for several reasons, including:

- **Performance:** Yarn is designed to be faster than NPM, with improved caching and parallel downloads of packages. This performance improvement can save developers time, especially in larger projects.
- **Workspaces:** Yarn introduced a "workspaces" feature, which allows

developers to manage dependencies for multiple projects in a mono repo more efficiently. This feature is beneficial for large-scale projects or organizations with multiple interdependent projects.

- **Lockfile:** Yarn introduced a deterministic lock file (yarn.lock) to ensure that identical dependency versions are installed across different environments, leading to more predictable builds.
- **Security:** Yarn added checksum verification and flat mode to improve package security and reduce dependency conflicts.

NPM and Yarn have advantages; developers often choose one based on their specific needs and preferences. However, both package managers are popular because they streamline dependency management, promote code reuse, and provide developers with a vast ecosystem of libraries and modules to leverage.

As these two package managers are the most used in the JavaScript community, we will use them both in the Cypress installation process to show readers how they can be used.

Before we can start using Cypress for web automation testing, we need to set up the development environment, and the first step is to install Node.js. This section will guide you through installing Node.js on various platforms, including Windows, macOS, and Linux. Cypress supports the following versions of Node.js: 14.x, 16.x, 18.x, and above.

As Cypress is a desktop application, it will be installed on your computer. It supports these operating systems:

- **macOS** 10.9 and above (Intel or Apple Silicon 64-bit (x64 or arm64))
- **Linux Ubuntu** 12.04 and above, **Fedora** 21, and **Debian** 8 (x86_64 or Arm 64-bit (x64 or arm64))
- **Windows** 7 and above (64-bit only)

Follow the given steps to install Node.js on your system:

Windows

1. Visit the Node.js official website (https://nodejs.org/en/) and download the Windows installer. Node.js provides two options to download. Choose the one that corresponds to the Cypress requirements mentioned above.
2. Run the installer and follow the prompts to complete the installation process. The installer will also install the Node Package Manager (npm), essential for managing JavaScript packages, including Cypress.

3. Once the installation is complete, open a Command Prompt and verify the installation by running the following commands:

   ```
   node -v
   npm -v
   ```

   These commands will display the installed versions of Node.js and npm, respectively.

macOS

To install Node.js on macOS, you can use the same approach as Windows by downloading Node.js from the official website and choosing the correct version. But there is an alternative solution:

1. You can install Node.js on macOS using the Homebrew package manager. If you haven't installed Homebrew, follow the instructions on the Homebrew website (https://brew.sh/) to set it up. You will receive a script that should be copied and pasted to the Terminal.

2. Once Homebrew is installed, run the following command to install Node.js:

   ```
   brew install node
   ```

After the installation is complete, open a Terminal window and verify the installation by running the following commands:

```
node -v
npm -v
```

These commands will display the installed versions of Node.js and npm, respectively.

Linux

You can install Node.js on Linux using a package manager specific to your distribution.

The following examples show how to install Node.js on Ubuntu and Fedora:

Ubuntu

```
sudo apt update
sudo apt install nodejs
sudo apt install npm
```

Fedora

```
sudo dnf install nodejs
sudo dnf install npm
```

After the installation is complete, open a Terminal window and verify the installation by running the following commands:

```
node -v
npm -v
```

These commands will display the installed versions of Node.js and npm, respectively.

If Yarn is the tool of your choice, it can be installed by the following command:

```
npm install --global yarn
```

To check that Yarn is installed, the following command should be executed:

```
yarn --version
```

With Node.js successfully installed on your system, you are now ready to install Cypress and configure your testing environment. In the following sections, we will detail the installation and configuration process to help you get started with Cypress as smoothly as possible.

Installing Cypress

This section will guide you through installing Cypress on Windows, macOS, and Linux. The installation steps are very similar across all platforms, as they involve using the Node Package Manager (npm), which comes with Node.js.

Cypress can be installed globally or as a local dependency in your project. For this guide, we will focus on installing Cypress as a local dependency, as it ensures that the version of Cypress used is consistent across different machines and developers working on the same project.

Follow the given steps to install Cypress on your system:

1. Create a new directory for your project (if you haven't already) and navigate to it using the terminal (Command Prompt on Windows, Terminal on macOS and Linux). For example:

   ```
   mkdir my-cypress-project
   cd my-cypress-project
   ```

2. Initialize a new npm project in the directory by running the following command:

   ```
   npm init -y
   ```

   This command will create a package.json file in your project directory, storing information about your project and its dependencies.

3. Install Cypress as a local dependency by running one of the following commands:

   ```
   npm install cypress --save-dev
   ```

   Or (if you choose Yarn)

   ```
   yarn add cypress -dev
   ```

   This command will download and install the latest version of Cypress as a development dependency in your project. The `--save-dev` or `-dev` flag ensures the dependency is saved to the package.json file under the `devDependencies` section.

4. Once the installation is complete, you can verify that Cypress has been installed by checking the `node_modules` directory in your project folder. You should find a `cypress` folder within the `node_modules` directory.

5. To open the Cypress Test Runner for the first time, you can run the following command in your terminal:

   ```
   npx cypress open
   ```

   `npx` is a command-line utility that comes with npm, which allows you to run locally installed packages.

   Or by using Yarn:

   ```
   yarn run cypress open
   ```

   Upon running the command, Cypress will open its Test Runner, and you will see a list of example tests that come with the default installation. You can now start writing your tests and using Cypress for web automation testing.

The installation process is complete, and Cypress has been successfully installed on your system, whether it's Windows, macOS, or Linux. The following section will discuss configuring Cypress to fine-tune its behavior and settings to suit your testing requirements better.

Configuring Cypress

After installing Cypress, it is essential to configure the testing environment according to your project requirements. In this section, the reader will be introduced to various aspects of configuring Cypress, such as setting up the project structure, understanding configuration files, and customizing settings.

The first configuration that will be useful is to write a specific script to the `package.json` file. It is much more straightforward than writing the full path to the Cypress executable every time. The command should be added to the `scripts` field of the `package.json` file.

```
{
  "scripts": {
    "cypress:open": "cypress open"
  }
}
```

Once the command is added, Cypress can be invoked from the project root:

```
npm run cypress:open
```

Installing Cypress through NPM also gives access to many other CLI commands. On top of that, as Cypress is a fully JavaScript library, it can be easily imported to the Node scripts.

When Cypress runs using the `npx cypress open` command for the first time, it creates a default project structure that includes several folders and files. Together with that, the user will be navigated to the Cypress Launchpad. It was built to guide users through the decisions and configuration tasks to be completed before writing the first tests.

It is a great tool that was added by the Cypress team together with the introduction of the Component testing feature. The Launchpad helps to configure E2E Testing and Component Testing. By default, both choices are greyed out. Depending on the project's needs, the user should choose one of the options: E2E Testing, if needed to run the whole application and visit pages to test them, or Component Testing, if necessary, to mount individual components of the application and test them in isolation.

The following sections will introduce these types of testing and Cypress capabilities. In this section, it will be more important to introduce the reader to the Cypress configuration with the assumption that both types of testing will be used.

Project structure

When Cypress runs using the `npx cypress open` command for the first time, it creates a default project structure that includes several folders and files. The following is a breakdown of the default project structure:

```
my-cypress-project/
├── cypress/
|.  ├── e2e/spec.cy.js
|   ├── fixtures/example.json
|   └── support/
|        ├── commands.js
|        ├── e2e.js
|        ├── component.js
|        └── component-index.html
├── src/
|   ├── components/Component.cy.js
├── cypress.config.js
└── package.json
```

Let's discuss them in detail:

- **`cypress/`**: This folder contains all Cypress-related files, including tests, fixtures, and configuration.
- **`fixtures/`**: This folder stores static data that users can use in their tests. By default, Cypress includes an example JSON file (example.json) demonstrating how to use fixtures. The fixtures are mainly used with `the` `cy.fixture()` command for stubbing network requests.
- **`support/`**: This folder includes support files that will be executed before test files. Depending on which testing type was selected (in our case, we are using both), Cypress automatically creates an example support file for each configured testing type. Each example file will include several commented examples. These files run before every single spec (test) file.

This was done intentionally to prevent users from importing this code to the test files. By default Cypress will create the type-specific support files:

`cypress/support/e2e.{js, jsx, ts, tsx}` - for E2E testing.

`cypress/support/component.{js, jsx, ts, tsx}` - for Component testing.

Meanwhile, the `support/` directory is a great place to store reusable behavior, such as custom commands or global overrides that will be applied and available to all spec files. For example, all reusable commands will be stored in the `cypress/support/commands.js` file.

- **`e2e/`**: This folder is the default location for storing end-to-end (E2E) tests. Cypress will only look for E2E tests in the `e2e/` folder by default. However, you can configure Cypress to look for E2E tests by your custom path.
- **`src/components`**: This folder is commonly used to store web components. The component tests will also be stored here using the next naming convention: `ComponentName.cy.js`
- **`cypress.config.js`**: This is a default place for Cypress configuration where all the properties on which and how Cypress tests should behave will be set. Configurations can be customized according to the project's needs. The default values of Cypress configurations can be found in the Settings folder of the Cypress Test Runner (as shown in *Figure* 2.1):

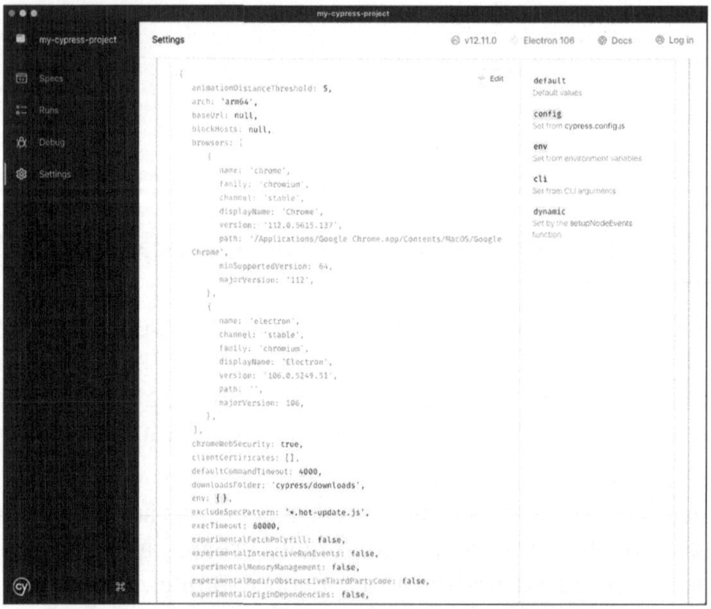

Figure 2.1: *Cypress configuration in the Settings folder*

- `package.json/`: The place where the information about the project and its dependencies will be stored.

This is the default structure suggested by the Cypress team. But readers should always remember that Cypress can be configured differently depending on the project's needs.

Together with the project structure described above, Cypress will generate the place where all spec files will be located. By default, they are located in the `cypress/e2e/` folder, but the spec directory can be configured differently according to the needs. The spec files can be written in various formats, including `.js, .jsx, .ts, .tsx, .coffee, and .cjsx.` Cypress supports ES2015 out of the box, allowing the use of either ES2015 modules or CommonJS modules. This means users can import or require npm packages and local relative modules.

Specific folders may be generated after a test run containing assets created during the test run. These folders include:

- Download Files: Files downloaded during tests are stored in the `cypress/downloads` folder by default.
- Screenshot Files: Screenshots taken via the `cy.screenshot()` command or automatically when a test fails are stored in the `cypress/screenshots` folder by default.
- Video Files: Videos recorded during test runs are stored in the `cypress/videos` folder by default.

Adding these folders to the .gitignore file is highly recommended to prevent them from being checked into source control.

As one of the advantages of Cypress is its customization with plugins, it will be helpful to provide readers with information about plugins. Before Cypress version 10, all plugins were stored in the `cypress/plugins/index.js` file. Since version 10.0.0, a new approach to working with plugins has been implemented.

Plugins are an essential aspect of Cypress that enable you to tap into, modify, or extend its internal behavior. In addition, they allow you to interact with the Node process running outside the browser, providing a "seam" for incorporating custom code during different stages of the Cypress lifecycle.

This chapter will explore the various use cases for plugins and how to install and use them.

1. Use cases for plugins.

    a. **Configuration**: Alter the resolved configuration and environment variables programmatically. This enables multiple environment configurations, swapping environment variables, reading in configuration files, and changing the list of browsers used for testing.

b. **Pre-processors**: Customize the transpilation and bundling of your test code using the `file:preprocessor` event. This allows for language and builds system customizations.

c. **Run Lifecycle**: Utilize the `before:run` and after:run events to execute code before and after a run.

d. **Spec Lifecycle:** Employ the `before:spec` and after:spec events to execute code before and after a single spec is run.

e. **Browser Launching**: Modify browser launch arguments with the `before:browser:launch` event.

f. **Screenshot Handling**: Employ the `after:screenshot` event to manipulate or save details about the screenshots taken during tests.

g. **`cy.task`**: Use the task event in conjunction with the `cy.task()` command to execute arbitrary Node code for accomplishing tasks impossible in the browser.

2. Install Plugins from the official list of npm modules:

```
npm install <plugin name> --save-dev
```

3. To use a plugin in Cypress, add it to the `setupNodeEvents` function in the Cypress configuration:

```
const { defineConfig } = require('cypress')

module.exports = defineConfig({
  // setupNodeEvents can be defined in either
  // the e2e or component configuration
  e2e: {
    setupNodeEvents(on, config) {
      // bind to the event we care about
      on('<event>', (arg1, arg2) => {
        // plugin stuff here
      })
```

```
        },
      },
    })
```

Plugins provide a powerful way to extend and customize the behavior of Cypress tests. Understanding the different use cases and implementing plugins in your test suite can create a more flexible and efficient testing environment.

Creating your first Cypress project

After getting familiar with the installation and configuration processes, this section will provide a step-by-step process for creating the first Cypress project. Next, we will explore the project structure, detailing each folder and file, and provide examples and code snippets to ensure a comprehensive understanding.

1. Initialize a ncw project. To start, create a new folder for your project and navigate to it using the following command line:

   ```
   mkdir my-cypress-project
   cd my-cypress-project
   ```

   Next, initialize a new Node.js project by running the following command:

   ```
   npm init -y
   ```

   This command will create a `package.json` file with default values.

2. Install Cypress as a development dependency by running:

   ```
   npm install cypress --save-dev
   ```

3. Configure `npm` scripts by adding the following scripts to your `package.json`:

   ```
   "scripts": {
     "cypress:open": "cypress open",
     "cypress:run": "cypress run"
   }
   ```

   These scripts will enable you to open the Cypress Test Runner using the command `npm run cypress:open` and run your tests heedlessly with `npm run cypress:run`.

4. Open Cypress for the first time by running the command:
   a. Using scripts from your `package.json`:

      ```
      npm run cypress:open
      ```

   b. Using `npx`:

      ```
      npx cypress open
      ```

   c. Using `yarn`:

      ```
      yarn run cypress open
      ```

Cypress will create a default folder structure and open the Cypress Launchpad (*Figure* 2.2) to help configure E2E or Component type of testing. For this chapter, only the E2E type of testing will be used for further examples. More detailed E2E and Component testing reviews will be done in the appropriate chapters.

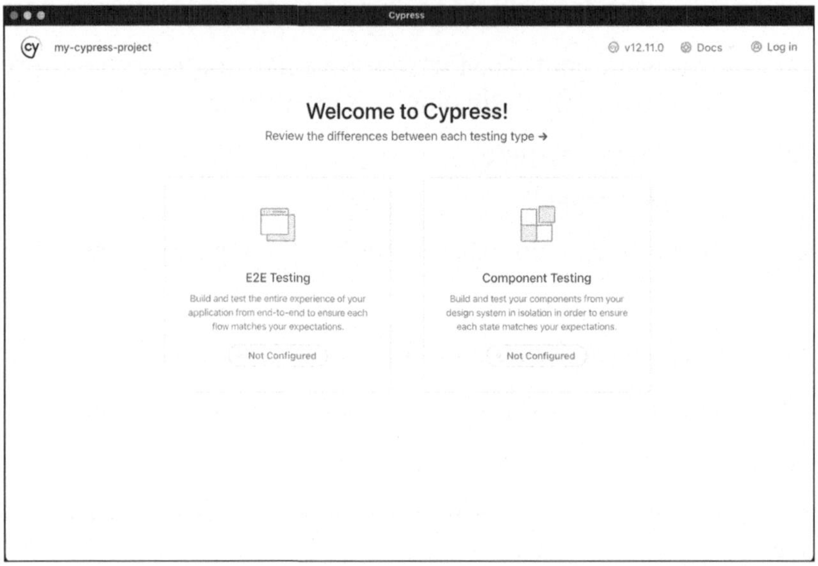

Figure 2.2: *Cypress Launchpad*

As shown in *Figure* 2.2, Cypress provides a Launchpad to help with configuration. For example, to configure E2E Testing, the user must click E2E Testing, which will trigger an E2E testing configuration, as shown here:

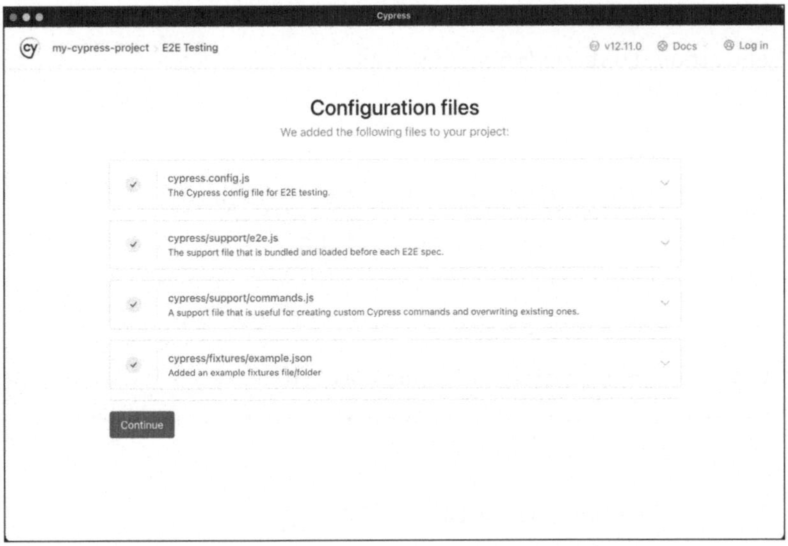

Figure 2.3: *Cypress Launchpad. E2E Configuration files*

As shown in *Figure* 2.3, Cypress has already added the following files to the project: `cypress.config.js`, `cypress/support/e2e.js`, `cypress/support/commands.js`, and `cypress/fixtures/example.json`. We can see what Cypress added to the project by expanding each configuration:

- **`cypress.config.js`**

```
const { defineConfig } = require("cypress");

module.exports = defineConfig({
  e2e: {
    setupNodeEvents(on, config) {
      // implement node event listeners here
    },
  },
});
```

- **`cypress/support/e2e.js`**

```
// ***********************************************************
// This example support/e2e.js is processed and
// loaded automatically before your test files.
//
```

```
// This is a great place to put global configuration and
//behaviour that modifies Cypress.
//
// You can change the location of this file or turn off
// automatically serving support files with the
// 'supportFile' configuration option.
//
// You can read more here:
// https://on.cypress.io/configuration
// ***********************************************************

// Import commands.js using ES2015 syntax:
import './commands'

// Alternatively, you can use CommonJS syntax:
// require('./commands')
```

- **cypress/support/commands.js**

```
// ***********************************************
// This example commands.js shows you how to
// create various custom commands and overwrite
// existing commands.
//
// For more comprehensive examples of custom
// commands, please read more here:
// https://on.cypress.io/custom-commands
// ***********************************************
//
//
// -- This is a parent command --
// Cypress.Commands.add('login', (email, password) => { ... })
//
//
```

```
// -- This is a child command --
// Cypress.Commands.add('drag', { prevSubject: 'element'}, (sub-
ject, options) => { ... })
//
//
// -- This is a dual command --
// Cypress.Commands.add('dismiss', { prevSubject: 'optional'},
(subject, options) => { ... })
//
//
// -- This will overwrite an existing command --
// Cypress.Commands.overwrite('visit', (originalFn, url, options)
=> { ... })
```

- **cypress/fixtures/example.json**

```
{
  "name": "Using fixtures to represent data",
  "email": "hello@cypress.io",
  "body": "Fixtures are a great way to mock data for responses to
routes"
}
```

Also, Cypress advises you to click the Continue button. By clicking it, Cypress will bring us to the next step, where we must choose the browser to execute tests. Cypress includes the Electron browser as a default and all the browsers installed on your machine. In *Figure* 2.4, Cypress has only two browsers: Electron as a default and Chrome, which was found in the device:

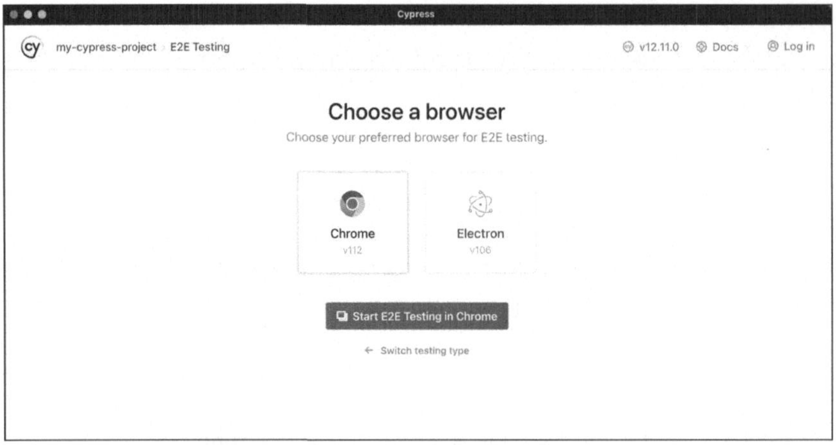

***Figure 2.4**: Cypress Launchpad Browser selection.*

Once the browser is selected, clicking the Start E2E Testing button can perform the next step. It will start the Test Runner with the following advice from the Cypress team. As the project is new, Cypress recommends selecting one of the options (as shown in *Figure* 2.5):

- **Scaffold example specs**: Cypress will generate several example specs to help guide users on how to write tests in Cypress. It is a great start to get familiar with Cypress. These example files showcase the different Cypress features and provide a starting point for your test cases. In addition, the examples help you understand how to write and structure tests, interact with web elements, and leverage various Cypress commands.
- **Create new spec**: Cypress will generate a template file that can be used to start testing the application.

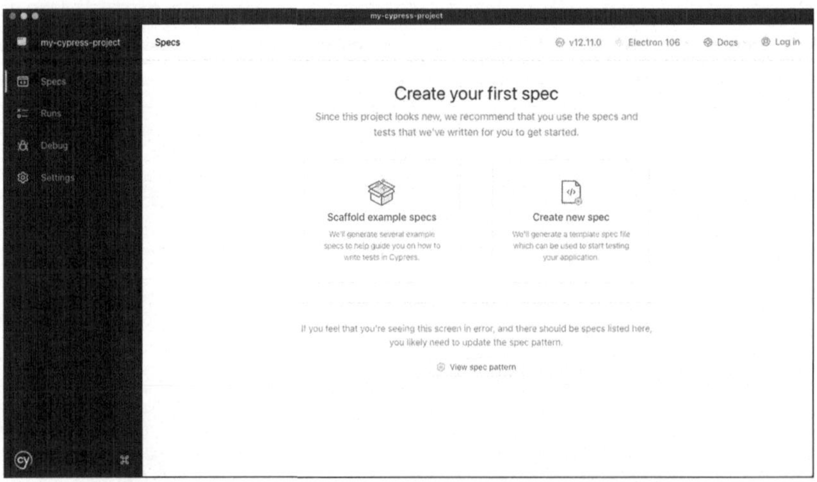

***Figure 2.5**: Cypress Test Runner - Create your first spec*

Regardless of the choice made by default, Cypress creates a `cypress/e2e/` folder to store the spec files. Of course, the path to the specs can be customized, but in this example, the default scenario will be used.

By selecting a Scaffold example spec, Cypress will add the example specs to the project (as shown in *Figure 2.6*):

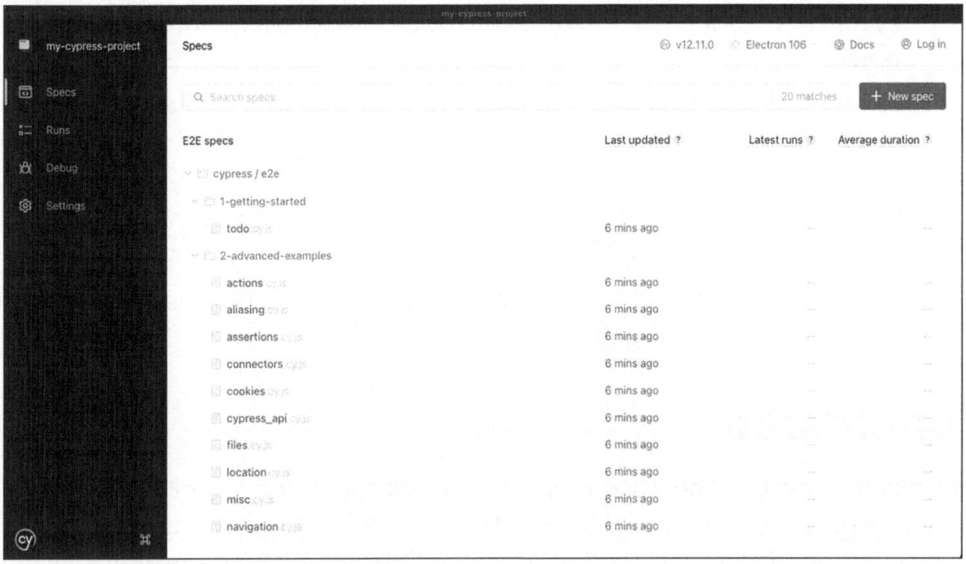

***Figure 2.6**: Cypress Test Runner - Scaffold example specs*

Some of the default example files include:

- **`actions.cy.js`**: This example demonstrates basic Cypress commands to interact with web elements, such as typing text into input fields, selecting dropdown options, and checking or unchecking checkboxes.
- **`aliasing.cy.js`**: This example showcases how to use aliases to store references to elements or responses for later use. Aliasing helps reduce redundancy and improves the readability of your test code.
- **`assertions.cy.js`**: This example explains how to write assertions to ensure your application behaves as expected. Assertions are used to verify elements, attributes, or values on a web page.
- **`connectors.cy.js`**: This example demonstrates how to use commands like `.each()`, `.its()`, and `.invoke()` to interact with collections of elements, access object properties, or call methods on elements.
- **`cookies.cy.js`**: This example covers how to work with browser cookies using Cypress commands such as `cy.getCookie()`, `cy.setCookie()`, and `cy.clearCookies()`.

- **cypress_api.cy.js**: This example overviews some common Cypress API commands, such as `Cypress.env()`and `Cypress.Commands.add()`.
- **files.cy.js**: This example shows how to work with files in your tests, including reading and writing data from files using commands like `cy.readFile()` and `cy.writeFile()`.
- **location.cy.js**: This example uses commands like `cy.location()` and `cy.url()` to assert the current URL or interact with the browser's location object.
- **navigation.cy.js**: This example demonstrates how to navigate between pages and interact with the browser's history using commands like `cy.visit()`, `cy.go()`, and `cy.reload()`.

At this stage, your project is good to start exploring Cypress's capabilities. It is strongly recommended to go through each spec file, run it, and explore the behavior. With this knowledge, you can dive deeper into more advanced topics and enhance your Cypress skills.

Conclusion

This chapter covers the essential steps to prepare for Cypress testing. The process begins with installing Node.js, the foundation for running Cypress. Next, the installation of Cypress itself is addressed, providing a comprehensive guide on how to set it up correctly.

Configuration is an integral part of the Cypress setup, and this section delves into the various aspects of the Cypress configuration file. Topics such as modifying the configuration file and using custom configurations are explored to help readers tailor the environment to their needs.

Lastly, the chapter walks through creating the first Cypress project, including the initial project setup, understanding the folder structure, and examining the default example test files in the `cypress/e2e/` folder. This chapter provides a solid foundation for readers to develop and execute their Cypress test cases.

In the upcoming chapter, we will venture into the exciting world of writing tests with Cypress. We will first familiarize ourselves with Cypress Test Runner, an essential tool for running the tests. The chapter will walk you through the process of crafting a simple test case to familiarize you with the basics. We will then delve into using Cypress commands and assertions, powerful tools that allow us to interact with web applications and verify their behavior. To round it all off, we will cover the concepts of hooks and aliases, which offer a more efficient way to manage and reuse parts of the tests. By the end of the chapter, readers will have a firm grasp of how to write and execute their own Cypress tests.

Further Readings

To deepen readers' understanding of the topics covered in this chapter, here are some resources that would be recommended:

1. **Node.js official documentation:** The official (https://nodejs.org/en/docs/) is a comprehensive resource to understand Node.js in-depth, from setup to advanced concepts.
2. **Cypress Real World App:** Cypress's Real World App (https://github.com/cypress-io/cypress-realworld-app) on GitHub is a full-fledged application meant for testing with Cypress. It could be a great reference for seeing how a Cypress project can be structured and configured in a real-world scenario.

Utilizing these resources will provide you with a broader understanding and practical examples of the concepts covered in this chapter.

CHAPTER 3

Writing Your First Test

Introduction

This chapter will guide readers through writing their first test using the Cypress Test Runner. It will explain the use of Cypress commands, hooks, and aliases and how to apply these concepts when creating test cases. By the end of this chapter, readers will have a solid foundation for writing and running Cypress tests.

Structure

In this chapter, we will discuss the following topics:

- Introducing Cypress Test Runner
- Writing a simple test case
- Using Cypress commands
- Using Cypress assertions
- Understanding hooks and aliases

Introducing the Cypress Test Runner

Before we can start writing tests, we first need to install Cypress. The installation process was fully covered in *Chapter* 2, "*Setting Up the Development Environment*" of this book. But anyway, it will be helpful to remind readers of the following steps that need to perform for every single Cypress project.

First, we will need Node.js installed on our machine. Once we have that, navigate to the project folder in the terminal and run the following command to install Cypress as a development dependency:

```
npm install cypress --save-dev
```

This command will install Cypress in the local project, and we can continue to discover Cypress to write our first test case.

Cypress itself will appear in the project after the first run. Once the installation is complete, we can open the Cypress Test Runner using the command:

```
npx cypress open
```

The initial view of Cypress Test Runner was already introduced to the readers in *Chapter* 2 in *Figure* 2.6. The Cypress Test Runner is a part of the Cypress testing framework, used for end-to-end and component testing of web applications. It's called a "test runner" because it's part of the testing framework that executes the tests, checking whether the conditions specified in the tests are met and then providing the results.

The Cypress Test Runner provides features like real-time reloading, automatic waiting, network traffic control, and capturing screenshots or videos of test runs. It is important to note that the Cypress Test Runner is part of the broader Cypress framework, including tools for writing our tests, integrating with continuous integration systems, and other features beyond just running the tests.

The Cypress Test Runner provides a visual interface to see all our spec files and the results of the tests. It's divided into several parts (*Figure* 3.1):

- **File Explorer:** On the left side, we will see a list of our spec files. Clicking any file will run the tests contained within it.
- **Command Log**: At the center of the Test Runner, this shows a running list of the commands executed in the currently running test. It includes assertions, network requests, and other actions. Each command is tied to a specific snapshot of the DOM at the time that command ran, so clicking a command will display what the app looked like at that point in time.
- **Application Preview**: The right side is the application preview. This is a live preview of our web application under test. It's a fully interactive, live view of our web page as the tests run.

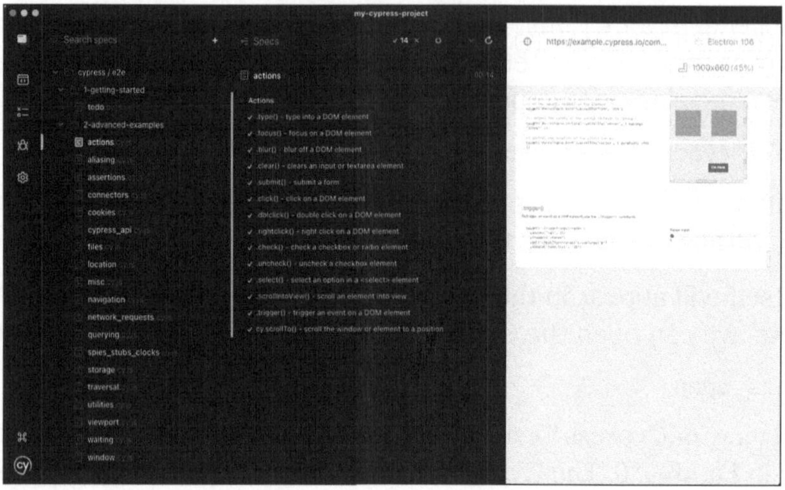

Figure 3.1: *Cypress Test Runner view*

The Cypress Test Runner is designed to be highly interactive and user-friendly:

- **Time-travelling**: We can hover over commands in the Command Log section to see the state of our application then. Cypress calls this "time-travelling" because we are essentially going back in time to see the exact state of the application when each command ran.
- **Debugging**: If a test fails, Cypress takes a snapshot of the application state and command log at the point of failure, which we can use to debug the issue. Also, it has built-in debugging support with the browser DevTools.
- **Automatic Waiting**: Cypress automatically waits for elements to become available. This means we don't have to guess how long to wait for elements to appear or commands to complete.
- **Real-Time Reloading**: Cypress automatically detects changes in our test files and reloads the test in real-time.
- **Test Statuses**: The Test Runner provides a clear, color-coded status of our tests at a glance. It shows which tests have passed (green), which have failed (red), and which are currently running (blue).
- **Videos and Screenshots**: The Test Runner can take screenshots automatically of test failures or videos of our entire test suite when run from the command line.
- **Cross-Browser Testing**: Cypress Test Runner supports testing in multiple browsers, including Chrome, Firefox, Edge, and Electron. We can choose which browser to run our tests in the Test Runner UI.
- **Open files in your IDE**: Some places in the Command Log display a link to the relevant file where the code is located.

The Cypress Test Runner provides a unique and valuable feature to help identify and locate elements in our application, which is the Selector Playground (*Figure 3.2*).

This is particularly useful when we are writing tests and need to find the best way to select a particular element or group of elements.

Here's how we can use it:

1. Click the "Open Selector Playground" button in the Test Runner's top bar.
2. The Application Preview pane will change to a selection mode where we can hover over elements in the application.
3. Selector Playground will automatically generate a unique selector for that element as we hover over elements.
4. Click an element, and the generated selector will be inserted directly into the clipboard. We can then paste this into the test code.

The Selector Playground also provides real-time feedback on our selectors. For example, we can type a selector into the input at the top of the Playground, and it will highlight matching elements in the Application Preview.

This feature makes interacting with our application's elements easier and provides a more efficient way to find manually and test selectors we would otherwise have to craft.

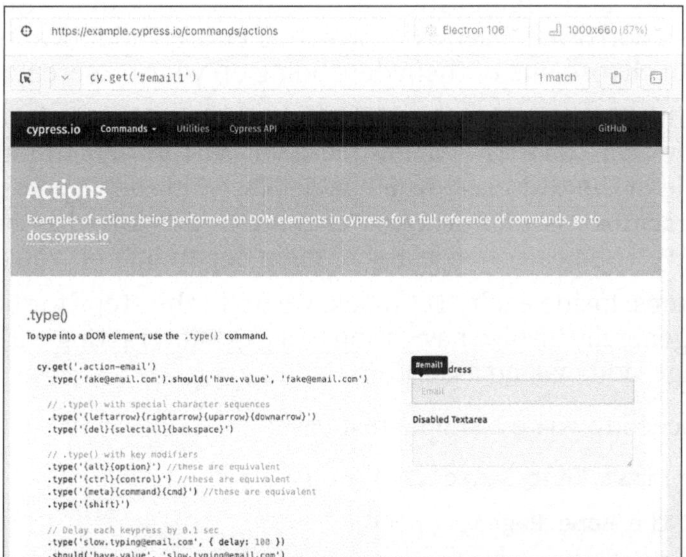

Figure 3.2: *Cypress Test Runner: Selector Playground*

Writing a simple test case

We've already introduced the Cypress Test Runner and some basic concepts. Now, let's delve deeper and write our first simple test case. We will navigate to a webpage, interact with elements on the page, and verify the application's behavior using assertions.

Before we start, let's explore the structure of a typical Cypress test. Cypress tests are primarily written in JavaScript and share similarities with other testing frameworks. Here is a skeleton of a basic test file:

```
describe('My Test Suite', () => {
  it('My Test Case', () => {
    // Test steps go here
  });
});
```

In the preceding code snippet:

- **`'describe'`**: This function, borrowed from Mocha, allows us to organize our tests into distinct suites or groups. Although it does not interact directly with our application, `'describe'` is crucial for maintaining readability and organization in the tests. Together with **`'describe'`**, Cypress borrowed **`'context'`**, which is entirely identical to **`'describe'`**. You can choose one of them depending on your preferences in syntax.
- **`'it'`**: This function also comes from Mocha. Each `'it'` function signifies a single test case. The string provided as the first argument denotes the title of the test case, which is displayed in the Cypress Test Runner. As **`'describe'`** is identical to **`'context'`**, **`'it'`** also has an alias called **`'specify'`**. You can choose any of them depending on your preferences.
- Test steps: Inside each `'it'` block, we write the steps for our test. These steps generally involve navigating to a page, interacting with elements on the page, and making assertions.

Now, let's proceed to write a simple test case:

```
describe('My First Test Suite', () => {
  it('Visits the Home Page', () => {
    cy.visit('http://example.com'); // Navigate to the home page
```

```
    cy.contains('Welcome to Example.com'); // Assert that the page con-
tains the text 'Welcome to Example.com'
  });
});
```

In this test case, we utilize two Cypress commands: `cy.visit()` and `cy.contains()`.

- **`cy.visit()`** is used for navigating to a URL. It accepts a single argument: the URL of the page to visit.
- **`cy.contains()`** is used to assert the existence of a particular piece of text on the page. It also accepts a single argument: the text to look for.

These commands are executed in the order they appear. For example, Cypress first navigates to `'http://example.com,'` then checks if the page contains the text 'Welcome to Example.com.'

Now, let's extend our understanding with a few additional Mocha functions that readers might find helpful in their testing journey:

- **`beforeEach`** and **`afterEach`**: These hooks run before and after each test in a suite, respectively. They're often used for setting up and tearing down test conditions:

```
describe('My Test Suite', () => {
  beforeEach(() => {
    // Runs before each test in the suite
  });

  afterEach(() => {
    // Runs after each test in the suite
  });

  it('My Test Case', () => {
    // Test steps go here
  });
});
```

- `before` and `after`: These hooks run before the first test and after the last test in the suite, respectively. They're usually used for setting up and tearing down conditions that apply to the suite as a whole:

```
describe('My Test Suite', () => {
  before(() => {
    // Runs before the first test in the suite
  });

  after(() => {
    // Runs after the last test in the suite
  });

  it('My Test Case', () => {
    // Test steps go here
  });
});
```

- `it.only` and `it.skip`: These are special variants of the `'it'` function. As the names suggest, `it.only` will ensure that only the specified test case will be run, whereas `it.skip` will exclude the specified test case from being run. These are very handy when debugging a failing test or having a test that we know will fail and don't want to run it:

```
describe('My Test Suite', () => {
  it.only('This is the only test that will run', () => {
    // Test steps go here
  });

  it('This test will be skipped', () => {
    // Test steps go here
  });

  it.skip('This test will also be skipped', () => {
```

```
        // Test steps go here
      });
    });
```

In the preceding example, only the test case `'This is the only test that will run'` will be executed. The other two test cases will be ignored.

Let's now consider a more complex test case. In this example, we'll navigate to a login page, fill out a form, and submit it:

```
describe('Login Page Tests', () => {
  it('Logs in a user', () => {
    cy.visit('http://example.com/login'); // Navigate to the login page

    // Fill out the form
    cy.get('input[name=username]').type('myUsername');
    cy.get('input[name=password]').type('myPassword');

    cy.contains('Submit').click(); // Click the submit button

    // Assert that we've been redirected to the home page
    cy.url().should('eq', 'http://example.com/home');
  });
});
```

This test case introduces four new Cypress commands as follows:

- **`cy.get()`**: This command is used to get one or more DOM elements by a selector (for example, class, id, or attribute). It is similar to jQuery's `'$'` function or `document.querySelector()` in vanilla JavaScript.
- **`.type()`**: This command types into a DOM element. It's typically chained onto a `cy.get()` command and accepts the text to type as its argument.
- **`.click()`**: This is a command that clicks a DOM element. Like `.type()`, it's typically chained onto a `cy.get()` command.
- **`.should()`**: This command is used to assert the current subject. For example, it's used here to assert that the current URL is `'http://example.com/home'` after clicking the submit button.

Remember, one of the critical aspects of Cypress is its ability to wait automatically. So, for example, Cypress will wait for the page to load after the `cy.visit()` command, it will wait for the DOM to become ready, it will wait for animations to complete, it will wait for the `cy.get()` command to yield elements, and it will retry the `.should()` assertion until it passes (or time out after a default of four seconds).

This test case demonstrates the power and expressiveness of Cypress. As a result, we can create complex and robust end-to-end tests for our web applications by chaining commands and assertions.

Using Cypress commands

Cypress commands are the heart of our tests. They simulate user interactions, control the flow of tests, make assertions about the application's state, and much more. This section will explore some of the most commonly used Cypress commands and learn how to use them effectively in our tests.

Navigating commands

Cypress provides commands for controlling the navigation and URL of the web application.

- **`cy.visit()`**

This command is used to visit a URL. It can be an absolute or relative URL. The `cy.visit()` command will automatically prepend `baseUrl` (defined in the `cypress.comfig.js` configuration) to the relative URL.

```
cy.visit('http://example.com/login'); // Visits the login page
```

- **`cy.url()`**

This command allows us to get the current URL of the application, which we can then use for assertions.

```
cy.url().should('include', '/login'); // Asserts that the current URL
includes '/login'
```

- **`cy.reload()`**

This command is used to reload the current page.

```
cy.reload(); // Reloads the current page
```

- **cy.go()**

This command is used to navigate the user's browsing history. It accepts either a string or a number. The string can be `'forward'` or `'back.'` The number is the number of pages to go forward or back.

```
cy.go('back'); // Goes back one page in the browsing history
cy.go(-1); // Goes back one page in the browsing history
```

Querying DOM commands

Cypress provides several commands to query and manipulate DOM elements, including:

- **cy.get()**

This command is used to get one or more DOM elements by selector. We can use any selector that's valid in `document.querySelector`.

```
cy.get('.my-class'); // Gets elements with class 'my-class'
```

- **cy.contains()**

This command is used to get a DOM element by its contents. It can accept a string, a regular expression, or a function that returns a string or a regular expression.

```
cy.contains('Submit'); // Gets elements that contain the text 'Submit'
```

- **.find()**

This command is used to find a descendant DOM element by a selector.

```
cy.get('.articles').find('.title'); // Finds elements with class 'title' within elements with class 'articles'
```

- **.closest()**

This command is used to find the closest ancestor DOM element by a selector.

```
cy.get('.title').closest('.articles'); // Finds the closest ancestor element with class 'articles'
```

Action commands

Cypress provides several commands to interact with DOM elements.

- **.click()**

This command is used to click a DOM element.

```
cy.get('button').click(); // Clicks a button element
```

- **.type()**

This command is used to type into a DOM element.

```
cy.get('input').type('Hello, World'); // Types 'Hello, World' into an input element
```

- **.select()**

This command is used to select an option in a select element.

```
cy.get('select').select('option1'); // Selects 'option1' in a select element
```

- **.selectFile()**

This command selects a file in an HTML5 input element or simulates dragging a file into the browser.

```
cy.get('input[type=file]').selectFile('file.json')
```

- **.check()**

This command is used to check checkboxes or radio inputs.

```
cy.get('input[type="checkbox"]').check(); // Checks a checkbox
```

- **.uncheck()**

This command is used to uncheck checkboxes.

```
cy.get('input[type="checkbox"]').uncheck(); // Unchecks a checkbox
```

- **.clear()**

This command is used to clear the value of an input or text area.

```
cy.get('input').clear(); // Clears an input element
```

Assertion commands

Cypress commands for assertions help ensure the application is in the correct state as follows:

- **.should()**

This command is used to assert that the previous subject satisfies a particular state. It can be used with a function or a string argument.

```
cy.get('button').should('be.disabled'); // Asserts that a button is disabled
```

- **.and()**

This command is like cy.should(), and it's used to chain multiple assertions together.

```
cy.get('button').should('be.visible').and('contain', 'Submit'); // Asserts that a button is visible and contains the text 'Submit'
```

- **expect()**

This command asserts that a particular value meets a set of criteria.

```
cy.wrap(5).should((num) => {
  expect(num).to.equal(5); // Asserts that num equals 5
});
```

Network requests commands

Cypress provides commands for controlling and asserting the behavior of network requests in our application. For example, it enables us to stub a response and control the body, status, headers, or delay.

- **cy.intercept()**

This command is used to control the behavior of HTTP requests. For example, we can statically define the body, HTTP status code, headers, and other response characteristics.

```
cy.intercept('GET', '/users', { fixture: 'users.json' }); // Intercepts all GET requests to '/users' and respond with 'fixture:users.json'
```

- **cy.request()**

This command is used to make an HTTP request.

```
cy.request('POST', 'http://example.com/users/admin', { name: 'Jane' }).then(
  (response) => {
    // response.body is automatically serialized into JSON
    expect(response.body).to.have.property('name', 'Jane') // true
  }
)
```

Cookies and local storage commands

Cypress provides following commands for managing cookies and local storage in the application:

- **cy.getCookie()**

This command is used to get a browser cookie by its name.

```
cy.getCookie('session_id'); // Gets the 'session_id' cookie
```

- **cy.setCookie()**

This command is used to set a browser cookie.

```
cy.setCookie('session_id', '12345'); // Sets the 'session_id' cookie to
'12345'
```

- **cy.clearCookies()**

This command is used to clear all browser cookies.

```
cy.clearCookies(); // Clears all cookies
```

- **cy.clearLocalStorage()**

This command is used to clear the browser's local storage.

```
cy.clearLocalStorage(); // Clears local storage
```

- **cy.session()**

This command is used to cache and restore cookies, localStorage, and sessionStorage (that is, session data) in order to recreate a consistent browser context between tests.

```
// Caching session when logging in via page visit
cy.session(name, () => {
  cy.visit('/login')
  cy.get('[data-test=name]').type(name)
  cy.get('[data-test=password]').type('s3cr3t')
  cy.get('form').contains('Log In').click()
  cy.url().should('contain', '/login-successful')
})
```

These are some of the most common Cypress commands that readers will find themselves as they write their tests. However, this is a partial list, and Cypress has many more commands that can be discovered in the official Cypress API documentation (https://docs.cypress.io/api/table-of-contents/).

Using Cypress assertions

Assertions are an integral part of any testing framework. They help us validate the state of our application and check whether it meets our expectations. This section explores how Cypress handles assertions and introduces some of the most commonly used assertion commands.

In Cypress, assertions are built on top of the popular JavaScript testing framework, Chai. Chai has two styles of assertions: BDD (behavior-driven development) and TDD (test-driven development). Cypress primarily uses the BDD style, which is more human-readable and intuitive.

An assertion in Cypress typically follows this pattern:

```
cy.get('selector').should('condition', 'value');
```

The `.should()` command is used to make assertions about the current subject. It can take two arguments: the first is the condition or matcher, and the second (optional) is the value against which the condition is evaluated.

Here's an example:

```
cy.get('h1').should('contain', 'Hello World');
```

In this case, the `.should()` command checks if the text of the `h1` element contains the string `'Hello World.'` If the condition is not met, the test will fail.

It's important to note that Cypress assertions automatically retry until they pass or time out. This retry-ability makes Cypress uniquely suited to handle the asynchronous nature of modern web applications.

Let's delve into some of Cypress's most commonly used assertion commands:

- **`.should()`**

As mentioned earlier, the `.should()` command is the cornerstone of Cypress assertions. It can take a string and an optional value or a callback function. Here are a few examples:

```
cy.get('button').should('be.disabled'); // Asserts that a button is dis-
abled
```

```
cy.get('input').should('have.value', 'Hello World'); // Asserts that an input has a certain value


cy.get('div').should(($div) => {
  expect($div).to.have.length(3); // Asserts that there are 3 div elements
});
```

- **.and()**

The `.and()` command is used in conjunction with `.should()` to chain multiple assertions together. It functions just like `.should()` and can take the same arguments.

```
cy.get('button').should('be.visible').and('contain', 'Submit'); // Asserts that a button is visible and contains the text 'Submit'
```

- **expect()**

The `expect()` command is used to make assertions about a particular value. This command is often used in callback functions passed to `.should()`. Here's an example:

```
cy.get('input').should(($input) => {
  expect($input).to.have.value('Hello World'); // Asserts that the input has a certain value
});
```

Cypress supports several styles of assertions that cater to different testing needs and preferences. These styles come from the Chai library and include the following:

BDD assertions

BDD assertions are the default style in Cypress and are based on Chai's `'expect'` and `.should` interfaces. They provide a readable and expressive language to write assertions.

```
// 'expect' style
expect(true).to.be.true;
```

```
// 'should' style
true.should.be.true;
```

TDD assertions

TDD assertions use Chai's `'assert'` interface, which provides a more traditional, function-based way to write assertions.

```
// 'assert' style
assert.isTrue(true);
```

Sinon-Chai assertions

Sinon-Chai assertions extend Chai with assertions for the Sinon.JS mocking framework. This is useful when asserting that certain functions are called or not called.

```
// 'sinon-chai' style
expect(mySpy).to.have.been.calledOnce;
```

Cypress includes Sinon-Chai so that we can use these assertions out of the box without any additional configuration.

Complex assertions

Cypress allows us to make complex checks with ease. Let's delve into some of them:

- **Checking Element's CSS**: Cypress allows us to check an element's CSS properties using the `'have.css'` assertion.

  ```
  cy.get('button').should('have.css', 'background-color', 'rgb(0, 123, 255)');
  ```

  This will assert that the `'button'` has a background color of `'rgb(0, 123, 255)'`.

- **Checking Element's Visibility**: With Cypress, we can easily check whether an element is hidden or visible using the `'be.visible'` and `'be.hidden'` assertions.

  ```
  cy.get('#my-element').should('be.visible');
  cy.get('#my-hidden-element').should('be.hidden');
  ```

- **Checking Existence**: To verify whether an element `'exists;` in the DOM, use the `exist` assertion.

```
cy.get('#my-element').should('exist');
```

Conversely, to check if an element does not exist, we can use the `'not.exist'` assertion.

```
cy.get('#my-nonexistent-element').should('not.exist');
```

- **Checking Length**: If we need to check the number of matching elements, use the `'have.length'` or `'have.length.greaterThan'` assertions.

```
cy.get('.my-class').should('have.length', 3);
cy.get('.my-class').should('have.length.greaterThan', 0);
```

Assertion timeout

By default, Cypress will automatically retry assertions until they pass or until the command's timeout expires (the default is 4 seconds). However, if our application has longer asynchronous behavior, we might need to use the `'timeout'` option to increase this timeout.

```
cy.get('#my-element', { timeout: 10000 }).should('contain', 'Hello World');
```

This will make Cypress wait up to 10 seconds for the element to contain the `'Hello World'` text.

In conclusion, assertions are a powerful tool in Cypress that allow us to validate the application's state and behavior. With a wide range of commands and styles at our disposal, we can write expressive, human-readable tests that ensure our application works as expected. As readers continue their journey with Cypress, they will likely find themselves reaching for these assertions repeatedly.

Understanding hooks and aliases

In Cypress, hooks and aliases are critical for more efficient and reusable tests. This section will delve into the concepts of hooks and aliases and demonstrate how they can be used to streamline our test suite.

Introducing hooks

Hooks in Cypress, inspired by Mocha, are blocks of code that can run at various stages of the test lifecycle, such as before all tests, before each test, after each test, and after all tests. They provide the ability to set up necessary conditions before tests are run and clean up after them. These are the available hooks in Cypress:

- **before()**: Runs once before all tests in the block
- **beforeEach()**: Runs before each test in the block
- **afterEach()**: Runs after each test in the block
- **after()**: Runs once after all tests in the block

These hooks are typically used for setting up and tearing down test contexts to keep the tests isolated and independent, which is a best practice in testing.

Here is an example showing how these hooks work in a test suite:

```
describe('Hooks Example', function () {
  before(function () {
    // Runs once before all tests in the block
    cy.log('Setting up the test suite prerequisites...');
  });

  beforeEach(function () {
    // Runs before each test in the block
    cy.log('Setting up the test prerequisites...');
  });

  afterEach(function () {
    // Runs after each test in the block
    cy.log('Cleaning up after the test...');
  });

  after(function () {
    // Runs once after all tests in the block
    cy.log('Cleaning up after the test suite...');
  });

  it('does something', function () {
    // Test logic goes here
  });
```

```
});
```

In this example, any setup code that needs to be executed before the entire test suite starts would be placed in the `'before'` hook. Likewise, code that prepares the necessary conditions for each test would go in the `'beforeEach'` hook.

After the tests have run, any cleanup operations required to bring the system back to its initial state would be placed in the `'afterEach'` and `'after'` hooks.

These hooks help to ensure each test is run in a predictable context, thereby preventing tests from being affected by the residue of previous tests.

Using aliases

Aliases in Cypress are shortcuts or identifiers to elements, routes, stubs/spies, or arbitrary objects. They can be created using the **`.as()`** command, which assigns an alias to the subject of the command chain. The alias can then be referenced later in the test using the **`'@'`** prefix.

Here is a simple example of creating and using an alias for a DOM element:

```
cy.get('#submit-button').as('submitButton');


// later in the test...
cy.get('@submitButton').click();
```

In this example, the button with the ID `#submit-button` is given the alias `'submitButton.'` Later in the test, instead of writing out the full selector to reference this button, we can simply use `@submitButton`.

Aliases can be handy when dealing with complex selectors or when the same element is used repeatedly in a test.

But aliases are not limited to elements. For instance, we can also alias network routes. This allows us to wait for these routes to complete before proceeding with the test:

```
cy.intercept('GET', '/users/1').as('getUser');


// later in the test...
cy.wait('@getUser').then((interception) => {
  expect(interception.response.statusCode).to.equal(200);
```

```
});
```

Scopes of hooks and aliases

Understanding the scope of hooks and aliases is crucial for their effective use in our test suite. Both hooks and aliases have their own scoping rules that dictate their visibility and lifetime within our tests.

Hooks scope

The scope of hooks in Cypress is determined by where they are defined within the `describe` and `context` blocks of the test suite.

- A `before` or `after` hook defined within a `describe` block will run before or after all tests within that `describe` block, respectively.
- A `beforeEach` or `afterEach` hook defined within a `describe` block will run before or after each test within that `describe` block, respectively.

Here's an example of a nested describe block where hooks are defined at various levels:

```
describe('Outer block', () => {
  before(() => {
    cy.log('Runs before all tests in the outer block');
  });

  beforeEach(() => {
    cy.log('Runs before each test in the outer block');
  });

  describe('Inner block', () => {
    before(() => {
      cy.log('Runs before all tests in the inner block');
    });

    beforeEach(() => {
      cy.log('Runs before each test in the inner block');
    });
```

```
    it('does something', () => {
      // Test logic
    });
  });

  it('does something else', () => {
    // Test logic
  });
});
```

In this example, before running the test in the `Inner block`, Cypress will run the `before` hook of the `Outer block`, the `beforeEach` hook of the `Outer block`, the `before` hook of the `Inner block`, and finally, the `beforeEach` hook of the `Inner block`.

Aliases scope

Unlike hooks, aliases are not scoped to the `describe` or `context` blocks. Instead, aliases are scoped to the test in which they are defined (`it` or `specify` block). This means an alias created in one test will not be available in another. Also, aliases created in `before`, `beforeEach`, `after`, and `afterEach` hooks will be available only in the specific test that comes after that hook.

Here is an example:

```
describe('Alias scope', () => {
  beforeEach(() => {
    cy.get('#submit-button').as('submitButton');
  });

  it('test one', () => {
    cy.get('@submitButton').click();
  });

  it('test two', () => {
```

```
    cy.get('@submitButton').click();
  });
});
```

In this example, the alias `submitButton` is defined in a `beforeEach` hook, so it is created anew before each test runs. This makes it available for use within each test.

Understanding the scoping of hooks and aliases is critical for structuring the tests effectively and ensuring that they run predictably.

Best practices for using hooks and aliases

As we delve deeper into Cypress testing, it's essential to remember the best practices that will keep our tests reliable, readable, and efficient. Here are some best practices for using hooks and aliases in the Cypress tests:

- **Avoid Side Effects in Hooks**: Hooks should be used for setting up and tearing down test conditions. Therefore, avoid performing assertions or actions that could affect the outcome of the tests in our hooks.
- **Use Aliases to Avoid Unnecessary DOM Queries:** If we repeatedly query the same DOM element in the test, consider using an alias to reference that element instead. This can improve the performance of the tests and make our test code cleaner.
- **Avoid relying on the state from previous tests**: Cypress recommends that each test be able to run independently. This means that tests should not rely on the state set up by previous tests. However, hooks, especially `beforeEach` and `afterEach`, can be instrumental in setting up and tearing down the state for each test.
- **Avoid Overusing `before` Hooks**: While it might be tempting to use the `before` hook to set up conditions for all our tests, it can make the tests hard to understand and debug if something goes wrong. Instead, consider using `beforeEach` hooks for the setup that needs to occur before each test, or move some setup into the individual tests themselves if they do not share a common setup.

Dealing with asynchronous operations

One common use case for hooks and aliases is dealing with asynchronous operations. Cypress handles asynchronous operations differently than other testing frameworks. All Cypress commands are asynchronous, but they are run in a chain, and each command returns immediately, passing the value to the following command once it's ready.

This is why we can't assign the result of a Cypress command to a variable and expect to use it immediately:

```
// This will NOT work!
let button;
cy.get('#submit-button').then(($btn) => {
  button = $btn;
});
cy.wrap(button).click(); // This will throw an error
```

Instead, we can use aliases to "store" the value and reference it later:

```
// This will work
cy.get('#submit-button').as('button');
cy.get('@button').click(); // This will work as expected
```

Here, we're storing the reference to the `#submit-button` element as an alias `button` and then using `cy.get('@button')` to retrieve and click the button.

By embracing Cypress's unique command execution and effectively using hooks and aliases, we can write clean, understandable, and efficient tests.

Understanding and utilizing hooks and aliases are integral parts of mastering Cypress. Hooks provide a way to arrange our tests in a structured and organized manner. Aliases can keep the test scripts DRY and increase readability and maintainability. By mastering these concepts, readers will be well on their way to becoming proficient in end-to-end testing with Cypress.

Conclusion

This chapter is a hands-on guide to writing our first test using Cypress. First, it introduces the Cypress Test Runner, a crucial tool for executing our tests. The chapter then leads readers through the process of creating a straightforward test case, ensuring a solid understanding of the basics. Next, we learned how to use Cypress commands and assertions, both powerful components for interacting with our web application and confirming its behavior. It also covered hooks and aliases, which are essential for managing and reusing parts of our tests effectively. By the end of this chapter, readers will have a strong foundation in writing and running tests with Cypress, equipped with the knowledge to apply these concepts in their projects.

In the next chapter, we will dive into end-to-end (E2E) testing with Cypress, focusing on simulating user interactions and working with various types of elements. The chapter also covers handling timeouts and retries, providing practical examples and best practices to create robust E2E tests.

Further readings

To further expand readers' knowledge on the topics discussed in this chapter, it is suggested to explore the following additional resources:

- **Cypress API Documentation**: This is an excellent resource for understanding the details of Cypress commands, assertions, hooks, and aliases. You can access it at https://docs.cypress.io/api/api/table-of-contents.html.
- **"Writing Your First Test" on the Cypress website**: This guide will walk you through the process of writing your first test using Cypress, reinforcing the material in the chapter. You can find it at https://docs.cypress.io/guides/getting-started/writing-your-first-test.

These resources will give you a broader understanding and practical examples of the concepts you've learned in this chapter.

CHAPTER 4

End-to-End (E2E) Testing

Introduction

This chapter will focus on end-to-end testing using Cypress. Readers will learn how to test user interactions, work with different types of elements, and handle timeouts and retries in their tests. In addition, the chapter will provide examples and best practices to help readers create effective and reliable E2E tests.

Structure

In this chapter, we will discuss the following topics:

- Overview of E2E testing
- Testing user interactions
- Working with different types of elements
- Handling timeouts and retries

Overview of E2E testing

End-to-end (E2E) testing is a comprehensive and meticulous testing methodology implemented to ensure an application's seamless functioning across all interconnected systems and their components. It seeks to verify that the integrated components of an application function as expected together, providing an unbroken, efficient, and effective system for the end user.

These tests are designed to simulate a user's behavior and interaction with the application, assessing the entire course of actions from start to finish. Thus, E2E testing reflects a real-world usage scenario, ensuring that the whole system, not just the individual features, functions correctly and cohesively.

E2E testing is an essential part of any software development process. Using Cypress, we can write E2E tests that are easy to write, maintain, and debug. This will help readers to ensure that the applications work as expected and meet the users' needs.

The crucial role of E2E testing

E2E testing is integral to developing and maintaining a high-quality, reliable application. In addition, it offers several unique benefits that contribute to its importance in testing.

- **Real User Simulation**: One of the primary benefits of E2E testing is its ability to mimic the behavior of real users. Interacting with the application, just like a user would, helps uncover issues that unit or integration tests may miss. This ensures that the application is not only functionally sound but also user-friendly and intuitive.
- **Data Integrity**: E2E testing is designed to test data flow across the application, ensuring that the data remains consistent and accurate throughout all systems and components. This is crucial in maintaining the reliability and trustworthiness of the application.
- **Dependency-Check**: E2E testing also helps identify issues related to system dependencies. It ensures that all systems and interdependencies communicate correctly, which is essential for the application's overall functionality.
- **Boosts Confidence**: E2E tests provide a robust safety net for developers, boosting their confidence in the product. With comprehensive testing, developers can be assured that the end product will function as expected, minimizing risks and potential problems down the line.

E2E testing with Cypress: A new age in testing

Cypress is a cutting-edge, open-source JavaScript E2E testing framework that offers a refreshing alternative to traditional testing tools. Unlike Selenium, which is often used for web application testing, Cypress operates directly on the web app's runtime. This direct operation allows for more reliable results and significantly faster test execution, making Cypress a highly efficient and effective tool for E2E testing.

A standout feature of Cypress that enhances its E2E testing capabilities is its real-time reloading. As developers write tests, Cypress automatically refreshes these tests every time a file is saved. This immediate feedback loop significantly improves productivity, enabling developers to quickly detect and rectify any issues that may arise during the testing.

Here's an example of a simple E2E test in Cypress:

```
describe('My First Test', () => {
  it('Visits the Kitchen Sink', () => {
    cy.visit('https://example.cypress.io')
    cy.contains('type').click()

    // Should be on a new URL which includes '/commands/actions'
    cy.url().should('include', '/commands/actions')

   // Get an input, type into it and verify that the value has been
updated
    cy.get('.action-email')
      .type('fake@email.com')
      .should('have.value', 'fake@email.com')
  })
})
```

This test visits a web page, `'https://example.cypress.io,'` interacts with an element `'type'` on the page by clicking it and asserts that the page's URL has changed. Then Cypress inputs the `'fake@email.com'` value into the `'.action-email'` field and asserts that the new value of the field is `'fake@email.com.'`

Here's an example of the `cypress.config.js` file for end-to-end testing in Cypress:

```
const { defineConfig } = require("cypress");

module.exports = defineConfig({
```

```
  e2e: {
    setupNodeEvents(on, config) {
      // implement node event listeners here
    },
  },
});
```

As you can see, the configuration file for E2E testing in Cypress doesn't require additional parameters or configurations.

The E2E test is not limited to a single interaction and assertion. Multiple steps may be required to interact with various elements and change the application state. For example, we can add another chain to manipulate elements on a new page to continue the interactions and assertions.

For instance, we can utilize the `cy.get()` command to select an element by its class, then use `.type()` to input text into the chosen input field. Finally, we can verify the input's value using another `.should()` assertion.

The test structure should follow the **query -> query -> command or assertion(s)** pattern as a general guideline. It's considered a best practice to avoid chaining anything after an action command.

In conclusion, E2E testing is an essential part of ensuring the quality and reliability of the application, and Cypress provides a powerful and user-friendly platform for performing these tests. With its comprehensive command library, robust support for assertions, and convenient features such as real-time reloading and automatic waiting, Cypress makes E2E testing more efficient, effective, and enjoyable. And with the improvements introduced in Cypress 10.0, it's now even easier to set up, write, and run our E2E tests.

Testing user interactions

We engage with applications through various user interactions as we navigate the digital landscape. These may range from clicking buttons, filling out forms, and navigating dropdown menus to more complex operations such as drag-and-drop actions. Ensuring these interactions work as expected is paramount to providing a seamless user experience, and this is where Cypress shines. This section explores how Cypress allows us to simulate and test various user interactions.

Clicking and double clicking

Two of the most fundamental user interactions on a webpage are clicking and double-clicking. Cypress provides `.click() and .dblclick() commands to simulate these actions`. Let's see an example:

In a user journey, a single click could be utilized for multiple functions like opening a dropdown menu, submitting a form, or triggering a particular action. The Cypress `.click()` command allows you to replicate this interaction.

Let's assume we have a button in our web application with the class `.my-button`. To simulate a click action on this button, you would use the following code:

```
cy.get('.my-button').click();
```

This command uses `cy.get('.my-button')` to select the button, and the `.click()` command is chained to it to simulate a click action.

Double-clicking is another standard user interaction, especially in applications where a double-click triggers a different action than a single click. The Cypress `.dblclick()` command allows you to simulate a double click.

Suppose we have an item in our web application with the class `.my-item` that requires a double click to trigger its action. To simulate a double-click action on this item, you would use the following code:

```
cy.get('.my-item').dblclick();
```

Like the previous example, `cy.get('.my-item')` is used to select the item, and the `.dblclick()` command is chained to it to simulate a double-click action.

These commands will search for the specified element in a web application and simulate the desired action. One of the main advantages of using Cypress for these interactions is its automatic assertion that the element is actionable before the interaction. This means Cypress ensures the element is visible and not disabled, leading to more reliable test results.

Remember that these interactions might trigger network requests or changes in your application's state. With its automatic waiting mechanism, Cypress ensures these actions are completed before moving on to the following command, reducing the likelihood of flaky tests.

Typing into input fields

Input fields are fundamental to most web applications, capturing user data such as names, emails, passwords, and so on. Therefore, simulating user typing in these input fields is a significant part of end-to-end testing. The `.type()` command in Cypress allows us to mimic this action.

Let's take a common scenario where we have an input field with the class `.my-input` in our web application. To simulate typing a phrase, say 'Hello, world!', into this input field, we would use the following code:

```
cy.get('.my-input').type('Hello, world!');
```

In this command, `cy.get('.my-input')` is used to select the input field, and the `.type()` command is chained to it to simulate typing 'Hello, world!' into the input field.

Cypress also allows us to simulate the typing of special characters. Cypress got you covered if your application reacts to special keystrokes, like arrow keys. Here's how to type special characters:

```
cy.get('.my-input').type('{leftarrow}{rightarrow}{uparrow}{downarrow}');
```

This example simulates the left, right, up, and down arrow keystrokes in succession.

In some scenarios, you should slow down the typing to simulate a real user's pace more accurately or to test how your application behaves when the user takes longer to enter their input. Cypress allows us to do this with the `delay` option. This option slows down typing by a specified delay in milliseconds. Here's an example:

```
cy.get('.my-input').type('Slow typing...', { delay: 100 }); // delay is
in ms
```

In this case, there will be a 100-millisecond delay between each keystroke when typing 'Slow typing...'.

Simulating user typing with Cypress provides powerful capabilities beyond simple input filling. It brings you closer to the actual user behavior, increasing the reliability of your end-to-end tests.

Checking and unchecking boxes

Web applications often use checkbox elements to allow users to select one or more options from a set. Cypress's `.check()` and `.uncheck()` commands can simulate checking and unchecking these checkbox elements.

You first need to get the checkbox element to interact with a single checkbox. You can then chain the `.check()` or `.uncheck()` command to perform the desired action. Let's look at an example:

```
// Checking a checkbox
cy.get('.my-checkbox').check();

// Unchecking a checkbox
cy.get('.my-checkbox').uncheck();
```

In these examples, Cypress locates the checkbox with the class `.my-checkbox`, then checks or unchecks it depending on the command.

Cypress isn't limited to interacting with single checkboxes; it can also handle multiple ones simultaneously. Let's assume we have a group of checkboxes, each with a unique value, and they all share the class `.my-checkboxes`. Here's how we can check or uncheck several checkboxes:

```
// Checking multiple checkboxes
cy.get('.my-checkboxes').check(['choice1', 'choice2']);

// Unchecking multiple checkboxes
cy.get('.my-checkboxes').uncheck(['choice1', 'choice2']);
```

In the `.check()` and `.uncheck()` commands, we pass an array of values corresponding to the checkboxes we want to interact with. Cypress will then check or uncheck the checkboxes with these values.

This ability to manipulate multiple checkboxes simultaneously allows you to create more comprehensive and practical end-to-end tests, increasing the reliability of your testing suite.

Selecting options in dropdowns

Dropdowns or `<select>` elements are common in web forms, allowing users to choose an option from a list. Cypress simplifies interacting with these elements through its `.select()` command.

To select an option in a dropdown, get the `<select>` element first and then chain the `.select()` command with the option's value or its text content. Here's an example:

```
// Selecting an option
cy.get('.my-select').select('Option 1');
```

In this example, Cypress finds the dropdown with the class `.my-select` and selects 'Option 1'. This selection can be made by the option's value attribute or its displayed text.

In some cases, dropdowns allow multiple selections. The `.select()` command in Cypress also supports this functionality. You can select multiple options by passing an array to the `.select()` command, like so:

```
// Selecting multiple options
cy.get('.my-select').select(['Option 1', 'Option 2']);
```

In this case, Cypress will select both 'Option 1' and 'Option 2' from the dropdown. Again, these selections can be made by the options' value attributes or their displayed text.

The ability to manipulate dropdown selections extends the range of forms and user inputs users can test with Cypress, contributing to comprehensive and robust end-to-end tests.

Working with events

Interactive web applications rely heavily on events: clicks, hovers, key presses, and even custom events unique to the specific application. These events are essential for triggering certain behaviors and functionalities. Cypress enables us to trigger these events in our tests using the `.trigger()` command.

The most common events include user interactions like 'click,' 'mouseover,' and so on. We can simulate these interactions by triggering these events:

```
// Triggering a click event
cy.get('.my-button').trigger('click');

// Triggering a mouseover event
cy.get('.my-link').trigger('mouseover');
```

In the preceding examples, Cypress finds the specified element and triggers the indicated event.

Some applications use custom events to control unique functionalities. For instance, a third-party JavaScript library might dispatch a custom event to signal that it's finished loading or that a particular action has occurred.

Cypress allows you to trigger these custom events. Here's how:

```
// Triggering a custom event
cy.get('.my-element').trigger('myCustomEvent');
```

In this example, Cypress triggers the 'myCustomEvent' on the element with the class of `'.my-element.'`

Triggering custom events can be powerful when testing the integration of third-party libraries or any part of your application that relies on custom events.

The `.trigger()` command expands the scenarios you can test with Cypress. Whether dealing with formal events like 'click' and 'mouseover' or custom ones, Cypress ensures you can simulate and test these interactions in your E2E tests.

Drag and Drop

Drag-and-drop operations are common in web applications, allowing users to interact with elements visually, engagingly and intuitively. Although Cypress does not support drag-and-drop operations out of the box, we can effectively simulate them using a combination of mouse events.

To simulate a drag-and-drop operation, we essentially need to mimic the sequence of events that occur during the operation: a mouse down event on the element we want to drag, a mouse move event to the desired drop location, and finally, a mouse up event to release the dragged item. Let's illustrate this with an example:

```
// Simulating drag-and-drop
cy.get('.drag-item')
  .trigger('mousedown', { which: 1 }); //{ which: 1 } means left click
cy.get('.drop-area')
  .trigger('mousemove', { clientX: x, clientY: y }) // we need to
specify location
  .trigger('mouseup', { force: true });
```

In the preceding code snippet, we first locate the element we want to drag – `.drag-item` – and trigger a `mousedown` event to simulate the beginning of the drag operation. Then we find the target location – `.drop-area` – and trigger a `mousemove` event to affect moving the dragged item to this location. Finally, we trigger a `mouseup` event to simulate releasing the dragged item, completing the drop operation.

This approach leverages Cypress's ability to control different types of mouse events, allowing us to simulate complex user interactions like drag-and-drop. Remember that the element selectors (`.drag-item` and `.drop-area` in our example) will depend on your application's HTML structure. The same applies to any data you must include with the triggered events.

Hovering

User interactions with a web application are not limited to clicks and input. Hovering over an element is another meaningful action, often used to display additional information, show hidden menus, or highlight interactive elements.

Cypress provides us with a `.trigger()` method to simulate different events. Among these, the 'mouseover' event allows us to simulate a hover action. Let's look at an example:

```
// Simulating hover
cy.get('.hover-item').trigger('mouseover');
```

In the preceding example, we target the element with the class 'hover-item' and trigger a 'mouseover' event. This will simulate the action of a user moving their mouse cursor over the '.hover-item' element.

Simulating hover can be a powerful tool for testing. For instance, it can be used to validate whether hovering over an element brings about the expected change in the application's UI. These changes could range from simple effects, such as a color change or the appearance of an underline, to more complex ones, like the opening of a drop-down menu.

Consider an element that changes color when hovered over:

```
cy.get('.hover-item').trigger('mouseover');
cy.get('.hover-item').should('have.css', 'color', 'red');
```

In this case, we're simulating a hover over '.hover-item' and then asserting that the color of '.hover-item' has changed to red.

Sometimes, you can simulate a hover-and-wait scenario - like when a tooltip takes some time to appear after the user hovers over an element. This can be achieved with the `.wait()` command in Cypress:

```
cy.get('.hover-item').trigger('mouseover');
cy.wait(500);  // Wait for 500ms
cy.get('.tooltip').should('be.visible');  // Assert that tooltip is visible after waiting
```

Here we simulate a hover over `'.hover-item,'` wait for 500ms, and then assert that the '.tooltip' element is visible.

File uploads

File upload functionality is a crucial component of many web applications. Whether allowing users to upload a profile picture or import data from an external file, properly handling file uploads is key to a smooth user experience. Thankfully, Cypress allows us to test this functionality straightforwardly and efficiently.

Cypress introduced the `.selectFile()` command in version 9.3.0, simplifying the process of testing file uploads. This command allows you to simulate selecting a file or files in an HTML5 input element or dragging a file or files into the browser. Let's look at an example:

```
// Simulating file upload
cy.get('.file-input').selectFile('file.json');
```

In the preceding code snippet, we target the file input element with the class `'file-input'` and use the `.selectFile()` command to attach a file named `'file.json.'` By default, Cypress looks for this file in the fixtures folder of your project, located at `'cypress/fixtures.'`

This simplicity is one of the reasons why Cypress is preferred for end-to-end testing. It abstracts away much of the complexity involved in setting up such a test, allowing you to focus on the logic of your application instead.

The `.selectFile()` command also supports a range of options that provide additional flexibility in your testing. For example, you can give a file path, a buffer, or a blob as the file to upload. Also, multiple files can be uploaded at once by passing an array of file paths.

```
// Uploading multiple files
cy.get('.file-input').selectFile(['file1.json', 'file2.json']);

// Using a buffer
const buffer = ... // Get or create the buffer
cy.get('.file-input').selectFile(buffer);

// Using a blob
const blob = ... // Get or create the blob
cy.get('.file-input').selectFile(blob);
```

After simulating the file upload, you'll typically want to verify that the upload was successful. This will depend on how your application handles the uploaded files. Some applications display the uploaded file name, while others show a preview of the uploaded file. Here's an example where we check if the uploaded file's name is displayed:

```
// Simulating file upload
cy.get('.file-input').selectFile('file.json');

// Verifying the file upload
cy.get('.file-name').should('contain', 'file.json');
```

Keyboard interactions

The interaction with web applications isn't limited to just the mouse. Users often utilize the keyboard for navigation, form filling, triggering shortcuts, and more. Therefore, testing these keyboard interactions becomes essential to ensure a comprehensive user experience.

Cypress provides a simple way to simulate keyboard key presses using the `.type()` command. This ability extends beyond input fields and can test keyboard shortcuts, navigations, and more.

Cypress's `.type()` command allows us to simulate typing into an element. While it's commonly used with input fields, it can also be utilized on other elements to simulate key presses. Let's look at an example:

```
// Simulating 'Ctrl + C' shortcut
cy.get('body').type('{ctrl}{c}');
```

In this example, we target the 'body' element and simulate pressing the 'Ctrl + C' keyboard shortcut. This is because `{ctrl}` and `{c}` are special characters in Cypress that represent the 'Ctrl' and 'C' keys, respectively.

Cypress supports a range of special characters representing various keys on the keyboard. For example, `{enter}`, `{esc}`, `{tab}`, `{uparrow}`, `{downarrow}`, `{leftarrow}`, `{rightarrow}`, and so on. These can be used to simulate key presses of the respective keys.

We can chain special characters together to trigger keyboard shortcuts as we did with `{ctrl}{c}`. This can be used to test if keyboard shortcuts in your application are working as expected.

```
// Simulating 'Ctrl + Alt + Delete' shortcut
cy.get('body').type('{ctrl}{alt}{del}');
```

Navigation within the application using the keyboard, particularly arrow keys, is a standard user interaction, especially in applications with complex interfaces or accessibility needs. Here is an example of how we could test such functionality:

```
// Simulating navigation with arrow keys
cy.get('.my-element').type('{uparrow}{uparrow}{rightarrow}');
```

In the preceding example, we're simulating two 'Up Arrow' key presses followed by a 'Right Arrow' key press.

Scrolling

Scrolling is a fundamental interaction that almost every web user performs, and ensuring your web application handles it correctly is vital. For example, different elements may become visible or hidden as a user scrolls, and this dynamic behavior needs to be tested. Also, infinite scrolling pages with 'Scroll to Top' or 'Scroll to Bottom' buttons are common, and testing these interactions is necessary to ensure they function as expected.

Cypress provides the `.scrollTo()` command to simulate scrolling, making it easy for us to write tests for such interactions.

The `.scrollTo()` command in Cypress allows us to scroll an element into view. This command scrolls the window or element to a specific position. Cypress can scroll to a particular position or part of the element like 'top,' 'center,' 'bottom,' 'left,' and 'right.'

Here's a simple example:

```
// Scrolling to the bottom of an element
cy.get('.scroll-item').scrollTo('bottom');
```

In this example, Cypress will find the `.scroll-item` element and scroll to the bottom of its scrollable ancestor element.

If you want to scroll to a specific position, you can pass coordinates (x, y) to the `.scrollTo()` function:

```
// Scrolling to a specific position
cy.get('.scroll-item').scrollTo(250, 450);
```

In this case, Cypress will scroll the `.scroll-item` element to its scrollable ancestor element's position (250, 450).

You can specify the direction of the scroll using the 'x' or 'y' options:

```
// Scrolling in the 'x' direction
cy.get('.scroll-item').scrollTo('center', { axis: 'x' });

// Scrolling in the 'y' direction
cy.get('.scroll-item').scrollTo('center', { axis: 'y' });
```

In the first example, Cypress will scroll the `.scroll-item` element horizontally to its center. In the second example, it will scroll vertically to its center.

Another command that simulates scrolling is `.scrollIntoView().` This is a Cypress command that scrolls an element into view. It can be used to scroll the window or a specific element, and it can be chained with other commands to create complex test cases.

To use `cy.scrollIntoView()`, you first need to get a reference to the element that you want to scroll to. This can be done using the `cy.get()` command. Once you have a reference to the element, you can call the `cy.scrollIntoView()` command on it.

The `cy.scrollIntoView()` command takes a number of options, which can be used to control how the scrolling is performed. The most common options are:

- `easing`: This option specifies the easing function to use for the scroll animation. The default value is `swing`, but you can also use `linear`.
- `duration`: This option specifies the duration of the scroll animation in milliseconds. The default value is `0`, which means that the scroll animation will be performed as quickly as possible.
- `offset`: This option specifies an offset to scroll by after the element has been scrolled into view. The offset is specified as an object with top and left properties: `{top: 0, left: 0}`

The following example shows how to use the `cy.scrollIntoView()` command to scroll to a footer element:

```
cy.get('footer').scrollIntoView();
```

This will scroll the window so that the footer element is visible.

You can also use the `cy.scrollIntoView()` command to scroll to a specific position within an element. For example, the following example shows how to scroll to the bottom of a scrollable element:

```
cy.get('.scrollable-element').scrollIntoView('bottom');
```

This will scroll the `.scrollable-element` element so that its bottom is visible.

Scrolling may seem trivial to test, but in complex web applications, incorrect scrolling behavior can lead to a poor user experience. By simulating and testing scrolling interactions using Cypress, we can ensure our application provides users with a smooth and expected scrolling experience.

Right clicking

Right-clicking is another typical interaction in web applications. The behavior upon right-clicking can vary based on the context, such as displaying context menus or additional options. For instance, right-clicking in a text editor could bring up options for copying and pasting text, while right-clicking a graphic element in a design tool might show options for resizing or repositioning the element. Ensuring your application responds correctly to right-click events is crucial for maintaining a seamless and intuitive user experience.

Cypress provides us with the `.rightclick()` command, allowing us to simulate a right-click action and test the resulting behavior.

Cypress's `.rightclick()` command can simulate a right-click action on a specific element. Here's a simple usage:

```
// Simulating a right click
cy.get('.context-menu-item').rightclick();
```

In this example, Cypress will find the `.context-menu-item` element and simulate a right-click.

Just like with the `.click()` function, you can also pass an options object to `.rightclick()` to simulate right-clicking with modifier keys:

```
// Simulating a right click with the control key pressed
cy.get('.context-menu-item').rightclick({ctrlKey: true});
```

In this case, Cypress simulates a right-click the `.context-menu-item` while the control key is pressed.

One common use of right-clicking in web applications is to open context menus. You can use Cypress to both simulate the right click to open the menu and then interact with the options in the menu:

```
// Simulating a right click to open a context menu and selecting an op-
tion
cy.get('.context-menu-item').rightclick();
cy.get('.context-menu-option').contains('Option 1').click();
```

In this example, after Cypress simulates the right click to open the context menu, it finds the option labeled 'Option 1' and clicks it. This allows you to thoroughly test the behavior and functionality of your application's context menus.

Just like left-clicking, right-clicking is a vital interaction in many web applications. Simulating and testing right-click behavior helps ensure your application behaves correctly and provides a seamless user experience. With Cypress's `.rightclick()` command, simulating and testing these interactions is straightforward and efficient.

Form interactions

Form interactions are critical to most web applications as they enable users to input data that your application can use. This could include anything from logging in to an account, submitting search queries, to completing an online purchase.

Form interactions typically involve various elements such as text inputs, checkboxes, radio buttons, dropdowns, and the submission of the form itself. As such, testing forms can be quite complex due to the various elements and scenarios involved, but Cypress makes this process much simpler and more efficient.

- **Text input:**

Text inputs are the most common form of data entry on the web. They allow users to input alphanumeric data.

In Cypress, you can simulate typing into a text input field using the `.type()` command:

```
// Typing into a text input field
cy.get('input[name="username"]').type('myUsername');
```

In this example, Cypress will find the input field with the `name` attribute equal to "username" and type "myUsername" into it.

- **Checkbox selection:**

Checkboxes are form elements that allow users to select one or multiple options from a list. The `.check()` command can be used to simulate checking a checkbox:

```
// Checking a checkbox
cy.get('input[name="terms"]').check();
```

In this example, Cypress will find the checkbox with the `name` attribute equal to "terms" and check it.

- **Radio button selection:**

Radio buttons are similar to checkboxes but only allow the user to select one option from a group. Cypress uses the `.check()` command to select a radio button:

```
// Selecting a radio button
```

```
cy.get('input[value="option1"]').check();
```

In this example, Cypress will select the radio button with the `value` attribute equal to "option1".

- **Form submission:**

Submitting a form is the final step in most form interactions. This is typically done using a submit button. Cypress can simulate this action with the `.submit()` command:

```
// Submitting a form
cy.get('form').submit();
```

In this case, Cypress will submit the form.

Forms are vital parts of most web applications, and testing them effectively is crucial to ensuring a good user experience. Cypress provides several commands that make testing form interactions straightforward and efficient, allowing you to simulate real user input and ensure your forms work as expected.

Dealing with popups and alerts

Web applications often use Popups and alerts to notify the user of some action, request confirmation or provide interactive feedback. Cypress enables us to handle JavaScript alerts, popups, and confirmations programmatically. In addition, it can automatically deal with these, which can be particularly handy when you are automating tests and want to ensure that your tests stay on track for manual input.

Alerts are a simple way for a web application to provide information to the user or ask for confirmation. They are usually shown using the JavaScript `alert()` function, and they show a small box with a message and an OK button. Cypress can intercept these alerts using the `cy.on()` command:

```
// Auto accept alert popups
cy.on('window:alert', (str) => {
  expect(str).to.equal('Expected alert text');
});
```

In this example, Cypress sets an event listener for the `window:alert` event. When an alert is triggered, Cypress intercepts the alert message and automatically clicks the OK button. The message in the alert is also tested to ensure it equals the expected string.

Confirmations are another type of popup that ask the user to confirm an action. They are usually shown using the JavaScript `confirm()` function, and they show a small box with a message and OK and Cancel buttons.

Cypress can also handle these using the `cy.on()` command. However, for confirmations, we can control the result of the confirmation (either OK or Cancel):

```
// Auto dismiss confirm popups
cy.on('window:confirm', () => false);
```

In this example, Cypress sets an event listener for the `window:confirm` event. When confirmation is triggered, Cypress automatically clicks the Cancel button (as indicated by the `false` return value).

Testing popup alerts and confirmations are made simple with Cypress. In addition, it controls how your test script should handle these events, allowing for more robust and complete end-to-end testing. This functionality is essential for ensuring your application behaves as expected in real-world usage scenarios.

Working with iframes

Iframes are used in web applications for various reasons, such as embedding third-party content like YouTube videos, loading content asynchronously, or segregating parts of the website for security or style isolation. However, testing elements within iframes can be more challenging than dealing with elements directly in the document body.

The primary reason is the same-origin policy, which restricts scripts running on pages from different sites. This policy is crucial for web security but can complicate things when writing end-to-end tests.

While Cypress doesn't have built-in commands to interact with elements inside an iframe, it provides enough flexibility to create custom commands to circumvent this. Here's an example:

```
Cypress.Commands.add('getIframeBody', () => {
  // getting the iframe body
  return cy
```

```
  .get('iframe')
  .its('0.contentDocument.body')
  .should('not.be.empty')
  .then(cy.wrap);
});

// usage
cy.getIframeBody().find('#button-inside-iframe').click();
```

In this example, we are defining a new command `getIframeBody`, that retrieves the body of an iframe. First, the `cy.get('iframe')` command fetches the iframe element. Then we use the `.its('0.contentDocument.body')` to get the iframe's body. Next, the `should('not.be.empty')` ensures that the iframe's body is not empty before proceeding, thereby avoiding errors if the iframe's content hasn't loaded when the command runs. Finally, we wrap the body element with `cy.wrap` to enable further chaining of Cypress commands.

This custom command can then interact with elements within the iframe, just as we would with elements in the main document. The `cy.getIframeBody().find('#button-inside-iframe').click();` line is an example of how to use this custom command to click a button inside an iframe.

It's worth noting that since Cypress 10.0, the framework has added native support for interacting with iframes, making it easier to handle iframes in your tests without the need for custom commands.

End-to-end testing often involves interacting with various elements and components within a web application. The ability to test user interactions even within iframes is a testament to the comprehensive nature of Cypress' API. With it, you can ensure your application's response to user interactions is as expected, creating a more reliable and enhanced user experience.

Working with different types of elements

Web applications are a melting pot of various elements, each playing a unique role in the overall functionality. As an end-to-end tester, you'll interact with an array of element types, mimicking the user's actions as closely as possible. This section delves deeper into the most common web elements and learns how Cypress can interact with them.

Text elements

Text elements form the basic building blocks of any web page and include elements like paragraphs (`<p>`), headings (`<h1>` through `<h6>`), and labels. These are static elements that convey information to the user. In end-to-end testing, we often need to validate the presence and correctness of such text elements.

In Cypress, the `.contains()` command primarily interacts with text elements. This command gets the first element that contains the given text content. Here's an example:

```
// Find an element containing 'Welcome to our website'
cy.contains('Welcome to our website');
```

In the preceding code snippet, Cypress will look for any web element in the Document Object Model (DOM) that contains the text 'Welcome to our website.'

You can also narrow down your search to a specific type of element by chaining the `.contains()` command with the `.get()` command:

```
// Find a heading h1 element containing 'Welcome'
cy.get('h1').contains('Welcome');
```

In this case, Cypress will only look within `h1` elements. The `.get()` command retrieves all instances of `h1` elements, and then `.contains()` is used to filter these instances down to those containing the text 'Welcome.'

These commands, along with the many other commands provided by Cypress, allow for precise and accurate interaction with text elements in a web application. By using these commands, you can ensure that the textual content of your application is displayed as expected, contributing to a seamless and intuitive user experience.

Remember, as with any command in Cypress, commands will automatically wait until the elements are available in the DOM, thereby handling any asynchronous behavior tied to the loading or rendering of these elements. This results in more reliable and robust tests.

Furthermore, Cypress' automatic retries ensure that transient states do not result in test flakiness. This can often be a concern when testing text elements that may update dynamically based on user interaction or other asynchronous events.

Input fields

Input fields are the primary means for users to interact with a web application. These include various elements such as text fields, password fields, checkboxes, radio buttons, select dropdowns, and file upload inputs. Each of these element types serves a unique purpose, and as a tester, you need to validate that each of these behaves as expected.

Let's start with the text and password fields. These are the most common interactive elements, allowing users to input text data. In Cypress, the `.type()` command allows you to simulate typing into these fields:

```
// Typing into a text field
cy.get('input[name="username"]').type('myUsername');


// Typing into a password field
cy.get('input[name="password"]').type('myPassword');
```

In these examples, Cypress will find the respective input fields and type the given text into them. The `.type()` command triggers the same events that a real user typing in a browser would, such as keydown, keypress, and keyup. This ensures that your application behaves precisely when interacting with an actual user.

Note, however, that you must ensure your test scripts' security when dealing with sensitive data such as passwords. For example, hardcoding sensitive information directly into your scripts exposes a security risk. Instead, consider using environment variables or Cypress's built-in mechanism for managing sensitive data.

It's also worth noting that the `.type()` command can be used to simulate special keypress events, like pressing enter:

```
// Typing text and then pressing enter
cy.get('input[name="username"]').type('myUsername{enter}');
```

In this example, Cypress will type '`myUsername`' into the username field and then simulate pressing the enter key. This could, for instance, submit a form or trigger auto-complete suggestions, depending on how your application is designed.

Sometimes the input field is already populated with some data, and you may want to clear the input field. The `.clear()` command in Cypress clears the value of an input element. It is a particularly useful command for testing forms, as it allows you to simulate the user clearing the value of an input field before entering a new value.

To use the `.clear()` command, you first need to get a reference to the input element that you want to clear. This can be done using the `cy.get()` command. Once you have a reference to the input element, you can call the `.clear()` command on it.

The `.clear()` command is an "action command," which means that it will automatically wait for the element to reach an actionable state before clearing it. This ensures that your test will not fail if the element is not yet ready to be cleared.

The `.clear()` command can also be chained with other commands. For example, the following example shows how to use the `.clear()` command to clear the value of an input element and then enter a new value:

```
cy.get('#name').clear().type('John Doe');
```

This will clear the value of the input element with the ID `name` and then enter the value `John Doe` into it.

Working with input fields also often involves validation including checking whether an input field contains the expected value. This can be done using the `.should()` command:

```
// Type into a field and then verify its value
cy.get('input[name="username"]')
  .type('myUsername')
  .should('have.value', 'myUsername');
```

In this case, Cypress types '`myUsername`' into the input field and then checks that the input's value is actually '`myUsername`.' The `.should()` command is a powerful tool for asserting your application's state, helping ensure that it behaves exactly as expected.

Buttons

Buttons are indispensable elements in any web application, crucial in user interactions. Whether it's to submit a form, open a modal window, trigger some functionality, or navigate through the application, buttons are essential in facilitating these user actions.

Typically, user interaction with buttons involves clicking. Cypress makes simulating this straightforward with the `.click()` command:

```
// Clicking on a button
cy.get('button[name="submit"]').click();
```

In this example, Cypress will find the button with the name attribute "submit" and simulate a click action. Like the `.type()` command for input fields, the `.click()` command triggers the same events that a real user clicking in a browser would, such as mousedown, mouseup, and click. Again, this ensures a realistic testing scenario, mirroring user interaction closely.

But what if you need to interact with a button that's not immediately clickable? Maybe it's disabled until certain conditions are met (like filling out a form), or it's hidden until you hover over a specific page area. Cypress provides powerful features to handle these scenarios.

If a button is disabled until certain conditions are met, you can simulate those conditions before clicking the button:

```
// Typing into a field, then clicking a button

cy.get('input[name="username"]').type('myUsername');

cy.get('button[name="submit"]').click();
```

In this scenario, we're simulating a typical pattern where a button remains disabled until a user types into a specific field. So we first use the `.type()` command to simulate typing into the username field, and then we use the `.click()` command to click the submit button.

For a button that's hidden until you hover over a specific area, you can use the `.trigger()` command to simulate a mouseover event before clicking the button:

```
// Hovering over a section to reveal a button, then clicking that button
cy.get('.some-section').trigger('mouseover');
cy.get('button[name="hidden-button"]').click();
```

Here, Cypress first triggers a mouseover event on '.some-section,' which makes the button with the name "hidden-button" visible. It then simulates a click action on the button.

Cypress also allows the chaining of commands, providing a way to sequence interactions in a readable manner:

```
// Chaining commands

cy.get('input[name="username"]').type('myUsername').get('button[name="-
submit"]').click();
```

In this example, we first find the input field with the name "username," simulate typing 'myUsername,' then find the submit button and simulate a click. This sequence of commands closely replicates the interactions a user would make in the application.

Remember, Cypress's automatic waiting solves most synchronization problems for you. For example, suppose an element isn't immediately available for interaction. In that case, Cypress will automatically wait for it to reach an actionable state (for example, not being covered by another element, not being disabled, and so on) before interacting with it. This powerful feature allows you to write more straightforward and intuitive tests, closely resembling how a user would interact with your application.

Links

Links, also known as anchor tags, are crucial navigation elements in any web application. They steer users through different parts of a website or direct them to completely different sites. These essential elements shape the user's journey, keeping them within the application or leading them elsewhere.

User interaction with links is straightforward, involving merely a click action. Thankfully, Cypress has a command specifically tailored for this: `.click()`. Let's look at a basic example:

```
// Clicking on a link

cy.get('a[name="home"]').click();
```

In the preceding code snippet, Cypress finds the link with the name attribute "home" and simulates a click action.

In the same way as it does for buttons, the `.click()` command triggers a realistic chain of events such as mousedown, mouseup, and click, accurately replicating a real user clicking in a browser.

But what if the link is not immediately available or hidden within a dropdown menu or behind a hover event? Just as with buttons, Cypress provides features to handle such scenarios.

For instance, if a link is hidden within a dropdown menu, you can use the `.click()` command to open the menu before clicking the link:

```
// Clicking to open a dropdown menu, then clicking a link within it
cy.get('.dropdown').click();
cy.get('a[name="dropdown-link"]').click();
```

Here, Cypress first clicks the element with the class "dropdown" to open the dropdown menu. Then, it finds the link with the name "dropdown-link" within the menu and simulates a click action.

Or, if a link is revealed when you hover over a certain part of the page, you can use the `.trigger()` command to simulate a mouseover event before clicking the link:

```
// Hovering over a section to reveal a link, then clicking that link
cy.get('.some-section').trigger('mouseover');
cy.get('a[name="hidden-link"]').click();
```

In this scenario, Cypress triggers a mouseover event on the element with the class "`some-section`," which results in the link with the name "`hidden-link`" becoming visible. Cypress then simulates a click action on the now-visible link.

It's worth noting that Cypress's powerful automatic waiting feature is also applicable here. For example, a link is not immediately available for interaction. In that case, Cypress will automatically wait for it to become actionable (for example, not being covered by another element) before interacting with it.

In short, Cypress provides a robust set of commands and features that allow you to interact with links in many ways, mimicking the user's actions when navigating your application.

Images

Images are often the centerpiece of the aesthetic appeal of a web application. However, their purpose isn't just about enhancing the visual experience. They can also play an active role in user interactions, serving as clickable elements that trigger events or navigation, much like buttons or links.

In other scenarios, an image's visibility or position can affect the layout and appearance of the application. As such, it might be essential to verify these images' correct rendering and placement in an end-to-end test.

In Cypress, you interact with an image similar to how you would handle a button or link. The first step is locating the image element. As with other elements, you can find an image using the `.get()` command and providing an appropriate selector. A good practice is to use the image's `alt` attribute as it improves the accessibility of your site:

```
// Locate an image using its alt attribute
cy.get('img[alt="Profile picture"]');
```

In this example, Cypress will find an image element with the alt text "`Profile picture`."

After you've selected the image, you can interact with it. For instance, if the image is meant to function as a link or button, you can simulate a click event on the image using the `.click()` command:

```
// Click on an image
cy.get('img[alt="Profile picture"]').click();
```

Cypress will simulate a click action on the image with the alt text "`Profile picture`," just as a user might do.

You can also check an image's visibility or position:

```
// Ensure an image is visible
cy.get('img[alt="Banner"]').should('be.visible');

// Check the position of an image
cy.get('img[alt="Icon"]').should('have.css', 'position', 'absolute');
```

In the first example, we're using the `.should()` command to verify that an image with the alt text "`Banner`" is visible in the viewport. In the second example, we're checking that an image with the alt text "Icon" is absolutely positioned.

You can effectively interact with and test image elements in your web application by leveraging Cypress's various commands and assertions. This will help ensure not only that your site functions correctly but also that it maintains its intended visual appeal and layout consistency.

Lists

Lists are commonplace in web applications, effectively presenting information in an organized and easily digestible format. The two most common types of lists in HTML are unordered lists (represented by `<ul>` tags) and ordered lists (represented by `<ol>` tags). Unordered lists are typically used to group related items in no particular order, whereas ordered lists are used when the sequence of items is essential.

As an end-to-end tester, you'll often need to verify the content of these lists, ensuring that the correct items are present, in the proper order, and with the correct hierarchy. Cypress offers a range of commands and assertions to help you interact with and test list elements.

For instance, suppose you have a to-do list application and want to verify that a certain item is on the list. You can do this using the `contains()` command. Here's an example:

```
// Check whether a list contains a certain item
cy.get('ul.todos').contains('Buy milk');
```

In this case, Cypress will search for an unordered list (`<ul>`) with the class `.todos` and check if it contains the item '`Buy milk`.' The `contains()` command in Cypress automatically makes an assertion about the element's content, and your test will fail if the expected text is not found.

If you want to check the order of items in a list or assert multiple items, you can chain multiple `contains()` calls together:

```
// Check the order of items in a list
cy.get('ol.shopping-list')
  .contains('1. Buy milk')
  .contains('2. Buy bread')
  .contains('3. Buy eggs');
```

Here, Cypress will look for an ordered list (`<ol>`) with the class `.shopping-list` and check if the items '`Buy milk`,' '`Buy bread`,' and '`Buy eggs`' appear in that order. This is a simple way to test whether the items in your list are rendered in the correct sequence.

Remember, testing with Cypress is not just about verifying the presence or order of items in a list. Depending on the functionality of your application, you might also need to interact with list items, such as clicking an item to mark it as done or dragging and dropping items to reorder them. Like other interactive elements, Cypress provides a comprehensive set of commands to simulate these interactions.

Tables

Tables are an integral part of many web applications, often used to display complex data in a structured and easily understandable format. For example, HTML tables are created using a combination of `<table>`, `<tr>` (table row), `<td>` (table data), and `<th>` (table header) elements.

As an end-to-end tester, you'll interact with tables in various ways, including:

- Verifying the content of specific cells
- Checking the order of rows or columns
- Interacting with buttons or links within cells
- Testing the functionality of table controls, such as pagination buttons and sorting headers

Cypress provides a range of commands to help you interact with and test tables. For example, you have a user management table and want to verify that a particular user is present. You can do this using the `contains()` command.

```
// Verify the content of a specific cell
cy.get('table').contains('td', 'John Doe');
```

In this case, Cypress will find a table and check whether it contains a table data cell (`<td>`) with the content `'John Doe.'` The `contains()` command in Cypress will automatically fail the test if the expected text is not found.

If you want to interact with a cell that contains an interactive element, such as a button or a link, you can use the `within()` command to scope your selectors to elements within a specific cell:

```
// Interact with a button within a specific cell
cy.get('table').contains('td', 'John Doe').within(() => {
  cy.get('button.delete').click();
});
```

In this example, Cypress will find a table data cell (`<td>`) that contains the text 'John Doe,' then look within that cell for a button with the class '.delete', and click it. This is a helpful way to simulate user interactions with interactive elements within tables.

Remember, working with tables can be complex, especially when dealing with large tables, dynamic data, or complex interactive features. However, by leveraging the powerful commands and assertions Cypress provides, you can effectively interact with and test virtually any table aspect in your web application.

Scalable vector graphics (SVGs)

Scalable Vector Graphics (SVGs) are an XML-based vector image format for two-dimensional graphics. They are used extensively in web applications due to their high-quality rendering at any size or resolution. They can be static images, but they can also be animated or interactive.

Like other web elements, SVG elements can be interacted with in Cypress. However, the approach might vary slightly due to the nature of SVGs and their XML structure.

Consider an example where you have an SVG circle element in your application and want to simulate a click event on it. Here's how you can do it:

```
// Interact with an SVG element
cy.get('svg').find('circle').click();
```

In this case, Cypress will find the parent `svg` element, locate a child `circle` element, and trigger a click event.

You might face scenarios where the SVG elements are not directly interactable due to pointer-events properties. In such cases, you might have to trigger events explicitly. Here's an example of triggering a mouseover event on a rectangle within an SVG:

```
// Trigger mouseover event on an SVG element
cy.get('svg').find('rect').trigger('mouseover');
```

In this example, Cypress will find a `rect` element within an `svg` parent and trigger a 'mouseover' event. This can be handy for testing SVG interactivity, such as hover effects or tooltips.

While working with SVGs can be slightly different due to their nature, Cypress provides a versatile set of commands to efficiently simulate user interactions with

SVG elements. Understanding the SVG structure and the unique characteristics of SVG elements is key to effective end-to-end testing of applications involving SVG graphics.

Forms

Forms are a critical part of many web applications, serving as the primary mechanism for users to input and submit data. Forms encompass a range of different element types, including text fields, checkboxes, radio buttons, dropdowns, and buttons. Cypress offers a range of commands to simulate user interactions with all of these form element types.

Let's consider a typical scenario of a user login form, which usually contains fields for a username, password, and a button to submit the form. Here's how you might use Cypress to simulate a user filling out and submitting this form:

```
// Fill out and submit a form

cy.get('input[name="username"]').type('myUsername');  // Type into the username field

cy.get('input[name="password"]').type('myPassword');  // Type into the password field

cy.get('button[type="submit"]').click();  // Click the submit button
```

In this scenario, the `type()` command is used to simulate typing into the username and password fields, and the `click()` command simulates clicking the submit button.

When working with checkboxes or radio buttons within a form, you can use the `check()` command to select a specific option:

```
// Check a radio button

cy.get('input[name="gender"]').check('female');
```

Here, Cypress will check the radio button with the name `'gender'` and value `'female.'`

Dropdowns within a form can be interacted with using the `select()` command, as shown in this example:

```
// Select an option from a dropdown

cy.get('select[name="country"]').select('United States');
```

This command will select the 'United States' option from the 'country' dropdown.

Validating form behavior also often involves verifying form validation errors. For example, to check that a validation message appears when the username field is left empty, you could use a test like this:

```
// Verify form validation

cy.get('button[type="submit"]').click();  // Try to submit the form
without filling it out

cy.contains('Please enter a username.');  // Check for the validation
error message
```

By chaining these commands, you can effectively simulate and test various form interactions, ensuring your forms behave as expected when users interact.

Dialog and pop-up windows

Sometimes, web applications use new browser windows (or tabs) to display content or request user input. However, because Cypress operates within a single tab, it doesn't natively support multiple browser tabs or windows.

While there isn't a straightforward way to interact with these new windows directly, you can use Cypress's stubbing and spying capabilities to intercept the window opening command. This allows you to prevent the window from opening and assert that the command was called:

```
// Preventing window.open and asserting it was called
cy.visit('/page', {
  onBeforeLoad(win) {
    cy.stub(win, 'open').as('windowOpen')
  },
})
cy.get('#open-window-button').click();
cy.get('@windowOpen').should('have.been.calledOnce');
```

In this example, we're intercepting the `window.open` command that would normally open a new browser window. We're then asserting that this command was called when the button with the id 'open-window-button' was clicked.

Canvas

HTML5 Canvas draws graphics and animations on a web page via scripting. Although Canvas is a bitmap and doesn't have built-in behavior like other HTML elements, reader can still trigger events on it:

```
cy.get('#my-canvas').click();
cy.get('#my-canvas').trigger('mousedown');
```

This will simulate a click or mousedown event on the Canvas with the id '`my-canvas`.' Note, though, that Cypress cannot validate the drawn content within the Canvas.

Audio and video elements

Audio and video elements are interactive but often do not require direct user interaction in automated testing. However, in some cases, you might need to interact with the controls of audio or video elements:

```
cy.get('audio').invoke('play');
cy.get('video').invoke('pause');
```

This will simulate play on an audio element and pause on a video element. Note that you may be unable to verify the audio or video output, but you can check whether the media element's state has changed.

Working with different types of elements requires a clear understanding of how they function and how users interact with them. As you write tests, strive to mimic user behavior as closely as possible to ensure your tests provide value and help maintain the quality of the application.

Shadow DOM

Shadow DOM is an influential web standard developers utilize to encapsulate their JavaScript, CSS, and templating. This encapsulation allows for better component reusability, isolation, and encapsulation.

The shadow DOM is challenging to work with when it comes to end-to-end testing due to its nature of encapsulation. However, Cypress provides the `.shadow()` command, allowing you to traverse into an element's shadow DOM.

```
cy.get('.shadow-host').shadow()
```

The `.shadow()` command should be chained off a command that yields a DOM element which is a shadow host (that is, has a shadow root directly attached to it).

Let's say you want to find and click a button inside the shadow DOM. Here's how you can do it:

```
<div class="shadow-host">
  #shadow-root
  <button class="my-button">Click me</button>
</div>


// yields [#shadow-root (open)]
cy.get('.shadow-host').shadow().find('.my-button').click()
```

This simulates a user finding and clicking on the button inside the shadow DOM of the div with the class `shadow-host`. For example, the command `// yields [#shadow-root (open)]` means that this sequence of commands results in accessing the open shadow root of the `div`.

Custom Elements

Custom elements are a part of the Web Components model. They allow authors to define their elements with custom tags and behavior. You can interact with custom elements as you would with standard HTML elements:

```
cy.get('my-custom-element').click();
```

In this example, we're simulating a click on the custom element 'my-custom-element.'

Map Elements

Maps embedded in web applications, like Google Maps, usually involve complex interactions that are difficult to simulate with E2E tests. However, you can interact with certain elements, like buttons or markers, on the map:

```
cy.get('.gm-style .gm-control-active').click();
```

In this example, we're clicking on an active control on a Google Map. Map testing often involves verifying visual aspects, which might not be fully testable with Cypress alone.

Understanding these varied element types and how to interact with them through Cypress ensures that you can effectively simulate real-world user behavior, providing robust test coverage across the web application. Remember that some elements might not be fully testable due to their complex nature, but their main interactions can still be simulated and tested to ensure a functional user interface.

Handling timeouts and retries

Understanding how to handle timeouts and retries effectively is vital for a successful end-to-end test suite. It enables the tests to be resilient against minor delays and intermittent issues. It can be advantageous when dealing with real-world scenarios, like network latency or slow-loading elements. This chapter will dive deep into handling timeouts and retries in Cypress.

Timeouts

In Cypress, the default command timeout is 4 seconds. This means that Cypress will automatically wait 4 seconds for an element to appear in the DOM or an HTTP request to complete before failing the test. This setting is generous and should be sufficient for most cases. However, if you're testing a slow application, you might need to adjust this timeout.

Here's how to increase the default command timeout globally in your cypress.config.js file:

```
{
  “defaultCommandTimeout”: 10000
}
```

This configuration will set the default command timeout to 10 seconds.

Using the `timeout` option, you can also adjust the timeout for a specific command. For instance, if you have a specific API that takes a long time to respond, you can increase the timeout just for that API call:

```
cy.request({
  url: ‘/slow-api’,
  timeout: 20000
});
```

In the preceding example, Cypress will wait up to 20 seconds for the API to respond before failing the test.

Here is an example of a UI element timeout:

```
// This test will fail if the element with the ID `login-button` is not visible within 5 seconds.
cy.get('#login-button', { timeout: 5000 }).should('be.visible');
```

This test will first try to find the element with the ID `login-button`. If the element is found within 5 seconds, the test will pass. However, if the element is not found within 5 seconds, the test will fail.

However, remember that while it might be tempting to set a very high timeout to avoid test failures, a high timeout can also mean that your tests will take a very long time to fail when something goes wrong. Therefore, finding a balance that works for your situation is essential.

Automatic retries

One of the significant advantages of Cypress over many other testing tools is its automatic retry-ability. When a command doesn't initially succeed, Cypress will automatically retry the command until the command passes or the timeout period is reached. This feature makes your tests more reliable and less flaky.

For instance, consider the following test:

```
cy.get('#my-element').click();
```

Cypress won't immediately fail the test if the element with the ID `my-element` doesn't immediately exist in the DOM when the `cy.get()` command is run. Instead, it will keep retrying to find the element and click until it succeeds or reaches the timeout period.

Custom retries

Cypress 5.0 introduced test retries, a feature that allows you to automatically retry failed tests. When a test fails, Cypress can retry the test up to a specified number of times. This feature helps mitigate the impact of flaky tests that might fail intermittently due to temporary issues like network glitches.

You can enable test retries globally by adding the following to your `cypress.config.js`:

```
{
  "retries": 2
}
```

In the preceding example, Cypress will retry tests twice before marking them as failed. This means each test will have a total of three attempts to pass: the initial run plus two retries.

You can also set the number of retries on a per-test or per-hook basis using the `retries()` function:

```
it('retries 3 times', {
  retries: 3
}, () => {
  // test code
});
```

Best practices for handling timeouts and retries

Handling timeouts and retries is crucial for creating stable and reliable tests. Here are some best practices to consider when working with timeouts and retries in Cypress:

- **Use default timeouts and retries settings when possible**: Cypress has sensible defaults that work well in most situations. Avoid overriding these defaults unless you have a specific reason to do so.
- **Avoid arbitrary wait times**: It's tempting to use `cy.wait()` with arbitrary wait times to solve flakiness or slow-loading elements. However, this approach can lead to unreliable tests and an increased test suite runtime. Instead, rely on Cypress's automatic retry-ability and adjust timeouts as needed.
- **Be cautious with high timeout values**: While increasing timeouts can help mitigate flakiness in some cases, excessively high timeouts can lead to long-running tests and make it difficult to identify real issues. Instead, strive to find a balance between reliability and test execution time.
- **Opt for targeted retries**: If a specific test or API call is prone to flakiness, consider using targeted retries by adjusting the timeout for that particular command or enabling retries for that specific test. This will help improve

the overall stability of your test suite without affecting the runtime of other tests.

- **Investigate the root cause of flakiness**: While retries and adjusted timeouts can help mitigate test flakiness, it's essential to investigate and address the root cause of flakiness to create truly reliable tests. This may involve fixing issues in your application, optimizing loading times, or addressing network latency.

In conclusion, understanding and effectively handling timeouts and retries in Cypress is essential for creating reliable and stable end-to-end tests. By following the best practices and utilizing the features available in Cypress, you can ensure that your tests are resilient and adaptable to real-world scenarios.

Conclusion

This chapter delves into End-to-End (E2E) testing with Cypress, focusing on practical techniques and strategies. Readers gained an understanding of E2E testing as a whole and how Cypress can be leveraged effectively. The chapter covers testing user interactions, enabling readers to simulate and validate complex user actions. It also explores working with different types of elements within web applications, providing insights on handling elements such as forms, buttons, and dropdowns. Additionally, the chapter addresses the critical aspect of timeouts and retries, equipping readers with knowledge on handling scenarios where elements may take longer to appear or interact with. By leveraging examples and best practices, readers will be empowered to create reliable and efficient E2E tests using Cypress, ensuring the comprehensive validation of their applications.

In *Chapter 5, Component Testing with Cypress*, we will delve into component testing with Cypress. This chapter focuses on testing individual web components in isolation, exploring the concepts of component testing and its distinctions from end-to-end testing. Readers will learn how to set up their environment for component testing with Cypress, and step-by-step instructions will be provided. The chapter will cover writing component tests for popular web frameworks such as React, Angular, and Vue.js, emphasizing the testing of functionality and behavior. Additionally, best practices for component testing, debugging and troubleshooting strategies, and integrating component tests into the overall testing workflow will be discussed, enabling readers to incorporate component testing into their projects effectively.

Further readings

To further expand readers' knowledge on the topics discussed in *Chapter* 4, I suggest exploring these additional resources:

- **Cypress Recipes**: The Cypress Recipes section of the official Cypress documentation (https://docs.cypress.io/examples/examples/recipes.html) provides a wide range of practical examples and solutions for common testing scenarios in E2E testing. It offers valuable insights and guidance for enhancing your test suite.
- **Cypress Real-World Examples**: The Cypress Real-World Examples repository on GitHub (https://github.com/cypress-io/cypress-realworld-app) offers a collection of real-world applications built with Cypress. Exploring these examples can provide insights into how E2E tests can be structured and implemented in practical scenarios.
- **Cypress Best Practices**: The Cypress Best Practices guide (https://docs.cypress.io/guides/references/best-practices) provides comprehensive recommendations and guidelines for writing maintainable and efficient Cypress tests. It covers various aspects, including organizing tests, handling test data, and optimizing test execution.

These resources will give you a broader understanding and practical examples of the concepts you've learned in this chapter.

CHAPTER 5

Component Testing

Introduction

In this chapter, we'll explore the concepts of component testing with Cypress, focusing on how to test individual web components individually. We introduce component testing and discuss the difference between component testing and end-to-end testing. The chapter guides the reader through setting up component tests with Cypress, providing step-by-step instructions for configuring the necessary tools and libraries.

Readers will dive into writing component tests for popular web frameworks such as React, Angular, and Vue.js and demonstrate how to test the functionality and behavior of individual components. The component testing best practices will be shared to help readers create maintainable and practical tests.

Additionally, we'll discuss debugging and troubleshooting strategies for component testing, ensuring readers know how to resolve any issues they may encounter. Finally, the chapter will explain how to integrate component testing into the overall testing workflow, allowing readers to take advantage of component testing and end-to-end testing in their projects.

Structure

In this chapter, we will discuss the following topics:

- Introduction to component testing
- Component testing vs. end-to-end testing
- Setting up component testing with Cypress
- Writing component tests
  - Testing React components
  - Testing Angular components
  - Testing Vue.js components
- Best practices for component testing
- Debugging and troubleshooting component tests
- Integrating component tests into your testing workflow

Introduction to component testing

As our digital world grows in complexity, so do the web applications that power it. These applications comprise numerous small parts working harmoniously to provide a smooth user experience. We call these parts "components," and each plays a vital role in the functionality of a web application.

In web development, component-based architecture has become the norm, especially with the rise of libraries and frameworks like React, Angular, and Vue.js. Instead of viewing an application as a monolithic structure, this architectural style breaks down the app into reusable, modular components. A component can be as simple as a button or as complex as an entire navigation bar.

However, just like any other part of an application, components are prone to bugs and errors. To ensure they function as expected, developers write component tests.

Component testing, also known as unit testing in the context of UI, is a testing method that focuses on verifying the functionality of individual components in isolation from the rest of the application. Each component is tested separately, outside its parent application, and in a controlled environment. This strategy helps ensure that components function correctly in any situation or state, regardless of the state of the rest of the application. This early detection reduces the time and effort developers and testers require in the later stages of application-wide testing. Component testing effectively roots out errors in the initial stages, bolstering confidence in individual modules.

Component testing serves a critical role before integration testing in the testing process. It allows the team to pinpoint and tackle issues at both the component and integration levels independently before subjecting the entire application to comprehensive QA testing. This structured and compartmentalized approach enables a more efficient and effective testing process, leading to a robust and reliable end product.

Component testing aims to confirm that each component correctly implements the specified behavior. For example, a component test for a button could verify that when the button is clicked, it triggers the appropriate function.

Component testing plays a critical role in building reliable web applications. By validating each component in isolation, developers can catch and fix issues at the earliest stages of the development process, long before they become problematic. Not only does this improve the quality of the code, but it also speeds up the development process by reducing the time spent on debugging and troubleshooting.

Types of component testing

The application of component testing can vary greatly depending on factors such as project complexity, the utilized software development methodology, and the interdependencies among various components.

Typically, based on the intricacy of the application, component testing can be broadly categorized into two types:

- Small-scale component testing
- Large-scale component testing

Small-scale component testing

In small-scale component testing, individual components are tested independently, without any reliance on other parts of the application. This form of testing is most suitable for less complex applications.

For instance, consider a web application that provides practice questions for various subjects across different grade levels for a school. Each subject page is developed and tested individually, devoid of any dependence on the other subject pages.

Large-scale component testing

In contrast, large-scale component testing involves validating individual components with other components. When the input or output of one component is needed for testing another component, we refer to it as large-scale component testing.

When a component still under development is needed for testing, placeholder code snippets, referred to as STUB or DRIVER, enable testing.

Stubs and Drivers

Let's delve deeper into the concepts of Stubs and Drivers.

Both Stubs and Drivers are employed in component and integration testing to enhance testing efficiency.

Driver

A driver is a placeholder code that mimics the behavior of an absent component required to initiate the testing of a lower-level component. It serves as a calling function for the lower-level module when the original calling function is unavailable. In this context, a driver is considered a higher-level module.

Stub

On the other hand, a stub is a placeholder code that emulates the behavior of a missing component necessary for testing a higher-level component. A stub is a lower-level module that accepts inputs from the high-level module and returns the output.

To put it simply, suppose we have an application with components A, B, C, and D. Component B is the output from A and input for D, but neither B nor C has been developed yet. However, A and D are ready for component testing. In this scenario, a stub is created to replicate component B, and a driver is designed to mimic component D.

Timing of component testing execution

During the development phase of the Software Development Life Cycle (SDLC), developers conduct unit testing on each component before releasing a build to the Quality Assurance (QA) team for further testing. The initiation of component testing hinges upon the completion of unit testing. Subsequently, the testers undertake exhaustive testing, scrutinizing the functionality against the requirements and reporting any identified bugs.

The sequencing of testing stages places component testing after unit testing but before Integration testing.

Imagine working on a project that involves the development of a website. Upon completion of the website's pages, the development team performs a unit test before releasing the build to the testing team. The testing team then executes tests on individual pages of the website and furnishes the test results.

In this scenario, it's worth noting that completing all web pages isn't a prerequisite for the testing team to begin their tests. This flexibility allows testing to proceed in tandem with development, promoting efficiency and early bug detection.

Differentiating component testing and unit testing

Component and unit testing play crucial roles in the software testing landscape, yet they cater to distinct aspects of the process. Here's how they differ:

- **Purpose:** Component testing focuses on verifying individual components in isolation or conjunction, ensuring they fulfill the desired functionality. On the other hand, unit testing targets the validation of specific code sections, generally at the program level, against design specifications.
- **Who performs the tests:** The responsibility of executing component tests typically falls on the Quality Assurance (QA) team. Conversely, unit testing is carried out by the developers themselves.
- **Timing in the test lifecycle:** Component testing is conducted post-unit testing before integration testing. Unit testing, however, precedes component testing.
- **Testing methodology:** Component testing follows a black-box testing approach where the tester's internal code structure remains unknown. In contrast, unit testing employs a white-box testing method, allowing developers, who conduct the tests, to have intimate knowledge of the internal code structure.
- **Development stage:** Component testing occurs once the component's entire development is completed. Unit testing, however, is performed iteratively after each developmental step of the component.
- **Basis of validation:** Validation is based on test scenarios and functional specifications in component testing. Unit testing relies on design specification documents for validations.

With its flexibility and ease of use, Cypress has become a popular choice for component testing. It supports testing components from several popular frameworks like React, Vue, and Angular, and it provides powerful features that make writing tests a breeze. In this chapter, we'll explore component testing with Cypress in more detail, showing you how to effectively set up, write, and debug component tests.

Let's consider a simple example of a React component we may want to test. It's a button component that increases a counter when clicked.

Here's our component:

```
// CounterButton.js
import React, { useState } from 'react';

function CounterButton() {
  const [count, setCount] = useState(0);

  return (
    <button onClick={() => setCount(count + 1)}>
      Clicked {count} times
    </button>
  );
}

export default CounterButton;
```

In component testing, we want to ensure this button behaves as expected in isolation from the rest of the application. We will write a test to verify that:

- The button displays the correct initial state ("Clicked 0 times").
- The button's count increases by one each time it is clicked.

These tests will help us catch any regressions in the CounterButton component's functionality as we continue to develop our application.

Here's an example of how you might test the CounterButton component:

```
describe('CounterButton', () => {
  it('displays the correct initial state', () => {
```

```
    cy.mount(<CounterButton />);
    cy.contains('button', 'Clicked 0 times');
  });

  it('increments the count when clicked', () => {
    cy.mount(<CounterButton />);
    cy.get('button').click();
    cy.contains('button', 'Clicked 1 times');
  });
});
```

In these tests, we use `cy.mount()` to render the CounterButton component in the test runner's DOM. Then we can use standard Cypress commands to interact with the component and make assertions about its behavior.

Component testing vs end-to-end testing

In the broad software testing ecosystem, two primary types of testing methodologies emerge component testing and end-to-end testing. They hold specific positions in the software testing life cycle, each offering unique insights into the application's performance, functionality, and reliability. To fully appreciate their roles, delving into their definitions, functionalities, and differences is essential.

Component testing

Component testing, often known as module testing, focuses on scrutinizing individual elements of a web application in an isolated environment. It's akin to examining the cogs of a machine one by one. These "components" could be single functions, user interface elements, or even whole web pages in the context of a web application.

Think about an e-commerce website, for instance. Component testing would entail a separate examination of each part of the site, such as the product catalogue, the shopping cart, the checkout process, and the payment gateway, in an isolated environment.

Component testing steps into the spotlight early in the testing life cycle, taking place after the unit testing phase. It identifies and rectifies issues within the components before the modules are integrated and subject to further tests.

End-to-end testing

As the name suggests, end-to-end testing ensures the application works seamlessly from start to finish, testing the data flow across the application and verifying that every integrated component interacts as it should in a real-world scenario.

Back to our e-commerce example, end-to-end testing would involve creating test scenarios that mimic a real user's behavior, such as logging into a user account, browsing products, adding items to the shopping cart, proceeding to checkout, making payment, and logging out. This comprehensive testing strategy mimics the user's experience to ensure the entire process functions as intended.

End-to-end testing assumes its role near the end of the testing life cycle, providing a safety net before the web application is introduced into the production environment.

The comparison of these two testing types is summarized in *Table* 5.1.

Criteria	**Component Testing**	**End-to-End Testing**
Main Focus	Verifying individual components in isolation	Testing the complete functionality of an application
Timing	Conducted early in the testing life cycle	Performed later in the testing life cycle
Scope	Limited to individual components	Broad, covering all components, integrated
Tester's Role	Requires understanding of the component's functionality	Requires comprehension of the entire application flow
Example	Testing the functionality of a Button	Testing the entire shopping process from browsing to checkout

Table 5.1: *Component Testing vs. End-to-End Testing: A Comparative Analysis*

We can create a robust testing strategy by grasping the purpose and unique benefits of both component testing and end-to-end testing. While component testing ensures that each part of the web application operates correctly in isolation, end-to-end testing verifies the seamless interaction between these components, delivering a flawless user experience. Together, these testing strategies form a cohesive, comprehensive approach to guarantee the quality and reliability of web applications.

Setting up component testing with Cypress

Cypress Component Testing employs the same test runner, commands, and API you are accustomed to for End-to-End testing; however, it explicitly targets individual components.

A notable distinction between component and end-to-end testing in Cypress lies in the environment setup. In Component Testing, your components are constructed using a development server instead of rendered within the entire website context. This strategy results in more rapid tests and reduces dependencies on the broader infrastructure, increasing efficiency compared to end-to-end tests traversing the same code paths.

The API of Cypress has been designed with a user-centric perspective in mind. It aims to test anything that can be rendered on a web page, making it widely applicable. Regardless of the testing framework you're coming from, you'll find the API approachable and intuitive.

Setting component testing with Cypress is a simple process. You don't need to do anything additional, as Cypress will automatically guide you through the setup process and configuration while you select this option.

I want to remind you how to get started with Cypress. To begin using Cypress, you need to install it in your project. If you haven't already done so, you can add it to your project with the following npm command:

```
npm install cypress --save-dev
```

After installation, you can open Cypress with the following command:

```
npx cypress open
```

This command opens the Cypress Test Runner, where you can manage and run your tests.

Cypress v10 introduces a more streamlined approach to setting up component testing. Unlike previous versions, it does not require additional libraries to set up component tests. This new approach allows you to write component tests like end-to-end tests, with a few extra steps for mounting components.

Each time you initiate Cypress, you'll be greeted with the familiar **`Welcome to Cypress!`** page. This page allows you to configure either End-to-End testing or Component testing. The process of setting up End-to-End testing was thoroughly explored in *Chapter 2, Setting Up the Development Environment* of this book. The procedure for configuring Component testing mirrors that of End-to-End testing. Upon encountering the **`Welcome to Cypress!`** page, selecting **`Component Testing`** will launch the configuration wizard.

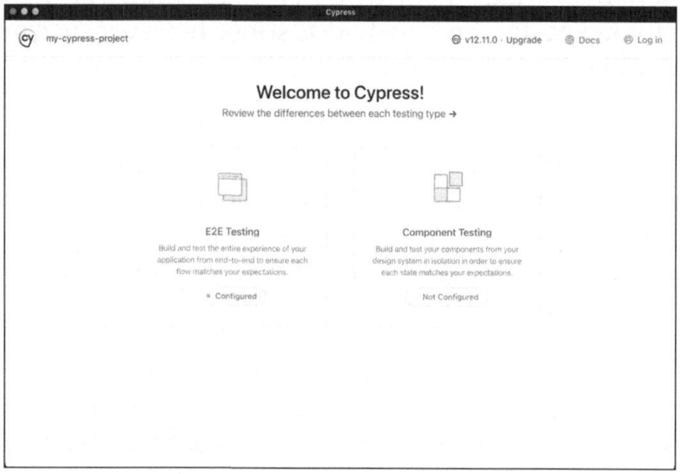

Figure 5.1*: "Welcome to Cypress!" page*

The Project Setup screen automatically detects your framework and bundler. In the next chapter, we will detail each configuration process for each Front-end framework like React, Angular, and Vue: "Writing Component Tests."

Writing component tests

Before embarking on writing component tests, it's imperative to have the application code readily available on your local machine. Component testing applies to applications built using any modern framework, such as React, Angular, and Vue. Cypress necessitates information about the Front-end framework and the bundler for the proper configuration of component testing.

In the realm of modern web applications, the bundler's role is indeed crucial. It performs the converter function, transforming the code you've crafted into syntax the browser can interpret and execute.

Typically, if your front-end framework has been established using the scaffold commands, Cypress will detect both the framework and the bundler automatically. However, if your team has integrated custom configurations, you'll need to fine-tune the Cypress configuration to align with your project for the correct setup of Cypress component testing.

In this book's context, we're assuming that you've utilized the scaffold commands to configure your Front-end framework and bundler. With this groundwork laid, we're set to delve into the process of writing component tests with the assistance of Cypress and contemporary frameworks.

Scaffold React Application

Before diving into the nuances of component testing, one must have a foundational grasp of the application structure and its intricacies. Cypress, being a versatile testing tool, can seamlessly integrate with applications constructed using prominent frameworks such as React, Angular, and Vue. However, the specifics of each framework bring about unique considerations. For the purpose of this chapter, we will predominantly focus on React, one of the most widely used frameworks today.

Let's embark on setting up a new React application. React provides a command-line tool named `create-react-app` that scaffolds a new application without the need for any build configuration.

```
npx create-react-app my-react-app
cd my-react-app
npm start
```

Executing the preceding commands will:

1. Create a new React application in a directory named `my-react-app`.
2. Change the current directory to the newly created application.
3. Start the development server to run the application.

Upon successfully running the commands, your default browser should automatically open, displaying a welcome screen of the React application.

The React App Structure

It's essential to familiarize yourself with the structure generated by `create-react-app`:

`public/`: This directory contains static files like index.html, which serves as the entry point of your application.

`src/`: This directory contains the main application code, including components, styles, and tests.

`node_modules/`: Houses the dependencies and libraries.

`package.json`: Enumerates the dependencies and scripts related to the project.

`README.md`: Offers a basic introduction and setup instructions.

Essential Configuration for Cypress Component Testing

Component testing in Cypress necessitates some essential configurations that are attuned to React. In the context of React, we often use Webpack as a module bundler and Babel for transpiling our JSX and ES6 code.

First, let's install Cypress:

```
npm install cypress --save-dev
```

Then open Cypress to continue component testing configuration.

```
npx cypress open
```

At first glance, preparing a React application for Cypress component testing may seem overwhelming, but it can become a seamless process if you break it down step by step. It is essential to have a proper understanding of the React framework and its structure. As you progress through this book, you will discover the power of component testing and learn how to ensure that your React application is robust and free of unforeseen glitches.

Testing React components

As previously stated, initiating React component testing requires selecting the **`Component Testing`** option on the **`Welcome to Cypress!`** page (refer to *Figure* 5.1). The subsequent page will be displayed once **`Component Testing`** is selected (*Figure* 5.2).

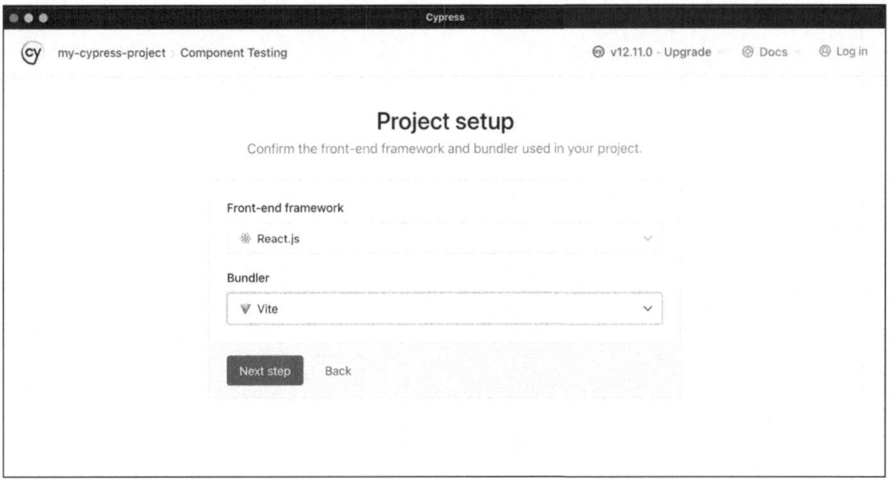

Figure 5.2: *"Project Setup" page with detected Front-end framework and Bundler*

As previously noted, Cypress can recognize the Front-end frameworks and Bundler in use. However, if your existing framework or bundler differs from what Cypress identified, you can adjust it by choosing from the dropdown options provided (refer to *Figure* 5.3).

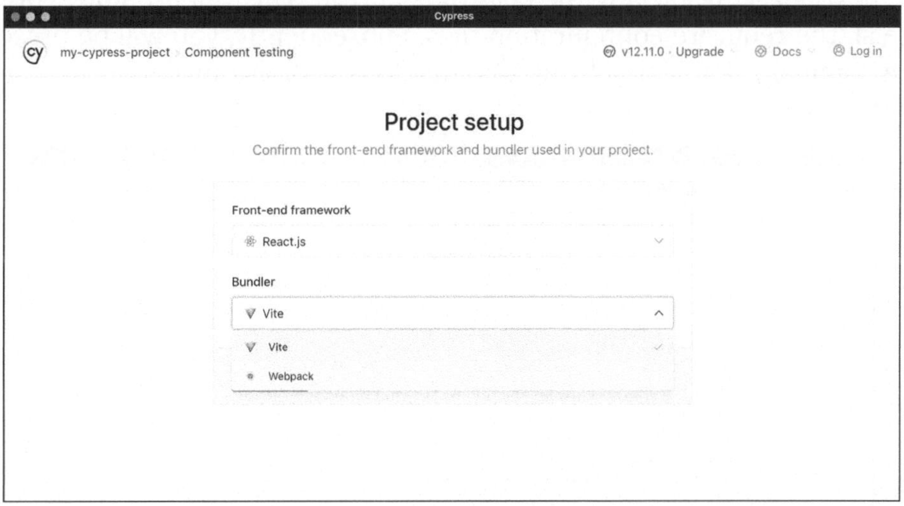

Figure 5.3: **`Project Setup`** *page with custom Bundler*

If you're sure about your chosen options, proceed by clicking the **`Next step`** button. Subsequently, you must patiently wait as the necessary dependencies are installed (*Figure* 5.4).

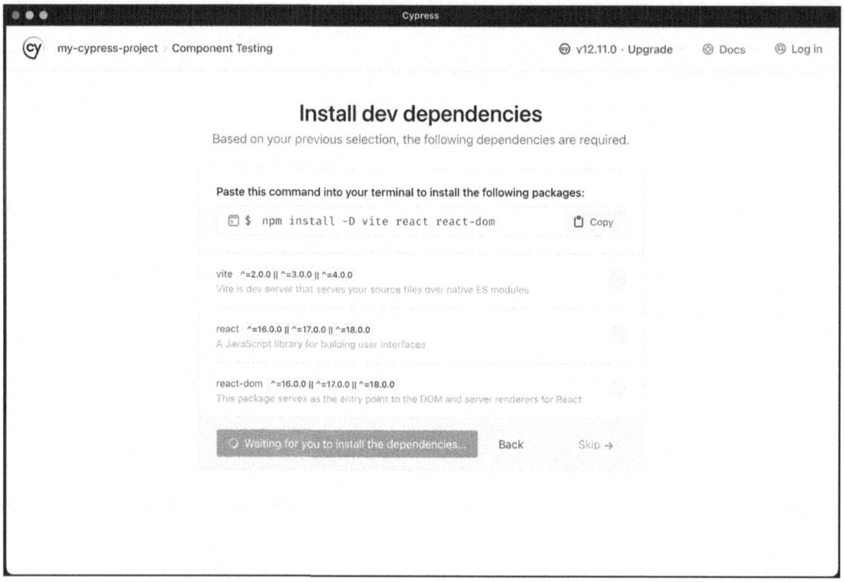

Figure 5.4: *"Install dev dependencies" page*

When all the required dependencies are completely installed, you can advance to the next phase by clicking the **`Continue`** button. This will prompt Cypress to create all the requisite configuration files. Subsequently, you will be presented with a summary detailing all the modifications Cypress made to your project (see *Figure* 5.5).

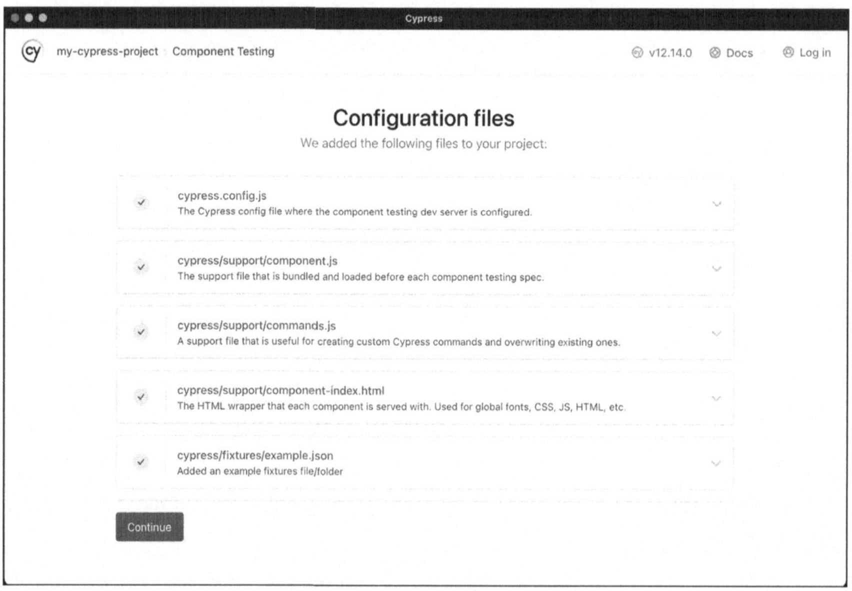

Figure 5.5: *Configuration files*

Upon the successful setup of component testing, your interaction with Cypress will proceed as during End-to-End testing. You will pick your preferred browser from the browser selection page and click **`Start Component Testing`** to launch the Cypress test runner.

At the moment, when the test runner comes into action, it won't discover any specs, primarily because we have yet to generate any thus far. Similarly, assume that we're yet to develop a component. Let's address that situation right away!

Crafting a component

With the project set up and Cypress primed for action, the stage is set for creating our first component to test.

We'll construct a `<Stepper/>` component, a simple and isolated piece with a single internal state aspect: a "counter" that users can increase or decrease.

Embark on this journey by launching your preferred code editor and setting up a new file in the following directory: `src/components/Stepper.jsx`.

```
import { useState } from 'react'

export default function Stepper({ initial = 0, onChange = () => {} }) {
  const [count, setCount] = useState(initial)

  const handleIncrement = () => {
    const newCount = count + 1
    setCount(newCount)
    onChange(newCount)
  }

  const handleDecrement = () => {
    const newCount = count - 1
    setCount(newCount)
    onChange(newCount)
  }
```

```
  return (
    <div>
      <button data-cy="decrement" onClick={handleDecrement}>
        -
      </button>
      <span data-cy="counter">{count}</span>
      <button data-cy="increment" onClick={handleIncrement}>
        +
      </button>
    </div>
  )
}
```

Our component's structure is relatively straightforward - a pair of buttons, one dedicated to decreasing the counter and another to increase it. A span tag proudly displaying the counter's current tally is nestled between these buttons.

First component test

With your component ready, it's time to pen our first test to affirm that the component can be mounted seamlessly.

To kick off the process, re-engage with the Cypress test application. In the **`Create your first spec`** page, select **`Create from component`**.

Subsequently, a modal window will make its presence felt, presenting a list of all the component files currently residing in your application (Cypress omits `*.config.{js,ts}` and `*.{cy,spec}.{js,ts,jsx,tsx}` files from this compilation). Expand the row for `Stepper.jsx` and opt for the Stepper component (*Figure* 5.6).

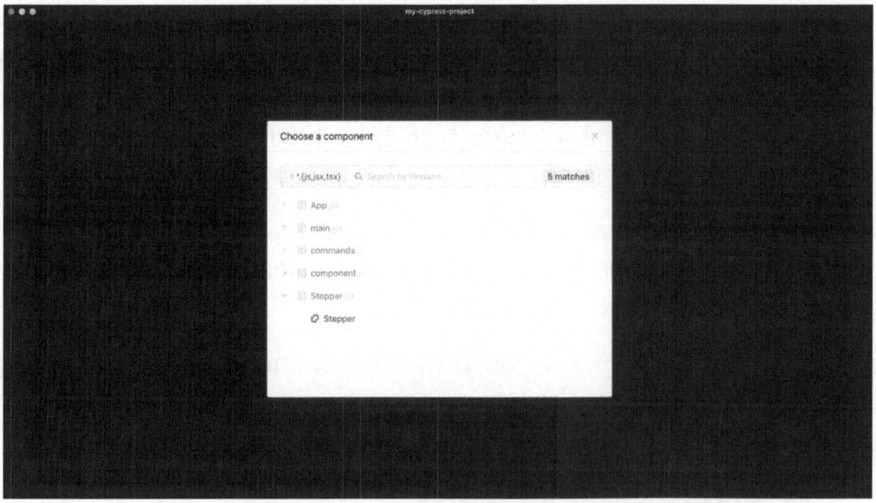

Figure 5.6: *Choose your Component*

A specification file is thus generated at `src/component/Stepper.cy.jsx`:

```
import React from ‘react’
import Stepper from ‘./Stepper’

describe(‘<Stepper />’, () => {
  it(‘renders’, () => {
    // see: https://on.cypress.io/mounting-react
    cy.mount(<Stepper />)
  })
})
```

Let's take a moment to dissect this spec. To start with, we import the **`Stepper`** component. Subsequently, we structure our tests utilizing the functions `‘describe’` and `‘it,’` which enable us to assemble tests into logical groupings within method blocks. These functions are supplied globally by Cypress. Hence there's no requirement to import them directly for usage. The top-tier describe block serves as a container for all the tests within a file, and each `‘it’` symbolizes an individual test. The `‘describe’` function receives two arguments, the first being the name assigned to the test suite and the second a function tasked with executing the tests.

Inside the `'describe,'` we've detailed a test employing the `'it'` function. The first parameter fed to it is a concise spec description, while the second is a function encompassing the test code. From the preceding example, we see that we've only put forward a single test, but shortly, we'll delve into how to incorporate multiple `'it'` blocks within a `'describe'` for a suite of tests.

The test runs a single command: `cy.mount(<Stepper />)`. The `cy.mount()` method mounts our component into the test application, setting the stage for us to begin conducting tests against it.

Transition back to the browser you previously launched for testing purposes, and you should now observe the `Stepper.cy.jsx` file in the spec list. Select it to watch the spec run its course (*Figure* 5.7).

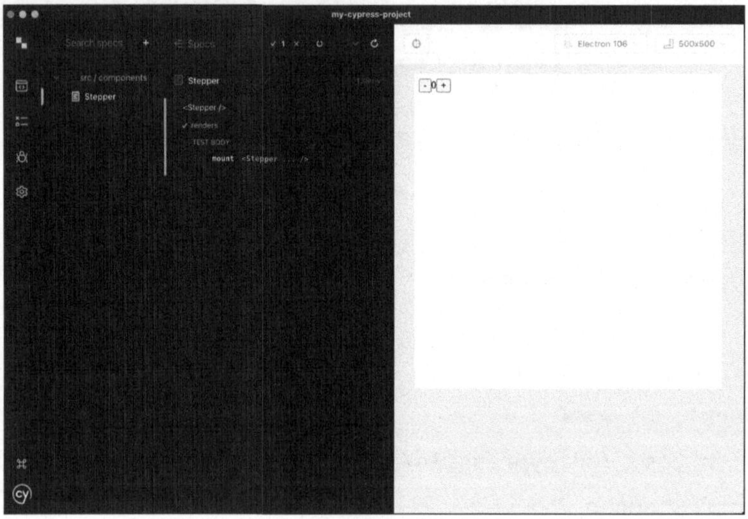

***Figure* 5.7**: *Running your first React component test*

Our initial test confirms the component can mount without issues in its default state. Should there be any runtime error during the test execution, the test will mark it as a failure, and you'll be presented with a stack trace leading you to the source of the issue.

A rudimentary test like the preceding one serves as a great kickoff point when testing a component. Cypress renders your component in a genuine browser, and you can employ all the usual techniques/tools you would use during the development process, such as interacting with the component within the test runner and utilizing the browser's development tools to inspect and debug both your tests and the component's code.

Now that we've successfully mounted the component, our subsequent step is to ensure the component's behavior is functioning as expected.

Locating elements and assertions

Starting with the core concepts, we'll look at how to select elements and perform assertions.

Imagine that the initial value of our Stepper's counter is "0". This can be changed by setting an initial count. We're going to create tests to verify these behaviors. This involves selecting the 'span' element displaying the counter value and ensuring that its textual content matches our expectations. In Cypress, we can select DOM items using methods like `cy.get()`, which allows us to provide a CSS-like selector.

Upon "getting" the element, we apply the 'should' assertion method to affirm that the textual content is correct. This can be achieved with the following code:

```
it('stepper should default to 0', () => {
  cy.mount(<Stepper />)
  cy.get('span').should('have.text', '0')
})
```

Here, `cy.get('span')` fetches all 'span' tags within our component. Given that we currently only have a single 'span,' this works perfectly. But, as our component evolves and we introduce other spans, this test could fail. So, we need to implement a more robust selector.

In the **`Stepper`** component, the 'span' tag includes a `data-cy` attribute:

```
<span data-cy="counter">{count}</span>
```

We use this attribute as a unique identifier for testing. We can adjust our test to employ a CSS attribute selector with `cy.get()`:

```
it('stepper should default to 0', () => {
  cy.mount(<Stepper />)
  cy.get('[data-cy=counter]').should('have.text', '0')
})
```

Now, even if we add more 'span' tags in the future, our test will continue to function correctly.

Incorporating props into components

Suppose we want to test a situation where the initial prop modifies the count from its default value of "0". We can pass props into the **Stepper** component through JSX in the `mount` method like so:

```
it('supports an "initial" prop to set the value', () => {
  cy.mount(<Stepper initial={100} />)
  cy.get('[data-cy=counter]').should('have.text', '100')
})
```

Here, we're passing an 'initial' prop with the value of '100' to the **Stepper** component when mounted. The test confirms that the counter's value is indeed '100'.

Testing interactions

But what about user interaction? So far, our tests have merely selected the element and mounted it. We should verify that the counter value adjusts appropriately when a user clicks the **increment** and **decrement** buttons. We'll simulate this user interaction using the `click()` command:

```
it('when the increment button is pressed, the counter is incremented',
() => {
  cy.mount(<Stepper />)
  cy.get('[data-cy=increment]').click()
  cy.get('[data-cy=counter]').should('have.text', '1')
})

it('when the decrement button is pressed, the counter is decremented',
() => {
  cy.mount(<Stepper />)
  cy.get('[data-cy=decrement]').click()
  cy.get('[data-cy=counter]').should('have.text', '-1')
})
```

In each test, we simulate a button press and then assert that the counter's value changes accordingly.

Testing React components with events

Finally, let's explore how we can use spies to test the `onChange` event. All state of the Stepper component is managed internally. Whenever the state changes, an `onChange` prop is used to notify the consumers of the changes.

While testing the components, we want to ensure that the **`onChange`** prop is called with the correct values when the increment and decrement buttons are clicked. Cypress Spies will help us accomplish this. A spy is a special function that tracks how often it's called and the parameters passed. We can pass this spy into the `onChange` event, simulate user interaction, and then check the spy to confirm it was called with the expected parameters.

Setting up the spies and binding them to the component would look like this:

```
it('clicking + fires a change event with the incremented value', () => {
  const onChangeSpy = cy.spy().as('onChangeSpy')
  cy.mount(<Stepper onChange={onChangeSpy} />)
  cy.get('[data-cy=increment]').click()
  cy.get('@onChangeSpy').should('have.been.calledWith', 1)
})
```

First, we create a spy using the `cy.spy()` method and give it an alias `'onChangeSpy.'` This alias allows us to reference the spy later in our test. Next, we mount the Stepper component and pass the spy into it. Then, we simulate a click on the increment button. Finally, we use the `cy.get()` method to retrieve our spy by its alias and assert that it has been called with the correct value. With this, our **`Stepper`** component is now thoroughly tested.

Testing Angular components

The Angular framework is known for its robustness and capability to build complex single-page applications (SPAs). Like any other application, testing Angular components is vital to the software development process.

The process of setting up the component testing for Angular components is similar to that described before for React components. We must select **`Component Testing`** on the **`Welcome to Cypress!`** page (*Figure* 5.1). And then, the Cypress Launchpad will guide us through the configuration process. But anyway, let's dive more profound as the Angular framework requires some additional steps to perform.

We must have an Angular app before diving into testing with Cypress. This section will guide you through the process of creating a new Angular application using the Angular CLI.

Angular CLI, or Angular Command Line Interface, is a powerful tool developed by the Angular Team to simplify the process of Angular development. With Angular CLI, you can easily create a new project, add different features to your existing project, or run various development tasks such as testing, bundling, and deployment. It provides a unified set of commands that act as a solid foundation for any Angular project, enabling you to focus more on the development than the setup.

To use the Angular CLI, you first need to install it globally on your machine. You can do this using the npm (Node Package Manager) command:

```
npm install -g @angular/cli
```

With the Angular CLI installed, you can now create a new Angular application. Use the `ng new` command followed by the name of your application, in this case, `my-angular-app`:

```
ng new my-angular-app
```

While creating the new application, you'll be asked a few questions regarding the setup. For our purposes, you can go ahead and select the default options.

After your new Angular project has been generated, navigate to the project's directory:

```
cd my-angular-app
```

Once our Angular application is set up, the next step is adding Cypress to our project. Installing Cypress in your project is as simple as installing any other npm package. We use the `-D` flag to install it as a development dependency:

```
npm install cypress -D
```

With Cypress successfully installed, let's go ahead and launch it for the first time:

```
npx cypress open
```

Running this command will open the Cypress Launchpad, a handy tool to guide you through configuring your project for Cypress, similar to what was described previously. Cypress will automatically detect the Angular framework and bundler used in the project and guide you through the configuration process:

install dev dependencies and generate all necessary configuration files. Once all configurations are done, you'll need to click on the **Start Component Testing** button to start building the component tests for the application. When the test runner appears, it won't find any existing specs as they haven't been created yet. However, there are no components as well.

Building an Angular component

Now that our project is set up and Cypress is installed, we still need a component to perform tests on. Let's create a simple component called **StepperComponent**. This component will have a simple counter-state that can be incremented and decremented by the user.

We will leverage Angular CLI to generate a new component. Run the following command in your terminal:

```
ng generate component stepper
```

After generating the component, let's modify it. Open the `stepper.component.ts` file and replace its contents with the following code:

```
import { Component, EventEmitter, Input, OnInit, Output } from
'@angular/core'

@Component({
  selector: 'app-stepper',
  template: `
    <div>
      <button data-cy="decrement" (click)="decrement()">-</button>
      <span data-cy="counter">{{ count }}</span>
      <button data-cy="increment" (click)="increment()">+</button>
    </div>
  `,
})
export class StepperComponent {
  constructor() {}
  ngOnInit(): void {}
```

```
  @Input() count = 0
  @Output() change = new EventEmitter()

  increment(): void {
    this.count++
    this.change.emit(this.count)
  }
  decrement(): void {
    this.count--
    this.change.emit(this.count)
  }
}
```

In this **Stepper** component, two buttons are included for incrementing and decrementing a counter and a span element to display the current value of the counter.

Now that our Angular component is ready, it's time to write some tests. We'll start with a simple test to ensure that the **Stepper** component can be successfully mounted.

Begin by creating a new spec file in the same directory as `stepper.component.ts`. Name this file `stepper.component.cy.ts`, and insert the following code:

```
import { StepperComponent } from './stepper.component'

describe('StepperComponent', () => {
  it('mounts', () => {
    cy.mount(StepperComponent)
  })
})
```

In this test, we first import the Stepper component. We then use the `describe`, and `it` functions to organize the tests. The `describe` block groups related tests together, while the `it` function represents individual tests. Note that Cypress provides these global functions, so you don't need to import them.

Within the `it` function, we briefly describe the test and define the test code within a function. Here, our test code involves just one command: `cy.mount(StepperComponent)`. This command mounts the **`Stepper`** component, preparing it for testing.

Now, it's time to put our test to work. Switch back to the browser you opened for testing, and you should see the `stepper.component.cy.ts` file in the spec list. Click on it to execute the spec.

Our initial test is a great start to ensure that the Stepper component successfully mounts without throwing any errors. If a runtime error is encountered during the test, the test fails, and Cypress will provide a stack trace that pinpoints the problem source. This basic test demonstrates the power of Cypress, it renders your component in a real browser, and you can interact with your component, use browser dev tools for inspection, and debug both your tests and your component's code just like you would during development.

With our component successfully mounted, it's time to examine its behavior to ensure it's functioning as expected.

Initially, the **`Stepper`** component's counter starts at "0". We can overwrite this initial count value and test the Stepper component in both scenarios: when the counter starts at "0" and when the counter starts at a different value.

To test these scenarios, we'll need to select the `span` element, which displays the counter value, and assert that the value is as expected. We'll use the `cy.get()` method to select items from the DOM and the `should` assertion method to verify that the selected element has the correct text value.

Insert the following test into your `describe` block right under the initial test:

```
it('defaults the stepper to 0', () => {
  cy.mount(StepperComponent)
  cy.get('span').should('have.text', '0')
})
```

Running this test should yield a passing result. Here, we select the span element using `cy.get('span')`, which targets all span tags within our component. However, if we add another span element in the future, this test might fail.

Let's mitigate this risk by using a less fragile selector. In our Stepper component, we've added a `data-cy` attribute to the span tag:

```
<span data-cy="counter">{{ count }}</span>
```

We can use the value assigned to the `data-cy` attribute, a unique id, for testing purposes. Update your test to select the span element by its `data-cy` attribute:

```
it('defaults the stepper to 0', () => {
  cy.mount(StepperComponent)
  cy.get('[data-cy=counter]').should('have.text', '0')
})
```

Component inputs

We should also test that the count input is properly reflected in the counter. This can be achieved by passing input to the `StepperComponent` through the mount method:

```
it('sets the initial counter value', () => {
  cy.mount(StepperComponent, {
    componentProperties: {
      count: 100,
    },
  })
  cy.get('[data-cy=counter]').should('have.text', '100')
})
```

Here, we're passing the input value of `100` for `count` to our `StepperComponent` through `componentProperties` in the mount method options.

Interactions with the component

Though we've successfully mounted our component and tested its initial state, we have yet to test user interactions with the component. For example, we need to ensure that the increment and decrement buttons function as expected.

We'll use the `click()` command, which simulates a user clicking on a DOM element. The tests for the **`increment`** and **`decrement`** buttons are as follows:

```
it('increments the counter', () => {
  cy.mount(StepperComponent)
  cy.get('[data-cy=increment]').click()
  cy.get('[data-cy=counter]').should('have.text', '1')
})

it('decrements the counter', () => {
  cy.mount(StepperComponent)
  cy.get('[data-cy=decrement]').click()
  cy.get('[data-cy=counter]').should('have.text', '-1')
})
```

Upon running these tests, you'll observe the counter incrementing and decrementing as expected.

Testing Angular component events

StepperComponent's state (the `count`) is managed internally. However, it also emits a `change` event whenever the state changes. As the developer, you want to ensure that this event is emitted with the correct values when the user interacts with the increment and decrement buttons.

We can use Cypress spies to validate this event. A spy is a special function that records how many times it was called and the parameters it was called with. We can use a spy to observe the `change` output, then interact with the component and examine the spy to verify it was called with the expected parameters.

Here's how you can set up a spy and bind it to your component:

```
import { createOutputSpy } from 'cypress/angular'

it('emits the change event upon incrementing', () => {
  cy.mount(StepperComponent, {
    componentProperties: {
      change: createOutputSpy('changeSpy'),
    },
  })
  cy.get('[data-cy=increment]').click()
```

```
  cy.get('@changeSpy').should('have.been.calledWith', 1)
})
```

In this test, `createOutputSpy()` creates an `EventEmitter` with a spy attached to its `emit` method. We pass the spied `EventEmitter` into our component when mounting it, then click the increment button. Finally, we use `cy.get()` to retrieve the spy (identified by its alias, `changeSpy`) and assert that it was called with the expected value of `1`.

Testing Vue.js components

Vue.js is a progressive JavaScript framework for building user interfaces. The framework is widely recognized for its simplicity and ease of use, making it an excellent choice for beginners and experienced developers.

One of Vue.js's core features is its reactive data binding system, which allows automatic and efficient updates of the rendered DOM when the underlying data changes. This is achieved through a system of reactive dependencies that only updates the DOM's necessary parts when data changes, making rendering highly efficient.

Vue.js uses a component-based architecture like other popular frameworks such as React and Angular. Components are reusable Vue instances with a name, allowing developers to create complex UIs by combining small, self-contained, and often reusable components.

Vue.js is suitable for a wide range of projects, from small interactive parts added to existing projects to complex, large-scale applications. It is open-source and has a vibrant and active community, ensuring its continued growth and development.

As we delve into this new journey of testing Vue.js components, our first step will be establishing a new Vue application. To swiftly get our app up and running, we'll utilize Vite, a build tool that significantly enhances the development experience. Vite is versatile and supports various frameworks, including Vue.js, React, and more. The setup remains consistent across these various frameworks.

To bootstrap a new Vue project using Vite, use the following command in your terminal:

```
npm create vite@latest my-vuejs-app -- --template vue
```

Once the command is executed, navigate into the newly created directory and install the dependencies:

```
cd my-vuejs-app
npm install
```

Having our Vue app ready, the following action on our agenda involves integrating Cypress into our project. Cypress is a robust end-to-end testing framework that ensures the reliability and stability of our application.

Let's install Cypress as a development dependency in our project:

```
npm install cypress -D
```

Now, it's time to open Cypress:

```
npx cypress open
```

The Cypress Launchpad will subsequently guide you through the steps of configuring your project, thus paving the way for thorough and efficient testing of your Vue components. The process will be similar to what was described before for React and Angular frameworks. The **`Project Setup`** screen automatically detects your framework and bundler, which, in our case, is Vue and Vite. Click **`Next Step`** to continue (*Figure* 5.2). Then Cypress installs all necessary dependencies and generates all configuration files. Once Cypress is set for component testing, we can run a test runner and start creating our first component (similar to React or Angular) and our first component test.

Building a Vue.js component

Now that our Vue project and Cypress are properly set up, we're ready to proceed, albeit with a tiny problem - we need components to test. To rectify this, let's construct a `<Stepper/>` component. This component will maintain a singular piece of internal state named **`counter`**, which users can either increment or decrement.

To create this component, open your project in your preferred code editor and navigate to `src/components/Stepper.vue`. Next, create a new file and input the following code:

```
<template>
  <div>
    <button data-cy="decrement" @click="decrement">-</button>
```

```
    <span data-cy="counter">{{ count }}</span>
    <button data-cy="increment" @click="increment">+</button>
  </div>
</template>

<script setup>
  import { ref } from 'vue'
  const props = defineProps(['initial'])

  const emit = defineEmits(['change'])

  const count = ref(props.initial || 0)

  const increment = () => {
    count.value++
    emit('change', count.value)
  }

  const decrement = () => {
    count.value--
    emit('change', count.value)
  }
</script>
```

Our component comprises a simple layout: two buttons flank a `span` tag. One button decrements the counter, the other increments it and the `span` tag displays the current value of the counter.

With our component ready, we can now focus on testing it to ensure that it mounts without any complications.

To embark on this process, return to the Cypress test application and select **`Create from component`** on the **`Create your first spec`** page (*Figure* 5.6). A modal will appear, showcasing all the components in your application. Choose the `Stepper.vue` component.

Doing so will generate a spec file at `src/component/Stepper.cy.js`:

```
import Stepper from './Stepper.vue'


describe('<Stepper />', () => {
  it('renders', () => {
    // see: https://on.cypress.io/mounting-vue
    cy.mount(Stepper)
  })
})
```

It's worth noting that you can also utilize JSX syntax to pen Vue tests. Refer to the Using JSX section for more information.

Let's deconstruct the spec file. Initially, we import the Stepper component. Following this, we structure our tests using the `describe`, and `it` functions. This approach enables us to categorize our tests into distinct sections. Since these functions are global within the Cypress ecosystem, there's no need for direct importation. The `describe` function operates as a container for our tests, and each `'it'` function embodies an individual test. The `describe` function requires two parameters: the name of the test suite and a function that executes the tests.

We employ the `'it'` function within `describe` to define a test. The `'it'` function also demands two parameters: a short description of the spec and a function containing the test code. Although our current example only has a single test, we will soon integrate multiple `'it'` blocks within the `describe` function for a comprehensive series of tests.

Our test contains a single command: `cy.mount(Stepper)`. This command will mount our component within the test application, enabling us to conduct tests against it.

The initial test we have constructed confirms that our component, in its default state, mounts without any issues. Should there be a runtime error while executing the test, the test will fail, and Cypress will provide a stack trace that leads you directly to the source of the problem.

Beginning your testing journey with a basic test, such as the preceding one outlined, is an ideal approach. Cypress brings your component to life in a real browser, permitting you to apply any techniques or tools you'd typically use during development. This includes engaging with the component through the test runner and utilizing the browser's developer tools to inspect and debug your tests, as well as the component's code.

Locating elements and assertions

In its default state, the Stepper component initializes the counter at "0". However, we have the option to override this initial value. To verify the functionality of both these states, let's devise a couple of tests.

We'll use a selector to access the span element encapsulating the counter to accomplish this. We'll then employ an assertion to confirm that the text value within the span corresponds to our expectations.

Cypress provides various ways to select elements from the DOM, including cy.get(), which we'll use here. This method allows us to provide a CSS-like selector.

Once we've procured the element, we apply the `should` assertion method to ascertain that it contains the correct text value.

Embed the following test within the `describe` block right after the initial test:

```
it('stepper should default to 0', () => {
  cy.mount(Stepper)
  cy.get('span').should('have.text', '0')
})
```

Upon returning to the test runner, you should notice that the test has passed successfully.

In this test, we use the `cy.get()` method with **span** as the argument, which will select all span tags within our component. As we currently only have one span, this works perfectly. Nevertheless, this test could fail if our component evolves and additional spans are introduced. It would be prudent to employ a selector robust to future alterations.

Notice that the `span` tag within the Stepper component comes with a data-cy attribute:

```
<span data-cy="counter">{{ count }}</span>
```

This attribute is assigned a unique ID for testing purposes. Update the test to utilize a CSS attribute selector with cy.get():

```
it('stepper should default to 0', () => {
  cy.mount(Stepper)
  cy.get('[data-cy=counter]').should('have.text', '0')
})
```

The test will pass as expected, and our selector is now future-proofed.

Incorporating props into components

It would be prudent to incorporate a test ensuring that the initial prop sets the count to a value other than its default "0". This can be achieved by passing in props to the Stepper component via the mount method:

```
it('supports an "initial" prop to set the value', () => {
  cy.mount(Stepper, { props: { initial: 100 } })
  cy.get('[data-cy=counter]').should('have.text', '100')
})
```

Props can be passed by utilizing the `props` property in the options.

Testing interactions

While we've successfully mounted and selected the element in our previous tests, we've yet to interact with it. It's essential to validate that the counter's value adjusts accordingly when the **increment** and **decrement** buttons are clicked.

This can be achieved by interacting with the component using the click() command, which simulates a real user clicking a DOM element.

Embed the following tests:

```
it('when the increment button is pressed, the counter is incremented', ()
=> {
  cy.mount(Stepper)
  cy.get('[data-cy=increment]').click()
  cy.get('[data-cy=counter]').should('have.text', '1')
})
```

```
it('when the decrement button is pressed, the counter is decremented', ()
=> {
  cy.mount(Stepper)
  cy.get('[data-cy=decrement]').click()
  cy.get('[data-cy=counter]').should('have.text', '-1')
})
```

Upon viewing the outcome of each test, you will observe the counter displaying "1" in the increment test and "-1" in the decrement test. This visualization confirms not only the successful execution of our tests but also allows us to view the results in a real-life browser context!

Refer to the guide Interacting with Elements for further insights into additional commands to interact with the DOM.

Testing Vue.js components with events

The entirety of the **Stepper** component's state (that is, the count) is internally managed. Consumers are alerted to state changes by listening for a change event.

As the developer of the **Stepper** component, it's crucial to ensure that upon clicking the increment and decrement buttons, the change event is emitted with the appropriate values.

Cypress Spies can be employed to validate the emission of the change event. A spy is a unique function that records the number of times it was invoked and the parameters it was called with. By binding a spy to the change event, interacting with the component, and then querying the spy, we can validate that it was invoked with the expected parameters.

Let's set up the spies and bind them to the component:

```
it('clicking + fires a change event with the incremented value', () => {
  const onChangeSpy = cy.spy().as('onChangeSpy')
  cy.mount(Stepper, { props: { onChange: onChangeSpy } })
  cy.get('[data-cy=increment]').click()
  cy.get('@onChangeSpy').should('have.been.calledWith', 1)
})
```

Initially, we create a new spy via the `cy.spy()` method, passing in a string that sets an alias for the spy. This alias allows us to reference the spy at a later stage. We initialize the component during `cy.mount()` and pass the spy into it. We then proceed to click the increment button.

The subsequent line differs slightly. While we've seen how the `cy.get()` method can be used to select elements, it can also be utilized to retrieve any aliases set up beforehand. We employ `cy.get()` to fetch the alias for the spy and assert that the method was invoked with the anticipated value.

Best practices for component testing

Component testing serves a crucial role in the software development cycle, ensuring that each part of your application functions as expected. With these best practices, you can further enhance the effectiveness of your component testing process.

Understand the component's functionality

Before writing tests, you need to understand the component's functionality thoroughly. What are its inputs (props, state)? What does it render based on those inputs? Does it have side effects (for example, API calls)? Knowing this information will guide you on what to test.

Before testing the `Stepper` component, we understand it has two main props: `initial` and `onChange`. Also, it internally handles a `count` state and two functions to increment and decrement the count.

```
it('calls onChange with new count after incrementing', () => {
  const mockOnChange = cy.spy()
  cy.mount(<Stepper initial={0} onChange={mockOnChange} />)
  cy.get('[data-cy=increment]').click()
  cy.wrap(mockOnChange).should('have.been.calledWith', 1)
})
```

Isolate the component

During testing, isolate the component as much as possible. This is known as unit testing. Isolated tests are easier to maintain and debug since they focus on one piece at a time. Use mocking and stubbing to isolate your component from dependencies such as network requests or child components.

In our test, we mount and interact with only the `Stepper` component, ensuring we are unit testing it in isolation.

Use descriptive test titles

Test titles should clearly state what is being tested and the expected outcome. Descriptive titles not only make tests easier to read and understand, but they also serve as documentation. Anyone reviewing your tests should be able to understand the component's functionality based on the test titles alone.

Our test title, `'calls onChange with new count after incrementing,'` clearly describes what is being tested.

Favor integration over snapshot tests

While snapshot tests can be helpful, they often need to be more robust as your application grows. Changes in a component often require snapshot updates, making them more of a chore than a help. Instead, focus on writing tests that mimic user interactions and verify outcomes.

Test different states

A component often has different states based on its props. Make sure to write tests that cover all these states. For instance, if you have a button that can be enabled or disabled based on a prop, write tests for both scenarios.

Here, we're testing the **`Stepper`** component in its initial state. But we could also write tests for when the initial prop is set to a non-zero value.

```
it('displays initial value', () => {
  cy.mount(<Stepper initial={5} />)
  cy.get('[data-cy=counter]').should('contain', '5')
})
```

Test events and side effects

If your component fires events or triggers side effects (like an API call), write tests for those. Mock the side effects to make your test reliable and faster. For events, ensure they fire when expected and carry the right payload.

After the increment button is clicked, we test that the `onChange` prop gets called with the correct value.

Keep tests DRY, but not at all costs

While it's generally good to adhere to the DRY (Don't Repeat Yourself) principle, more abstraction can make tests easier to understand in testing. Repeating your tests is okay if it makes them more straightforward and easier to read.

Our tests are focused and avoid unnecessary abstraction. We repeat the process of mounting the component and selecting the button in each test, making them easier to understand.

Incorporate accessibility checks

Accessibility is crucial, and you should make it a part of your testing process. Tools like Cypress-axe can help you automate accessibility checks in your tests.

For the `Stepper` component, we could add tests to check that the buttons are accessible.

```
it('has accessible increment and decrement buttons', () => {
  cy.mount(<Stepper />)
  cy.get('[data-cy=increment]').should('be.visible')
  cy.get('[data-cy=decrement]').should('be.visible')
})
```

It is always great to use additional tools to test accessibility. In the following example, the Cypress-Axe plugin helps us to check accessibility violations:

```
it('has no detectable accessibility violations', () => {
  cy.mount(<Stepper />)
  cy.injectAxe()
  cy.checkA11y()
})
```

We utilize the `cy.injectAxe()` and `cy.checkA11y()` methods to perform an accessibility audit on the Stepper component. We mount our `Stepper` component and inject the `axe` accessibility checker into the page using `cy.injectAxe()`. Lastly, we use `cy.checkA11y()` to run the `axe` and check for accessibility violations.

The `checkA11y` command will fail the test if there are any violations. In your Cypress Test Runner, you can click on the failed test for more details about the violations.

This approach allows you to integrate accessibility checks into your component testing process, ensuring your components are functional and well-tested and accessible.

Continuously run tests in your development environment

Use test runners that can watch your file system for changes and run tests automatically. This will provide you with instant feedback and speed up your development process.

Use a test-first methodology (TDD/BDD)

Consider using a test-first approach like Test-Driven Development (TDD) or Behavior-Driven Development (BDD). Writing tests before the code helps you thoroughly think through the requirements and design. It can lead to better-designed, more reliable components.

In a test-first approach, we might write a test like the following before implementing the increment functionality.

```
it('increments count when increment button is clicked', () => {
  cy.mount(<Stepper initial={0} />)
  cy.get('[data-cy=increment]').click()
  cy.get('[data-cy=counter]').should('contain', '1')
})
```

In this way, we would first see the test fail ('red'), then implement the functionality to make the test pass ('green'), and finally refactor if needed ('refactor').

Debugging and troubleshooting component tests

Component tests, like any other kind of test, will not always go the way we plan. We may encounter failing tests for several reasons, like unexpected behavior, syntax errors, or logic flaws. The ability to efficiently debug and troubleshoot is vital for any developer. This chapter will discuss some standard practices and tools you can leverage when debugging and troubleshooting your component tests in Cypress.

Utilize Cypress's time traveling and real-time reloading

One of the main selling points of Cypress is its time-travelling debugger. As you run tests, Cypress takes snapshots at every stage, allowing you to hover over commands in the Command Log to see exactly what happened at each step.

For instance, consider the `Stepper` component test:

```
it('supports an "initial" prop to set the value', () => {
  cy.mount(<Stepper initial={100} />)
  cy.get('[data-cy=counter]').should('have.text', '100')
})
```

If the test fails, you can look at the Command Log on the left side of the Test Runner. Hover over each command, and you'll see a snapshot of the DOM at that point in time on the right.

Furthermore, Cypress automatically reloads every time you save a file, making it quicker and easier to see the result of your changes.

Use `cy.log` for custom logging

Sometimes, it's helpful to log out certain information during the test execution. You can use `cy.log` for that:

```
it('supports an "initial" prop to set the value', () => {
  cy.mount(<Stepper initial={100} />)
  cy.log('Mounted with initial count of 100')
  cy.get('[data-cy=counter]').should('have.text', '100')
})
```

`cy.log` will add a log to the Command Log. You can use it to output any information that may help you understand the test flow.

Use `cy.pause` for pausing execution

When a test runs into an error, Cypress will automatically pause execution and let you inspect the state of your application at the moment of failure. However, you can also manually pause execution using `cy.pause`:

```
it('supports an "initial" prop to set the value', () => {
```

```
  cy.mount(<Stepper initial={100} />)
  cy.pause()
  cy.get('[data-cy=counter]').should('have.text', '100')
})
```

When Cypress hits the `cy.pause` command, it will pause and allow you to step through the rest of the commands one by one. You can use this to inspect the state of your application at each step.

Use Cypress's built-in debuggability

Cypress commands are built to be debuggable. You can use the `debugger` statement or use `.debug()`:

```
it('supports an "initial" prop to set the value', () => {
  cy.mount(<Stepper initial={100} />)
  cy.get('[data-cy=counter]').debug().should('have.text', '100')
})
```

This command will pause execution and allow you to inspect the state of your application at that point in the test.

Reviewing test artifacts

Cypress automatically records videos of your test runs when running them via `cypress run`. These videos are incredibly useful when debugging, as you can see exactly what happened during the test run. Cypress also captures screenshots when a test fails, which can help diagnose visual issues.

To sum up, efficiently debugging and troubleshooting component tests are crucial to maintaining a healthy test suite. Cypress offers a rich set of features like time-travelling, logging, pausing, debugging, and testing artifacts that make this task easier. Utilize these features, and you'll have more robust and reliable tests.

Integrating component tests into your testing workflow

Once you have a firm grasp on writing and debugging component tests, the next step is integrating these tests into your overall testing workflow. Doing so allows you to consistently check your components for bugs and regressions as part of your development cycle in this chapter, we'll discuss how to run your component tests, how to include them in your continuous integration (CI) process, and when you should write and run these tests.

Running component tests locally

Running your component tests locally should be as straightforward as possible. Cypress makes this easy with its interactive test runner. You can start it by running `npx cypress open` in your terminal. This will open the test runner, where you can run all tests or a single test file. Changes in your test files will automatically trigger a re-run of the tests, making the feedback loop very tight.

For the **`Stepper`** component, running the tests would look something like this:

```
# Start the test runner

npx cypress open
```

Now select the file `` `Stepper.spec.js` `` in the test runner to run the tests.

Running component tests in continuous integration

Having your component tests run in your CI environment ensures that your components remain in a good state, even when multiple people work on them. Cypress can be run in the command-line mode, which is perfect for CI environments. You can use the `cypress run` command to run all tests:

```
# Run all tests in command-line mode

npx cypress run
```

Setting up your CI environment to run the component tests whenever a change is pushed is recommended. This topic will be discovered in *Chapter 10, Integrating with GitHub,*

GitLab, and Cucumber of this book.

Writing component tests

A good rule of thumb is to write component tests for all of the critical components in your app. Critical components are those that, if broken, would severely affect the user experience. For the Stepper component, you would write tests whenever you create the component or modify its behavior.

Running component tests

It's good practice to run your component tests frequently. It would be best if you run the following:

- Before pushing your changes, ensure you didn't break anything
- After pulling changes, make sure your coworkers' changes didn't break your components
- Whenever you modify a critical component, check that the changes didn't introduce bugs

Integrating component tests into your workflow ensures that your components stay robust and reliable, making for a better user experience and less time spent on bug fixes and support.

Conclusion

This chapter focuses on component testing with Cypress, emphasizing the testing of individual web components in isolation. The chapter begins by introducing the concept of component testing and highlighting its distinctions from end-to-end testing. It provides step-by-step instructions for setting up the necessary tools and libraries for component testing with Cypress. Readers will learn how to write component tests for popular web frameworks like React, Angular, and Vue.js, enabling them to effectively validate the functionality and behavior of individual components. The chapter also shares best practices for creating maintainable and practical component tests. Additionally, it covers debugging and troubleshooting strategies specific to component testing and provides insights on integrating component tests into the overall testing workflow. By the end of this chapter, readers will have the knowledge and skills to perform robust component testing with Cypress, ensuring the quality and reliability of their web components.

The next chapter delves into the realm of API testing with Cypress. Readers will be introduced to the concept of API testing and will learn how to utilize Cypress for testing both RESTful and GraphQL APIs. The chapter focuses on validating API responses and ensuring the correctness and reliability of the data received. Practical examples and tips will be provided to guide readers in creating comprehensive API tests using Cypress, empowering them to enhance the quality and stability of their API-driven applications.

Further readings

To further expand readers' knowledge on the topics discussed in this chapter, I suggest exploring these additional resources:

- **Cypress component testing guide:** The official Cypress documentation provides a comprehensive guide on component testing (https://docs.cypress.io/guides/component-testing/introduction), offering detailed explanations and examples to help you master component testing with Cypress.
- **React testing library:** The React Testing Library (https://testing-library.com/docs/react-testing-library/intro) offers guidance and best practices for testing React components, including approaches that align well with component testing principles. This resource can enhance your understanding of testing components in a React application.
- **Angular testing guide:** The official Angular documentation on testing (https://angular.io/guide/testing) provides detailed guidance on testing Angular components, including techniques specific to Angular's testing ecosystem. It can serve as a valuable resource when writing component tests for Angular applications.
- **Vue test utils:** Vue Test Utils (https://vue-test-utils.vuejs.org/) is the official testing utility library for Vue.js applications. It offers comprehensive documentation, including examples and best practices, to assist you in effectively testing Vue.js components.
- **Component testing with Cypress component testing getting started app**: This GitHub repository (https://github.com/cypress-io/cypress-component-testing-apps) contains real-world examples of component testing using Cypress. It provides practical insights and code samples for testing components in different scenarios.

These resources will give you a broader understanding and practical examples of the concepts you've learned in this chapter.

CHAPTER 6
API Testing

Introduction

In this chapter, readers will learn how to use Cypress for API testing. It will cover testing RESTful and GraphQL APIs and validating API responses. The chapter will provide practical examples and tips to help readers create comprehensive API tests using Cypress.

Structure

In this chapter, we will discuss the following topics:

- Introduction to API testing
- Testing RESTful APIs
- Testing GraphQL APIs
- Validating API responses

Introduction to API testing

API, or Application Programming Interface, is a set of rules allowing different software applications to communicate. It defines methods and data formats a program can utilize to perform tasks requiring resources or functionalities from another service or application.

API testing involves examining these APIs directly, going beyond the conventional user interface testing to validate the software's performance, reliability, and security. It allows for more comprehensive testing since it can access the application without a user interface.

In web development, APIs often come in two main types: REST and GraphQL (as shown in *Table* 6.1).

REST	GraphQL
Stands for Representational State Transfer.	A query language for your API and runtime for executing those queries.
Uses standard HTTP methods like GET, POST, PUT, and DELETE.	Uses a single endpoint and HTTP POST method to access data.
It provides a straightforward approach for developers, as each URL corresponds to a specific resource.	GraphQL gives more power to the client, allowing it to aggregate responses, ask for specific data, and others.
To get different data, you have to make different requests to different endpoints.	You can get all the data you need in a single request with GraphQL.

Table 6.1: *Introduction to REST and GraphQL Characteristics.*

API testing is a critical part of the development process. A well-functioning API ensures that different software components can communicate effectively, while a faulty API can lead to bugs, crashes, and security vulnerabilities. Some of the key reasons to conduct API testing are:

- **Efficiency:** Testing at the API level can be more efficient than UI testing. You can isolate the component and do not need to wait for the UI to be ready, making it possible to detect and fix issues early in the development cycle.
- **Broad Coverage:** API tests can cover request and response data, HTTP status codes, response times, error codes, and so on, providing a comprehensive view of the application's performance.
- **Language Independence:** APIs can be tested irrespective of the programming language used for development.
- **Integration Readiness:** API testing helps verify if the software is ready for integration. This ensures that the different components of a system work together as expected.
- **Security:** APIs are a common point of attack. Testing can help identify vulnerabilities before the product goes live.

As a developer, you should make API testing an integral part of your workflow. Using Cypress, you can leverage a robust and friendly ecosystem explicitly built for developers and QA professionals, making creating and managing your tests easier.

Understanding RESTful APIs

REST (Representational State Transfer) is an architectural style for designing networked applications. A REST API breaks down a transaction into create, read, update, and delete (CRUD) operations and applies them to resources, such as objects in a database. These operations correspond to HTTP methods as follows:

HTTP Method	CRUD	Action
`GET`	`Read`	Retrieve a specific resource(s) from a server
`POST`	`Create`	Send data to the server to create a new resource
`PUT`	`Update`	Update a specific resource on a server
`DELETE`	`Delete`	Remove a specific resource from a server

***Table 6.2**: Common HTTP Methods.*

These four HTTP methods make REST a powerful style for working with APIs. However, RESTful APIs have their limitations. For instance, they can lead to over-fetching or under-fetching of data. Over-fetching happens when the client downloads more information than is necessary for a single API request. Conversely, under-fetching occurs when a specific endpoint doesn't provide enough information, forcing the client to make additional requests to fetch everything it needs.

Let's delve into the different HTTP methods used in RESTful APIs with examples and their main differences.

- **`GET`:** This HTTP method retrieves or reads data from a server. It should only retrieve data and should have no other effect. This is considered a safe method, meaning it's read-only and doesn't modify resources.

```
cy.request({
  method: 'GET',
  url: '/api/users'
}).then((response) => {
  expect(response.status).to.eq(200) // Successful response
})
```

In this example, we send a **GET** request to retrieve a list of users. If successful, it should return a status of 200.

- **POST:** This HTTP method sends data to the server to create a new resource. The data is included in the body of the request. This can result in the creation of a new resource or the updates of existing resources.

```
cy.request({
  method: 'POST',
  url: '/api/users',
  body: {
    name: 'John Doe',
    email: 'john.doe@example.com'
  }
}).then((response) => {
  expect(response.status).to.eq(201)
})
```

In this example, we send a **POST** request to create a new user. The user's details are sent in the body of the request. A successful **POST** request usually returns a status of 201, indicating that a new resource was created.

- **PUT:** This HTTP method updates a specific resource on the server. The data is included in the body of the request. This could potentially change the resource entirely or update parts of the resource.

```
cy.request({
  method: 'PUT',
  url: '/api/users/1',
  body: {
    email: 'new.email@example.com'
  }
}).then((response) => {
  expect(response.status).to.eq(200)
})
```

In this example, we are sending a **PUT** request to update the user's email address with ID 1. A successful **PUT** request usually returns a status of 200, indicating that the resource was successfully updated.

- **DELETE:** This HTTP method deletes a specific resource from the server. It should delete the specified resource and have no additional effect.

```
cy.request({
  method: 'DELETE',
  url: '/api/users/1'
}).then((response) => {
  expect(response.status).to.eq(200)
})
```

In this example, we send a **DELETE** request to remove the user with ID 1. A successful **DELETE** request usually returns a status of 200, indicating that the resource was successfully deleted.

In summary, the main difference between these HTTP methods is the type of operation they perform on the server's resources. **GET** retrieves data, **POST** sends new data, **PUT** updates existing data, and **DELETE** removes data. All these methods are crucial for manipulating resources in a RESTful API.

Exploring GraphQL

GraphQL is an open-source data query and manipulation language developed and open-sourced by Facebook. Its primary purpose was to address the efficiency issues in mobile applications when dealing with data loading.

In contrast to REST, which can result in over-fetching or under-fetching data due to its fixed data structure, GraphQL allows clients to specify exactly the data they need. This reduces the amount of data that needs to be transferred over the network, which can result in improved app performance.

Another differentiator is that unlike REST APIs, which expose multiple endpoints for different resources, a GraphQL API exposes just a single endpoint. This endpoint processes queries and mutations to read and write data, respectively.

A key feature of GraphQL is its type system. GraphQL APIs are organized in terms of types and fields, not endpoints. The server declares the resources available, and the client asks what it needs. This makes the data-fetching process more efficient.

Take a look at this example of a GraphQL query:

```
{
  user(id: "1") {
    name
    email
  }
}
```

This query retrieves the name and email of the user with an ID of 1. Unlike with REST, the client doesn't have to fetch any unnecessary data. We describe our data needs (the user's name and email), and GraphQL assembles that data for us.

Now, let's explore how we can perform a GraphQL query using Cypress with the `cy.request()` method:

```
cy.request({
  method: 'POST',
  url: '/graphql',
  body: {
    query: `
      {
        user(id: "1") {
          name
          email
        }
      }
    `
  },
}).then((response) => {
  expect(response.status).to.eq(200)
  expect(response.body.data.user).to.have.property('name')
  expect(response.body.data.user).to.have.property('email')
})
```

In this example, we are making a **`POST`** request to the `'/graphql'` endpoint with a body that contains our query. This query requests the `user's 'name' and 'email' fields` with an ID of 1. Once the request is complete, we assert that the response has a status of 200 and that the `'name'` and `'email'` properties exist within the response data. This confirms that our query succeeded and that we got the exact data we requested.

GraphQL provides a more efficient and powerful alternative to RESTful APIs, especially for complex systems and data structures, as it allows the client to specify exactly what data it needs. Its use can result in significant performance improvements and a better developer experience overall.

Comparing REST and GraphQL

Here is a detailed comparison between REST and GraphQL along some critical dimensions:

Aspect	**REST**	**GraphQL**
Endpoint Usage	REST uses multiple endpoints, each of which corresponds to a specific resource. For example, `/users` to get a list of users and `/users/{id}` to `get` a specific user.	GraphQL uses a single endpoint, usually `/graphql`. The data needed is determined entirely by the client's request rather than by the server's pre-defined endpoints.
Data Fetching	REST can result in over-fetching or under-fetching of data. Over-fetching occurs when the client downloads more information than is necessary, which can waste bandwidth. Under-fetching occurs when a client needs to make additional requests because an endpoint doesn't provide all the required information.	GraphQL eliminates over-fetching and under-fetching by allowing the client to specify exactly what data is needed. This can significantly reduce bandwidth usage and improve app performance.
Versioning	REST APIs often require versioning (like `/v1/users`, `/v2/users`) when changing the API, as changes to the structure of an endpoint can break existing clients.	GraphQL doesn't require versioning. New fields can be added to the server-side API, and they won't affect existing clients. Clients can simply add the new fields to their queries as they start needing them.

Error Handling	REST uses HTTP status codes to indicate the status of a response. There's a wide range of HTTP status codes, each indicating a specific type of error.	GraphQL always sends `'200 OK'` status, even if errors were processing the request. Errors are handled within the response body under the `errors` field, and successful data under the `data` field.

***Table 6.3**: Comparison of REST and GraphQL.*

From this comparison, it's clear that both REST and GraphQL have their strengths and weaknesses. While GraphQL offers several advantages over RESTful APIs, such as efficient data fetching and elimination of versioning, it's also more complex to set up. It has less widespread support among libraries and tools.

Conversely, REST is simple, widely adopted, and has excellent support in numerous languages and frameworks, but it can be less efficient for complex applications with diverse data needs. As a developer, it's essential to understand the characteristics of both REST and GraphQL to make the best decision for your application's specific needs.

Cypress for API Testing

Though widely acclaimed for its capabilities in end-to-end testing of user interfaces, Cypress isn't confined to merely UI testing. It comes packed with robust features that make API testing simpler, efficient, and seamlessly integrated into your testing workflow.

Cypress's fluent and intuitive API enables you to author tests for your HTTP endpoints easily, validating the behavior, performance, and reliability of both RESTful and GraphQL APIs. The ability to make HTTP requests and assert the responses is integral to ensuring your API's contract remains intact and functions as expected.

Let's look at a detailed example where we test a RESTful API with Cypress:

```
describe('API Test', () => {
  it('Validate the header', () => {
    cy.request('https://jsonplaceholder.typicode.com/posts/1')
      .its('headers')
      .its('content-type')
      .should('include', 'application/json; charset=utf-8');
```

```
  });
});
```

In the preceding example, we make a **GET** request to the `'posts/1'` endpoint. The response is inspected to ensure the `'content-type'` in the response header correctly indicates `'application/json; charset=utf-8'`. This ensures that the server correctly informs the client of the response's content type.

The `cy.request()` function makes this simple. It allows us to send HTTP requests to a server and receive responses. The `'its'` method enables us to drill down effortlessly into the response object, and the `'should'` method allows us to make assertions about the values we find.

In addition to `cy.request()`, Cypress also provides the `cy.intercept()` function, which gives more control over the behavior of network requests in your application. `cy.intercept()` can capture and optionally change the behavior of any network request (including XMLHttpRequests, Fetch API, page loads, and more). It can be used to wait for responses, stub responses, or dynamically modify responses or requests.

For instance, you might want to stub a response during a test to isolate your client-side application from the server as follows:

```
cy.intercept('GET', '/users', { fixture: 'users.json' })
```

In the preceding example, we're intercepting all GET requests to the `'/users'` endpoint, and instead of allowing the request to hit the server, we're returning a fixture stored locally in the `'users.json'` file. This allows us to control the data used during the test and makes tests more deterministic.

Overall, Cypress's features for API testing make it a powerful tool in your testing toolkit, capable of handling various testing scenarios and catering to different needs that arise during API testing.

Testing RESTful APIs

Building on the understanding of APIs and their crucial role in software development, we will now take a deep dive into the practical aspects of API testing with Cypress. As discussed, RESTful APIs revolve around performing operations (CRUD - Create, Read, Update, Delete) on URL-identified resources. These operations are tied to the HTTP methods: GET, POST, PUT, and DELETE, respectively. Now, when testing a RESTful API, you're essentially validating that these HTTP methods behave as expected when interacting with the resources on your server.

Regarding Cypress, its capabilities are not limited to end-to-end testing of user interfaces; it's also a powerhouse for API testing. The `cy.request()` function is your main point of interaction with your server's resources when writing Cypress API tests. You can use this function to send HTTP requests and receive HTTP responses, allowing you to write assertions based on the properties of those responses.

Let's look at a basic example of testing a GET request:

```
describe('GET Request Test', () => {
  it('Validate the status code', () => {
    cy.request('https://jsonplaceholder.typicode.com/posts/1')
      .its('status')
      .should('eq', 200);
  });
});
```

In this example, we're making a **GET** request to the endpoint `'https://jsonplaceholder.typicode.com/posts/1'`, which should return the post with the ID of 1. We then check the response's status code to ensure it's 200, which signifies a successful request. This is a straightforward example but a stepping stone toward more complex tests.

If you want to add authentication to your Cypress test, you would typically pass an authentication token or credentials as headers in the `cy.request()` method. Here's how you can modify your example to include authentication.

Let's assume you're using a Bearer token for authentication:

```
describe('GET Request Test', () => {
  it('Validate the status code', () => {
    const authToken = 'YOUR_AUTH_TOKEN_HERE'; // Replace with your token

    cy.request({
      method: 'GET',
      url: 'https://jsonplaceholder.typicode.com/posts/1',
      headers: {
        'Authorization': `Bearer ${authToken}`
      }
```

```
    })
    .its('status')
    .should('eq', 200);
  });
});
```

Replace `'YOUR_AUTH_TOKEN_HERE'` with your actual authentication token.

In this example, we're sending an `Authorization` header with the request, which contains the authentication token. If your API uses a different form of authentication, like Basic Auth or API key, you would adjust the headers accordingly.

Remember to never hard-code sensitive data such as tokens, directly into your code. In a real-world scenario, you might fetch this token dynamically or store it in environment variables or configuration files and then reference it in your tests.

Now, let's move forward and test a **`POST`** request:

```
describe('POST Request Test', () => {
  it('Validate the creation of a new resource', () => {
    const authToken = 'YOUR_AUTH_TOKEN_HERE'; // Replace with your token

    cy.request({
      method: 'POST',
      url: 'https://jsonplaceholder.typicode.com/posts',
      body: {
        title: 'Test Title',
        body: 'Test Body',
        userId: 1
      },
      headers: {
        'Authorization': `Bearer ${authToken}`,
        'Content-type': 'application/json; charset=UTF-8'
      }
```

```
    })
    .its('status')
    .should('eq', 201);
  });
});
```

In this case, we're making a **POST** request to the endpoint `'https://jsonplaceholder.typicode.com/posts'` to create a new post. We're sending a JSON object in the request's body with the new post's details. We then check the response's status code to ensure it's 201, which signifies that a new resource was successfully created.

The **PUT** method is used to update a specific resource on the server. Let's see an example of a Cypress test for a **PUT** request:

```
describe('PUT Request Test', () => {
  it('Validate the update of an existing resource', () => {
    const authToken = 'YOUR_AUTH_TOKEN_HERE'; // Replace with your token

    cy.request({
      method: 'PUT',
      url: 'https://jsonplaceholder.typicode.com/posts/1',
      body: {
        id: 1,
        title: 'Updated Title',
        body: 'Updated Body',
        userId: 1
      },
      headers: {
        'Authorization': `Bearer ${authToken}`,
        'Content-type': 'application/json; charset=UTF-8'
      }
    })
    .its('status')
    .should('eq', 200);
  });
```

```
});
```

In this test, we're making a **PUT** request to update a post with the ID of 1. We send a JSON object with the new details of the post and then validate the response's status code to ensure it's 200, meaning the resource was successfully updated.

The **DELETE** method is used to remove a specific resource from the server. Here's an example of a Cypress test for a **DELETE** request:

```
describe('DELETE Request Test', () => {
  it('Validate the deletion of a resource', () => {
    const authToken = 'YOUR_AUTH_TOKEN_HERE'; // Replace with your token

    cy.request({
      method: 'DELETE',
      url: 'https://jsonplaceholder.typicode.com/posts/1',
      headers: {
        'Authorization': `Bearer ${authToken}`
      }
    })
    .its('status')
    .should('eq', 200);
  });
});
```

In this example, we're making a **DELETE** request to remove the post with the ID of 1. We then validate the response's status code to ensure it's 200, indicating the resource was successfully deleted.

Cypress's `cy.intercept()` function is a powerful tool for controlling the behavior of network requests and responses in your tests. It can stub, spy on, and even modify network requests and responses on the fly.

A basic usage of `cy.intercept()` can be as follows:

```
describe('Test with cy.intercept()', () => {
  it('Modify the response', () => {
    cy.intercept('https://jsonplaceholder.typicode.com/posts/1', {
      body: {
```

```
        id: 1,
        title: 'Mock Title',
        body: 'Mock Body',
        userId: 1
      }
    }).as('getPost')

    cy.visit('your website url') // replace with the URL of your web app

    cy.wait('@getPost').then((interception) => {
      assert.isNotNull(interception.response.body, 'API call has data')
    })
  })
});
```

In this test, we intercept a **GET** request to the endpoint and modify the response body. We then visit our web application and wait for the intercepted request to complete before validating the response.

While journeying through the testing world, you will frequently encounter the terms Mocks and Stubs. These are essential strategies used in testing to gain more control over the behavior of functions or methods within your application. Cypress brings built-in support for all these techniques, making it a powerful tool for comprehensive testing.

- **Mocking** in testing parlance is the process of replacing a real system entity with a fake one. This fake entity mimics the behavior of the real one, enabling tests to run without any dependency on external factors. An example of mocking with Cypress using `cy.request()` and `cy.intercept()` is:

```
// Mocking with cy.request()
cy.request({
  url: 'https://jsonplaceholder.typicode.com/posts',
  method: 'POST',
  body: { title: 'Mock title', body: 'Mock body', userId: 1 },
  headers: { 'Content-type': 'application/json; charset=UTF-8' },
  response: { title: 'Mock title', body: 'Mock body', userId: 1, id: 101 }
```

```
})


// Mocking with cy.intercept()
cy.intercept('GET', '/posts/1', { fixture: 'post.json' }).as('getPost')
```

- **Stubbing** is similar to mocking in the sense that it involves replacing real functions or methods with fake ones. The difference, however, lies in the level of control it provides. Stubs allow you to dictate the behavior of the fake function or method, including specifying what it should return or if it should throw an error. Here's an example of stubbing with Cypress:

```
cy.window().then((win) => {
  cy.stub(win, 'fetch').returns(Promise.resolve({
    json: () => ({ message: 'Stubbing successful' }),
    ok: true
  })).as('fetchStub')
})
cy.get('#fetch-button').click() // replace with the selector of your
button
cy.get('@fetchStub').should('be.calledOnce')
```

In the preceding examples, we've covered how to stub the window's fetch method while leveraging Cypress's capabilities.

Harnessing these techniques effectively is a vital part of writing solid tests. They offer immense power and control, but with great power comes great responsibility. Use mocks and stubs judiciously to prevent your tests from becoming too complex or unwieldy.

Testing GraphQL APIs

Building on our previous discussion of RESTful APIs, let's focus on GraphQL. Introduced by Facebook in 2015, GraphQL has garnered immense popularity due to its efficiency and precision. It allows clients to fetch exactly what they need, drastically reducing data transfer over the network.

Unlike REST, based on an architectural style, GraphQL is a query language for APIs and a runtime for executing those queries with your existing data. GraphQL APIs are organized in terms of types and fields, not endpoints. This organization makes it possible for the client to dictate the shape of the responses.

GraphQL uses a single endpoint that receives HTTP POST requests. The requested data is defined in the body of the POST request, enabling flexible and efficient data retrieval. Let's illustrate this with a simple example of a GraphQL query.

```
{
  user(id: "1") {
    name
    email
  }
}
```

This query retrieves the name and email of the user with an ID of 1. Unlike a REST API, the client doesn't need to fetch unnecessary data.

Cypress's built-in capabilities make it an excellent choice for testing GraphQL APIs. We can leverage the `cy.request()` method to send a POST request to a GraphQL endpoint. Let's consider an example:

```
describe('GraphQL API Test', () => {
  it('Fetch User Data', () => {
    const authToken = 'YOUR_AUTH_TOKEN_HERE'; // Replace with your token

    const query = `
      {
        user(id: "1") {
          name
          email
        }
      }
    `;

    cy.request({
      url: '/graphql', // replace with your GraphQL endpoint
      method: 'POST',
      body: { query },
```

```
      headers: {
        'Authorization': `Bearer ${authToken}`,
        'Content-Type': 'application/json'
      }
    }).then((response) => {
      expect(response.status).to.equal(200);
      expect(response.body.data.user.name).to.exist;
      expect(response.body.data.user.email).to.exist;
    });
  });
});
```

In the preceding example, we used `cy.request()` to send a GraphQL query and validated the response.

We can also use `cy.intercept()` to mock GraphQL requests. This is particularly useful when you want to isolate your client-side application from the server or control the response from the server. Here's an example:

```
describe('Mock GraphQL Response', () => {
  it('Mock User Data', () => {
    const mockUser = { name: 'John Doe', email: 'john@example.com' };

    cy.intercept('POST', '/graphql', (req) => {
      if (req.body.query.includes('user')) {
        req.reply({ data: { user: mockUser } });
      }
    });

    cy.visit('/'); // visit your page that sends the GraphQL request
    cy.contains(mockUser.name); // assert that the page shows the mocked
data
  });
});
```

In this test, we used `cy.intercept()` to intercept the GraphQL request and respond with our mock data. We then assert that our page correctly displays the mocked data.

When dealing with GraphQL, error handling is also a crucial aspect to consider. Unlike REST APIs, which use HTTP status codes to indicate the status of a response, GraphQL always returns a 200 OK status, and errors are handled within the response.

```
describe('GraphQL Error Handling', () => {
  it('Handle Error', () => {
    const authToken = 'YOUR_AUTH_TOKEN_HERE'; // Replace with your token

    const query = `
      {
        user(id: "1") {
          name
          nonExistentField
        }
      }
    `;

    cy.request({
      url: '/graphql', // replace with your GraphQL endpoint
      method: 'POST',
      body: { query },
      headers: {
        'Authorization': `Bearer ${authToken}`,
        'Content-Type': 'application/json'
      },
      failOnStatusCode: false
    }).then((response) => {
      expect(response.body.errors).to.exist;
    });
```

```
  });
});
```

In this example, we request a non-existent field, which should return an error. Since GraphQL always responds with a status code of 200, we set `failOnStatusCode: false` in our request to prevent Cypress from automatically failing the test. Then, we assert that an error is present in the response.

Aliasing Multiple Queries or Mutations

Now, we need to explore how to designate multiple aliases for GraphQL queries or mutations for a series of tests, how to supersede existing intercepts to adjust the response of a query or mutation, and how to formulate assertions against a GraphQL query or mutation response.

The strategies we'll look at are rooted in well-established practices for pausing and formulating assertions against GraphQL queries and mutations.

Setting aliases for different queries or mutations in API testing is often helpful. This allows us to conveniently intercept, modify, and assert against these operations in our tests. Here is how we can achieve this with Cypress.

First, let's create a few utility functions that will help us to match and alias our queries and mutations. We need to create `utils/graphql-test-utils.js.`

```
// utils/graphql-test-utils.js


export const hasOperationName = (req, operationName) => {
  const { body } = req;
  return (
    body.hasOwnProperty('operationName') && body.operationName === oper-
ationName
  );
};


export const aliasQuery = (req, operationName) => {
  if (hasOperationName(req, operationName)) {
    req.alias = `gql${operationName}Query`;
  }
```

```
};

export const aliasMutation = (req, operationName) => {
  if (hasOperationName(req, operationName)) {
    req.alias = `gql${operationName}Mutation`;
  }
};
```

In our test file, we can import these utilities to alias the queries and mutations for our tests.

```
// our-test-file.cy.js
import { aliasQuery, aliasMutation } from '../utils/graphql-test-utils';

context('Tests', () => {
  beforeEach(() => {
    cy.intercept('POST', 'http://localhost:3000/graphql', (req) => {
      // Queries
      aliasQuery(req, 'GetLaunchList');
      aliasQuery(req, 'LaunchDetails');
      aliasQuery(req, 'GetMyTrips');

      // Mutations
      aliasMutation(req, 'Login');
      aliasMutation(req, 'BookTrips');
    });
  });
  // ...
});
```

Expectations for Query or Mutation Results

We can make assertions against the response of an intercepted GraphQL query or mutation using `cy.wait()` as follows:

```
// our-test-file.cy.js
import { aliasQuery } from '../utils/graphql-test-utils';

context('Tests', () => {
  beforeEach(() => {
    cy.intercept('POST', 'http://localhost:3000/graphql', (req) => {
      // Queries
      aliasQuery(req, 'Login');
      // ...
    });
  });

  it('should verify login data', () => {
    cy.wait('@gqlLoginQuery')
      .its('response.body.data.login')
      .should('have.property', 'id')
      .and('have.property', 'token');
  });
});
```

Modifying a Query or Mutation Response

Sometimes we want to modify the response of a GraphQL operation. For instance, we could test how our UI behaves when it receives a limited data set. Here's how we can do that:

```
// our-test-file.cy.js
import { hasOperationName, aliasQuery } from '../utils/
graphql-test-utils';

context('Tests', () => {
  beforeEach(() => {
    cy.intercept('POST', 'http://localhost:3000/graphql', (req) => {
      // Queries
      aliasQuery(req, 'GetLaunchList');
```

```
      // ...
    });
  });

  it('should not display the load more button on the launches page', ()
=> {
    cy.intercept('POST', 'http://localhost:3000/graphql', (req) => {
      const { body } = req;
      if (hasOperationName(req, 'GetLaunchList')) {
        req.alias = 'gqlGetLaunchListQuery';
        req.reply((res) => {
          // Modify the response body directly
          res.body.data.launches.hasMore = false;
          res.body.data.launches.launches =
            res.body.data.launches.launches.slice(5);
        });
      }
    });

    cy.visit('/');

    cy.wait('@gqlGetLaunchListQuery')
      .its('response.body.data.launches')
      .should((launches) => {
        expect(launches.hasMore).to.be.false;
        expect(launches.launches.length).to.be.lte(20);
      });

    cy.get('#launch-list').its('length').should('be.gte', 1).and('be.
lte', 20);
    cy.contains('button', 'Load More').should('not.exist');
  });
});
```

Validating API responses

Having thoroughly discussed testing RESTful and GraphQL APIs, we now pivot to another critical aspect of API testing - validating API responses. Testing the response of an API call is fundamental because it allows us to ensure that the API is functioning as expected and that it's returning the correct data.

When we talk about API response validation, we usually consider the following components:

1. **HTTP status codes:** The server responds with a status code to inform the client about the result of its request. For example, a status code 200 indicates a successful GET request, while a 404 status means that the requested resource could not be found.
2. **Response payload:** This is the data returned by the server in response to the client's request. Depending on the API, this data could be in various formats, though JSON is the most common.
3. **Response headers:** Headers can provide additional information about the server's response, such as its content type, encoding, caching rules, and so on.

Let's examine how we can validate these components using Cypress.

Validating HTTP status codes is straightforward with Cypress. When we use the `cy.request()` function, Cypress automatically asserts that the status code is 2xx or 3xx. The test will automatically fail if the status code is 4xx or 5xx.

```
describe('API Test', () => {
  it('Validate HTTP status code', () => {
    cy.request('https://jsonplaceholder.typicode.com/posts/1')
      .its('status')
      .should('equal', 200);
  });
});
```

In the preceding example, we assert that the response's status code equals 200.

We can also validate the response body's content to ensure that it contains the data we expect. Here's an example:

```
describe('API Test', () => {
  it('Validate response payload', () => {
    cy.request('https://jsonplaceholder.typicode.com/posts/1')
      .its('body')
      .should('contain', { id: 1 });
  });
});
```

In this test, we assert that the response body contains an object with an id of 1.

Cypress also allows us to validate the response headers. We might want to check the `'content-type'` header, for example, to confirm that we're getting a JSON response:

```
describe('API Test', () => {
  it('Validate response header', () => {
    cy.request('https://jsonplaceholder.typicode.com/posts/1')
      .its('headers')
      .its('content-type')
      .should('include', 'application/json; charset=utf-8');
  });
});
```

In this test, we're checking that the `'content-type'` in the response header is `'application/json; charset=utf-8'`.

Like with `cy.request()`, we can also use `cy.intercept()` to validate API responses. `cy.intercept()` also allows us to intercept a request and change the response, making it a powerful tool for testing edge cases. Here's an example:

```
describe('Mock and validate API response', () => {
  it('Should display mocked data', () => {
    const mockResponseBody = { title: 'Cypress is awesome!' };

    cy.intercept('GET', '/api/posts/1', mockResponseBody).as('getPost');
```

```
    cy.visit('/'); // visit your page that makes the request

    cy.wait('@getPost')
      .its('response.body')
      .should('deep.equal', mockResponseBody);
  });
});
```

In this test, we intercept a GET request to '/api/posts/1' and change the response to our mocked data. We then visit our page, wait for the request to happen, and validate that the response body equals our mocked data.

For the sake of thoroughness, let's add a discussion about error handling and validating error responses from an API. APIs may return various error messages with different HTTP status codes, and validating these responses is also an important part of API testing.

Here's how you can do it:

```
describe('API Test', () => {
  it('Validate error response', () => {
    cy.request({
      url: 'https://jsonplaceholder.typicode.com/posts/123456', //
Non-existing resource
      failOnStatusCode: false // Prevents Cypress from failing the test
    })
      .its('status')
      .should('equal', 404);
  });
});
```

In this test, we request a non-existing resource and expect a 404 status code in the response. We use the `failOnStatusCode: false` option to prevent Cypress from automatically failing the test due to a non-2xx or non-3xx status code.

Testing and validating error responses are essential to help ensure your application can handle errors correctly. It's crucial to validate that your API works well under perfect conditions and fails gracefully when things go wrong.

Validating GraphQL API responses is similar to validating RESTful API responses. However, due to the nature of GraphQL, there are some specific characteristics that you should be aware of.

In GraphQL, a successful request will always return a 200 OK HTTP status, even if there are errors in the response. GraphQL will still try to return as much data as possible, even if some fields have errors. Therefore, the primary validation in GraphQL API testing lies in the response body.

Here is an example of a Cypress test that validates a GraphQL API response:

```
describe('API Test', () => {
  it('Validate GraphQL response', () => {
    const query = `
      {
        user(id: "1") {
          id
          name
          email
        }
      }
    `;

    cy.request({
      url: 'https://graphql.example.com', // replace with your GraphQL
endpoint
      method: 'POST',
      body: { query },
      headers: {
        'Content-Type': 'application/json'
      }
    })
      .its('body')
      .should('deep.equal', {
        data: {
          user: {
```

```
            id: '1',
            name: 'John Doe',
            email: 'john.doe@example.com'
          }
        }
      });
  });
});
```

In this example, we're making a POST request to a GraphQL API with a query to fetch a user's information. We then validate the response body to ensure it matches the expected result. Notice how we're using the `deep.equal` assertion to compare the response body with the expected result. This is because GraphQL responses can be complex objects and `deep.equal` allows us to compare them correctly.

Let's consider a situation where you expect an error from your GraphQL API. Here's how you can validate the error:

```
describe('API Test', () => {
  it('Validate GraphQL error', () => {
    const query = `
      {
        user(id: "1") {
          id
          name
          nonexistentField
        }
      }
    `;

    cy.request({
      url: 'https://graphql.example.com', // replace with your GraphQL
endpoint
      method: 'POST',
      body: { query },
```

```
      headers: {
        'Content-Type': 'application/json'
      },
      failOnStatusCode: false // Since GraphQL returns 200 even on er-
rors
    })
      .its('body.errors.0.message')
      .should('equal', 'Cannot query field "nonexistentField" on type
"User".');
  });
});
```

In this example, we're querying a nonexistent field on a user. Since this field doesn't exist, GraphQL will return an error in the response. We then validate the error message to ensure it matches the expected error.

As you can see, validating GraphQL API responses involves checking the response body more than the status code or headers. This is due to the unique nature of GraphQL, where the client specifies precisely what data it needs and how it should be structured.

Conclusion

This chapter focuses on utilizing Cypress for API testing. It begins by introducing readers to the importance of API testing and its role in validating the functionality and behavior of APIs. The chapter then delves into the specifics of testing RESTful APIs, guiding crafting tests that simulate requests and validate responses. It also covers testing GraphQL APIs, showcasing how Cypress can be leveraged to send GraphQL queries and assertions. Furthermore, the chapter emphasizes the significance of validating API responses, ensuring the expected data and structure are present. Through practical examples and helpful tips, readers will gain the knowledge and skills to create robust and effective API tests using Cypress. By the end of the chapter, readers will be equipped with the tools and techniques to perform comprehensive API testing and ensure the reliability of their API endpoints.

In the upcoming chapter, we will delve into data-driven testing and how it can be effectively implemented with Cypress. We will start with an overview of data-driven testing, introducing you to the idea and its benefits in ensuring the robustness and versatility of your test cases. We will then look into utilizing

JSON files for test data, demonstrating how to structure and reference them in your Cypress tests. This will provide a quick, straightforward method to input and manage test data. Next, we will expand on this concept and explore how to read data directly from databases, providing you with the skills to handle more complex and dynamic testing scenarios. The chapter will wrap up with a practical guide on implementing data-driven test cases, ensuring you have the knowledge and the confidence to create reusable and flexible test cases using various data sources. By the end of this chapter, you will have a solid understanding of how to incorporate data-driven approaches into your Cypress testing workflows.

Further Readings

To further expand readers' knowledge on the topics discussed in this chapter, we suggest exploring these additional resources:

- **GraphQL Documentation:** The official GraphQL documentation (https://graphql.org/learn) provides a comprehensive resource to understand the GraphQL query language and its concepts. It can help readers better understand GraphQL APIs and how to test them effectively.
- **REST API Testing with Cypress:** This tutorial on the Cypress Real World App GitHub repository (https://github.com/cypress-io/cypress-realworld-app/tree/main/cypress/tests/api) demonstrates practical examples of testing RESTful APIs using Cypress. It offers hands-on experience and showcases different testing scenarios.
- **"Make GraphQL Calls from Cypress Tests":** Gleb Bahmutov's blog post (https://glebbahmutov.com/blog/request-graphql) is an in-depth guide offering step-by-step instructions on setting up, constructing, and validating GraphQL queries and mutations within a Cypress test suite.

These resources will give you a broader understanding and practical examples of the concepts you've learned in this chapter.

CHAPTER 7
Data-Driven Testing

Introduction

This chapter will introduce readers to data-driven testing with Cypress. It will explain how to use JSON files, read data from databases, and implement data-driven test cases. By the end of this chapter, readers will understand how to create flexible and reusable test cases using various data sources.

Structure

In this chapter, we will discuss the following topics:

- Overview of data-driven testing
- Using JSON files for test data
- Reading data from databases
- Implementing data-driven test cases

Overview of data-driven testing

Data-driven testing is an integral part of modern testing methodologies that enables the creation of flexible, reusable, and scalable test cases. This approach allows us to test the same functionality with various input data, enhancing our test scenarios' coverage.

Data-driven testing is typically executed by setting up a collection of test data outside the test scripts. This test data can be stored in various formats, including but not limited to databases, CSV files, Excel files, or JSON files. This chapter will focus specifically on utilizing JSON files and databases for data-driven testing with Cypress.

Data-driven testing comes with the following multiple advantages, and understanding these can underline its necessity in a robust testing strategy:

- **Enhanced Test Coverage:** By testing the same functionality with various sets of data, we can increase our test coverage and ensure our application behaves as expected under different conditions.
- **Code Reusability:** Instead of writing a new test case for each data set, we can use the same test code and feed it different data. This results in less code, which is easier to maintain and debug.
- **Efficiency:** A separate data source allows us to easily update, add, or delete test data without touching the test scripts. This approach makes managing and controlling the data we're testing against easier.
- **Early Bug Detection:** More data often means more edge cases, which improves the chances of catching a bug earlier in the testing process.

The following table summarizes the main differences between traditional testing and data-driven testing:

	Traditional Testing	**Data-Driven Testing**
Data	Embedded in the test scripts	Stored externally (for example, JSON files, databases)
Test Coverage	Limited by the hard-coded data	Can be increased by adding more data to the data source
Code Maintenance	Need to modify test scripts to change test data	Test data can be updated independently from test scripts
Bug Detection	It depends on how many test cases are manually written	Increased possibility of finding edge cases

Table 7.1: *Comparison of Traditional and Data-Driven Testing*

Data-Driven Testing in Action

Before we dive into more complex examples with JSON files and databases, let's start with a simple example of a data-driven test in Cypress.

Imagine testing a login form with multiple username and password data sets. Instead of writing a new test for each set of data, we can write a single test and iterate over an array of test data:

```
describe('Data-Driven Login Test', () => {
  const testData = [
```

```
    {username: 'user1', password: 'pass1'},
    {username: 'user2', password: 'pass2'},
    {username: 'user3', password: 'pass3'},
  ]

  testData.forEach((data) => {
    it(`Login test for ${data.username}`, () => {
      cy.visit('/login')
      cy.get('#username').type(data.username)
      cy.get('#password').type(data.password)
      cy.get('#login-button').click()
      cy.contains('Login Successful').should('be.visible')
    })
  })
})
```

In the preceding example, we define our test data in an array of objects, each representing a set of test data. We then use the `forEach` function to iterate over our test data and run our test case for each data set.

This is a simplistic illustration, but it demonstrates the core idea of data-driven testing. In the following sections, we'll discuss how to use more complex data sources like JSON files and databases for data-driven testing in Cypress.

As we move forward, we'll uncover how to store and manage our test data more efficiently and explore the power of data-driven testing in detail. So let's dive deeper into the world of data-driven testing with Cypress.

Using JSON Files for Test Data

One popular method for organizing and managing test data is using JSON (JavaScript Object Notation) files. JSON is a lightweight data-interchange format that is easy to read and write for humans and easy to parse and generate for machines. JSON is language-independent and can be combined with most modern programming languages.

Reasons for Using JSON Files

Several features make JSON an attractive option for storing test data as follows:

- **Human-readable:** JSON files are easily understood by people due to their clean, text-based format.
- **Lightweight:** JSON files require minimal space, and JSON data is easily transmitted between servers and web applications.
- **Structured Data:** JSON data is stored in key-value pairs, similar to JavaScript objects, making the data easy to access and manipulate.
- **Language-independent:** JSON data can be integrated and used with numerous programming languages, including JavaScript, which is the language of choice for Cypress.
- **Direct Support in Cypress:** Cypress has built-in commands for reading JSON files, so fetching and using data from JSON files in your tests is simple.

Structuring JSON Files for Test Data

JSON files for test data are typically organized in an array of objects, each representing a unique test case. Consider the following example of test data for a registration form:

```
[
    {
        "firstName": "John",
        "lastName": "Doe",
        "email": "john.doe@example.com",
        "password": "strongpassword"
    },
    {
        "firstName": "Jane",
        "lastName": "Doe",
        "email": "jane.doe@example.com",
        "password": "anotherstrongpassword"
    },
    ...
]
```

In this JSON file, each object represents a user with different data to register on a website. We can easily add more test cases by adding more objects to this JSON file.

Reading JSON Files in Cypress

Cypress provides the `cy.fixture()` command to read files from the `fixtures` directory. By default, the `fixtures` folder is located at the root level of the Cypress project directory. Here is an example of how we can use it to read our JSON file:

```
cy.fixture('testData.json').then((testData) => {
  // we can access the content of the JSON file within this callback
function
  console.log(testData)
})
```

In this example, `testData.json` is the name of our JSON file. `cy.fixture()` reads the file and parses the JSON content into a JavaScript object. We can access this object within the callback function passed to the `then()` method.

Implementing Data-Driven Tests with JSON Files

Let's combine everything and write a data-driven test case for the registration form using the JSON test data:

```
describe('Data-Driven Registration Test', () => {
  before(() => {
    cy.fixture('testData.json').as('testData'); // Alias the testData
  });

  it('Register new users from testData', function () {
    // The function notation allows you to use 'this.testData'
    // which is set by the use of the alias in the before hook.
    this.testData.forEach((data) => {
      cy.visit('/register');
      cy.get('#first-name').type(data.firstName);
```

```
      cy.get('#last-name').type(data.lastName);
      cy.get('#email').type(data.email);
      cy.get('#password').type(data.password);
      cy.get('#register-button').click();
      cy.contains('Registration Successful').should('be.visible');
    });
  });
});
```

We first read the JSON file using the `cy.fixture()` command in this example. We then use the `forEach()` function to iterate over our test data and create a test for each user.

Incorporating JSON files into our testing strategy has streamlined our testing process, enhancing flexibility and scalability. We can now easily add more test scenarios simply by appending them to our JSON files, eliminating the need to touch our test script code.

Reading Data from Databases

While using JSON files for test data offers simplicity and convenience, there are scenarios where more complex, dynamic data sets are required. This is where the ability to read data directly from databases becomes crucial.

This section will guide you through configuring Cypress to read data from databases. We will focus on using SQLite as a sample database, but the principles we discuss can be adapted to other databases with appropriate libraries and drivers.

Reasons for Using Databases for Test Data

Several reasons make databases a compelling source of test data as follows:

- **Realism:** Using actual data from your development or staging database makes your testing more realistic and robust.
- **Dynamic Data:** Databases allow you to work with dynamic data sets that can change over time, enabling you to cover more diverse scenarios in your testing.
- **Data Relationships:** Databases support complex data relationships, something not easily handled with flat file structures like JSON.

Setting up the Database Connection

The first step to reading data from a database is setting up the connection. This generally involves installing a suitable database driver or ORM (Object-Relational Mapping) tool, setting up your connection parameters, and testing the connection.

For SQLite, we can use the SQLite3 package in Node.js. First, install it as a devDependency:

```
npm install --save-dev sqlite3
```

Next, we create a helper file, `db.cjs`, that will create a database for us:

```
// db.cjs
const sqlite3 = require('sqlite3').verbose();


// Replace 'database.db' with the path to the file you want to create.
const DB_PATH = 'database.db';


// Connect to the database. If the file does not exist, it will be
created.
let db = new sqlite3.Database(DB_PATH, (err) => {
  if (err) {
    console.error(err.message);
    throw err;
  } else {
    console.log('Connected to the SQLite database.');
    db.run(`CREATE TABLE users (
      id INTEGER PRIMARY KEY AUTOINCREMENT,
      username text,
      password text,
      email text UNIQUE,
      active INTEGER
    )`, (err) => {
      if (err) {
        // Table already created
```

```
          console.log("Table already exists.");
        } else {
          // Table just created, creating some rows
          const insert = 'INSERT INTO users (username, password, email, active) VALUES (?,?,?,?)';
          db.run(insert, ["user1","password1","user1@example.com",1]);
          db.run(insert, ["user2","password2","user2@example.com",1]);
        }
      });
    }
  });

  // Close the database connection
  db.close((err) => {
    if (err) {
      console.error(err.message);
    }
    console.log('Close the database connection.');
  });
```

Use Node.js to run the script which will create the database and the users table with some initial data:

```
node db.cjs
```

Once you run this script, you should have a new file called `database.db` (or whatever you named it) in your project directory. This file is your SQLite database. The script also attempts to create a user's table and insert a couple of rows into it. If the table already exists, it will print a message and not attempt to create the table or insert the rows again.

Remember that every time you run this script, it will try to create the table and insert the initial rows, so you might want to modify it as needed for your use case.

Cypress test code must be written in a way that respects the Cypress asynchronous execution queue. The native database queries using Node.js libraries like sqlite3 don't return Cypress chainable objects, which means they're not managed by Cypress's internal promise chain.

Here's how to resolve this issue:

1. **Move Database Interaction to a Task**: Database interactions must be defined in a task within the cypress.config.js file because this is where Node.js code can run.

2. **Use Cypress Tasks in Test Files**: In your test files, you call the task you've set up to interact with the database.

Step 1: Define a task in the `cypress.config.js`

```
import { defineConfig } from "cypress";
import sqlite3 from 'sqlite3';
const { verbose } = sqlite3;
const db = verbose().Database;
const DB_PATH = 'database.db';

export default defineConfig({

  e2e: {
    setupNodeEvents(on, config) {
      // implement node event listeners here
      let database = new db(DB_PATH, sqlite3.OPEN_READONLY, (err) => {
        if (err) {
          console.error(err.message);
        }
        console.log('Connected to the SQLite database.');
      });

  on('task', {
    getActiveUsers() {
      return new Promise((resolve, reject) => {
        const sql = 'SELECT * FROM users WHERE active = 1';
        database.all(sql, [], (err, rows) => {
          if (err) {
            reject(err);
```

```
          }
          resolve(rows);
        });
      });
    }
  });

    },
  }
});
```

Step 2: Call the task in your Cypress tests

```
// Cypress test file
describe.only('Data-Driven Tests with Database Data', () => {
  it('should perform some data-driven tests', () => {
    cy.task('getActiveUsers').then((users) => {
      users.forEach((user) => {
        cy.visit('https://example.cypress.io');
        cy.get('#username').type(user.username);
        cy.get('#password').type(user.password);
        cy.get('#login-button').click();
        cy.contains('Login Successful').should('be.visible');
      });
    });
  });
});
```

Remember, the `cy.task()` command is used to send data from your Node.js environment to the browser-based tests. This way, you can keep your database operations in the Node.js context where they are synchronous and predictable, while still making use of the results in your asynchronous Cypress tests.

This example fetches a list of active users from our SQLite database and uses this data to drive a set of login tests. Each user's username and password are used to complete and submit the login form. The test then verifies that the login was successful.

Now, let's explore how to read data from MongoDB and MySQL databases for our Cypress tests.

Setting up MongoDB Connection

Let's start with MongoDB, a popular NoSQL database. To interact with MongoDB, you can use the native MongoDB Node.js driver or an Object Data Modeling (ODM) like Mongoose.

First, install MongoDB as a devDependency:

```
npm install --save-dev mongodb
```

Next, create a helper file, `dbMongo.js`, to manage the MongoDB connection and define a function to execute queries:

```
const { MongoClient } = require('mongodb');

async function getMongoDbData(collectionName, query) {
  const uri = 'your_mongodb_uri';
  const client = new MongoClient(uri);

  try {
    await client.connect();
    const database = client.db('your_database_name');
    const collection = database.collection(collectionName);
    return await collection.find(query).toArray();
  } finally {
    await client.close();
  }
}

module.exports = { getMongoDbData };
```

In this example, we connect to a MongoDB instance running locally and execute queries using MongoDB `find()` method.

Setting up MySQL Connection

For MySQL, we can use the mysql12 Node.js package which is a drop-in replacement for mysql and supports Promises.. Start by installing it as a devDependency:

```
npm install --save-dev mysql12
```

Then, like with MongoDB, we create a helper file `dbMySQL.js`:

```
// dbMySQL.js
const mysql = require('mysql2/promise');

async function getMySqlData(sql) {
  const connection = await mysql.createConnection({
    host: 'localhost',
    user: 'your_username',
    password: 'your_password',
    database: 'your_database'
  });

  try {
    const [rows] = await connection.query(sql);
    return rows;
  } finally {
    await connection.end();
  }
}

module.exports = { getMySqlData };
```

The `getMySqlData()` function creates a new connection to the MySQL server every time it is called, runs a query against the database, and returns a promise that resolves with the query results. After the query is completed, the function ensures that the connection is closed properly

Using MongoDB and MySQL Data in Cypress Tests

To use these functions in Cypress, you would typically not call them directly in your test files because Cypress commands run in the browser context, while Node.js code (like database connections) runs in the Node context.

Instead, you can use Cypress tasks to bridge this gap. Here's an example of setting up a task in your `cypress.config.js` file:

```
const { getMongoDbData } = require('../../path_to_your_mongo_helper');
const { getMySqlData } = require('../../path_to_your_mysql_helper');


module.exports = (on, config) => {
  on('task', {
    async getMongoData({ collectionName, query }) {
      return await getMongoDbData(collectionName, query);
    },
    async getMySqlData(sql) {
      return await getMySqlData(sql);
    }
  });
};
```

For MongoDB:

```
it('retrieves data from MongoDB', () => {
  cy.task('getMongoData', { collectionName: 'users', query: {} }).then(users => {
    // Use users data for the test
  });
});
```

For MySQL:

```
it('retrieves data from MySQL', () => {
  cy.task('getMySqlData', 'SELECT * FROM users').then(users => {
```

```
    // Use users data for the test
  });
});
```

This setup allows you to execute Node.js code, including database interactions, from your Cypress tests. Always make sure to handle sensitive information such as database credentials securely and not expose them in your codebase.

By extending the use of databases to MongoDB and MySQL, we demonstrate the adaptability of Cypress in handling different data sources. Following the established pattern of setting up a connection and querying data, you can use virtually any database with Cypress, making your data-driven tests more flexible and representative of real-world applications.

Implementing Data-Driven Test Cases

As we continue to delve into data-driven testing with Cypress, it's crucial to understand some of the best practices for conducting Cypress database testing effectively and efficiently. These practices will help improve the quality and reliability of your tests and ensure a smooth testing experience.

Segregation of Test Data and Production Data

An essential rule to abide by when conducting tests is to keep test data distinct from production data. The potential for data corruption, inconsistency, or loss is too great a risk. The following are a few methods to maintain this segregation:

- **Distinct Test Database:** Deploy a separate test database distinct from the production one. This helps protect your production data from any accidental modifications during testing. An alternative could be using the same database server with a distinct name for testing purposes.
- **Database Migration Scripts:** Use these scripts to define the test database schema and seed the initial data. This ensures your test data's consistency and known state across different test runs.
- **Test-specific Seed Data:** Employ test-specific seed data to ensure each test is self-contained and reproducible. This also aids in troubleshooting potential issues during testing.
- **Transactional Testing:** Every test should execute in a separate database transaction and should roll back once the test completes. This helps ensure that your test data does not interfere with production data.

- **Cleanup after Testing:** Post-testing, clear all the test data created in the database. Database migration scripts or cleanup functions in your tests can handle this task.

Leveraging Realistic Data in Tests

Utilizing realistic data during Cypress testing can help identify bugs that might not surface with artificial test data:

- **Real-world Scenarios:** Design test cases to emulate real-world scenarios your customers frequently encounter. This could involve multiple users, diverse user roles, or different data sets.
- **Production-like Data:** Test with data that closely mirrors production data. This includes data volume, types, and distribution.
- **Anonymized Data:** Always anonymize sensitive customer data to maintain customer privacy when testing.
- **Test Data Generators:** Use tools to automate the creation of realistic data, especially when dealing with large data sets.
- **Data Randomization:** Generate a broad range of test data values and edge cases using randomization techniques to uncover potential bugs.
- **Data Visualizations:** Use data visualization techniques to analyze test results better and identify patterns or trends indicating areas of improvement.

Minimizing Test Data Duplication

Reducing test data duplication in Cypress can increase the readability and reliability of your tests while avoiding unnecessary maintenance:

- **Fixtures:** Use fixtures to load test data into your tests. These external data files can be reused across multiple tests, thus avoiding test data duplication within your test files.
- **Data Factories:** Use these to generate test data dynamically. This allows each test to have unique data, reducing the need for duplicate data.
- **Database Migrations:** Leverage database migrations to populate the test database with initial data, helping avoid test data duplication in your test files.
- **Test-specific Data:** Make each test independent with its unique data set to avoid data duplication across multiple tests.
- **Shared Data:** Shared data can be used across multiple tests to improve readability and maintainability. However, avoid overusing shared data

as it might introduce complexities in understanding the dependencies between tests.

Employing Cypress Plugins for Database Testing

Cypress plugins are a robust feature that extends Cypress's functionality through custom code. With regard to database testing, plugins can simplify and automate the testing process as follows:

- **Database Plugins:** Cypress supports plugins that interact with databases, simplifying operations like create, read, update, and delete. For instance, the 'cypress-firebase' plugin for Firebase database interactions or the 'cypress-mongo-seed' for seeding a MongoDB database.
- **Test Data Generation Plugins:** These plugins help swiftly create large sets of realistic data, which is beneficial when dealing with large data sets. For example, the 'cypress-faker' for generating realistic test data or the 'cypress-data-session' for unique test data per test run.
- **Cypress Tasks:** Tasks allow you to execute custom Node.js code during your Cypress tests. This could be used for database interactions or other operations. For instance, a task could run a database migration script before your tests or seed your test database with initial data.
- **Assertion Plugins:** These plugins add custom assertions to your tests, helping to validate data retrieved from the database against specific criteria. For example, the 'chai-firebase' plugin can add Firebase-specific assertions to your tests.

Moving forward in our journey to master data-driven testing with Cypress, we are ready to execute test cases directly against our data sources. This section will guide you through setting up a test database, connecting Cypress to this database, implementing CRUD operations tests, verifying data integrity, and testing database transactions and migrations.

Setting up a Test Database

First, you need a database designated exclusively for testing. This database should mirror your production database structure but should operate independently to avoid any inadvertent modifications to production data.

Let's assume you're working with MySQL. You can use a tool like MySQL Workbench to set up a new database or use the MySQL command-line interface.

```
CREATE DATABASE cypress_test;
```

This SQL command will create a new database named `cypress_test`.

Connecting Cypress to the Test Database

Cypress doesn't directly interact with databases as it operates in the browser context. However, you can use Cypress tasks to run server-side code, thus interacting with your database.

First, install a suitable Node.js database client. For MySQL, you can use the **`mysql2`** library. Install it with npm:

```
npm install --save-dev mysql2
```

Next, create a new task in your `cypress.config..js` file to connect to the database:

```
const { defineConfig } = require('cypress')
const mysql = require('mysql2');
const connection = mysql.createConnection({
  host: 'localhost',
  user: 'root',
  database: 'cypress_test'
});

module.exports = defineConfig({
  // setupNodeEvents can be defined in either
  // the e2e or component configuration
  e2e: {
    setupNodeEvents(on, config) {
on('task', {
        'queryDatabase': query => {
          return new Promise((resolve, reject) => {
                  connection.query(query, (error, results) => {
                  if (error) reject(error)
                  else resolve(results)
                  })
        })
      }
```

```
    });
  };
```

The `'queryDatabase'` task allows you to execute any SQL query against your MySQL test database.

Test Cases for CRUD Operations

With the database connection in place, you can now write test cases for CRUD (**Create**, **Read**, **Update**, **Delete**) operations.

Here is an example of a simple test case for a **CREATE** operation:

```
describe('CREATE Operation', () => {
  it('creates a new record', () => {
    // Arrange
    const sqlInsert = `INSERT INTO users (name, email) VALUES
('John Doe', 'john@example.com')`;

    // Act & Assert
    cy.task('queryDatabase', sqlInsert).then(() => {
      const sqlSelect = `SELECT * FROM users WHERE email = 'john@
example.com'`;
      cy.task('queryDatabase', sqlSelect).then(result => {
        expect(result[0].name).to.equal('John Doe');
        expect(result[0].email).to.equal('john@example.com');
      });
    });
  });
});
```

Similar test cases can be written for **READ**, **UPDATE**, and **DELETE** operations.

The **READ** operation retrieves data from the database. Here is an example:

```
describe('READ Operation', () => {
  it('reads an existing record', () => {
    // Arrange
    const sqlInsert = `INSERT INTO users (name, email) VALUES
```

```
('John Doe', 'john@example.com')`;

    // Act & Assert
    cy.task('queryDatabase', sqlInsert).then(() => {
      const sqlSelect = `SELECT * FROM users WHERE email = 'john@
example.com'`;
      cy.task('queryDatabase', sqlSelect).then(result => {
        expect(result[0].name).to.equal('John Doe');
        expect(result[0].email).to.equal('john@example.com');
      });
    });
  });
});
```

The **UPDATE** operation changes existing data in the database. Here is a test case:

```
describe('UPDATE Operation', () => {
  it('updates an existing record', () => {
    // Arrange
    const sqlInsert = `INSERT INTO users (name, email) VALUES
('John Doe', 'john@example.com')`;

    // Act & Assert
    cy.task('queryDatabase', sqlInsert).then(() => {
      const sqlUpdate = `UPDATE users SET name = 'Jane Doe' WHERE
email = 'john@example.com'`;
      cy.task('queryDatabase', sqlUpdate).then(() => {
        const sqlSelect = `SELECT * FROM users WHERE email =
'john@example.com'`;
        cy.task('queryDatabase', sqlSelect).then(result => {
          expect(result[0].name).to.equal('Jane Doe');
        });
      });
    });
  });
```

```
});
```

The **DELETE** operation removes existing data from the database. Here is a test case:

```
describe('DELETE Operation', () => {
  it('deletes an existing record', () => {
    // Arrange
    const sqlInsert = `INSERT INTO users (name, email) VALUES
('John Doe', 'john@example.com')`;
    // Act & Assert
    cy.task('queryDatabase', sqlInsert).then(() => {
      const sqlDelete = `DELETE FROM users WHERE email = 'john@
example.com'`;
      cy.task('queryDatabase', sqlDelete).then(() => {
        const sqlSelect = `SELECT * FROM users WHERE email =
'john@example.com'`;
        cy.task('queryDatabase', sqlSelect).then(result => {
          expect(result).to.have.length(0);
        });
      });
    });
  });
});
```

These examples are straightforward and show the basic structure of CRUD operations. Of course, your actual test cases may be more complex depending on the specifics of your application.

Test Case to Verify Data Integrity

Data integrity is critical in any application. The **queryDatabase** task you've implemented can also help write test cases to verify data integrity. Here's an example test case:

```
describe('Data Integrity', () => {
  it('should have consistent data for a user', () => {
    const sqlSelect = `SELECT * FROM users WHERE email = 'john@
example.com'`;
```

```
      cy.task('queryDatabase', sqlSelect).then(result => {
        expect(result[0].name).to.equal('John Doe');
        expect(result[0].email).to.equal('john@example.com');
        expect(result[0].status).to.equal('active');
      });
    });
  });
```

Testing Database Transactions

Testing database transactions helps ensure that multiple related operations succeed or fail as a unit:

```
describe('Database Transactions', () => {
  it('should rollback transaction if an operation fails', () => {
    const sqlTransaction = `
      START TRANSACTION;
      INSERT INTO users (name, email) VALUES ('Jane Doe', 'jane@example.
com');
      INSERT INTO users (name, email) VALUES ('Jane Doe', NULL);  //
This should fail
      COMMIT;
    `;

    // Use .then() to handle fulfilled and rejected promises
    cy.task('queryDatabase', sqlTransaction).then(
      () => {
        // If the transaction is successful (which we don't expect)
        throw new Error('Transaction should have failed');
      },
      (error) => {
        // Transaction failed as expected, now check if the rollback was
successful
        const sqlSelect = `SELECT * FROM users WHERE name = 'Jane Doe'`;
        cy.task('queryDatabase', sqlSelect).then((result) => {
```

```
          expect(result).to.have.length(0); // Asserts that the transac-
tion was rolled back
        });
      }
    );
  });
});
```

Testing Database Migrations

Database migrations are a way to version control your database changes. Testing these migrations ensures that your database upgrades and downgrades work as expected. Here's an example:

```
describe('Database Migrations', () => {
  it('should apply migrations successfully', () => {
    const sqlMigrate = `
      ALTER TABLE users ADD COLUMN phone VARCHAR(20) AFTER email;
    `;

    cy.task('queryDatabase', sqlMigrate).then(() => {
      const sqlSelect = `SHOW COLUMNS FROM users LIKE 'phone'`;
      cy.task('queryDatabase', sqlSelect).then(result => {
        expect(result).to.have.length(1);
      });
    });
  });
});
```

This test case asserts that a new **phone** column was successfully added to the **users** table.

Data-driven test cases bring accuracy, efficiency, and robustness to your testing strategy. As you have seen, Cypress provides an excellent platform to create and manage these tests, making your applications reliable and bug-free.

Conclusion

This chapter focuses on data-driven testing with Cypress. This chapter overviews data-driven testing and its benefits in creating flexible and reusable test cases. Readers will learn how to leverage JSON files as a source of test data, enabling them to populate test scenarios dynamically. Additionally, the chapter covers reading data from databases, expanding the possibilities for data-driven testing. By the end of the chapter, readers will have a solid understanding of how to implement data-driven test cases, utilizing various data sources to enhance the effectiveness and versatility of their tests.

In the upcoming chapter, we will delve into advanced techniques in Cypress, empowering readers to enhance their test automation workflow. The chapter starts by exploring the creation of custom commands, allowing readers to encapsulate reusable test logic and simplify test code. It then introduces using videos and screenshots for debugging, aiding in identifying and resolving issues effectively. The chapter also covers working with Cypress plugins, enabling readers to extend Cypress's functionality and integrate additional tools seamlessly. Furthermore, advanced topics such as handling authentication and authorization, parallel test execution, cross-browser testing, network stubbing and mocking, and visual regression testing are discussed in detail. By leveraging these advanced techniques, readers will be able to optimize their test suite, increase efficiency, and ensure high-quality test coverage.

Further Reading

To expand readers' knowledge on the topics discussed in this chapter, it is recommended to explore these additional resources:

1. **Cypress Fixtures:** The Cypress documentation on fixtures (https://docs.cypress.io/api/commands/fixture) explains how to use JSON files as fixtures to provide test data for your Cypress tests. It covers how to load and use fixture data in your tests.
2. **Database Testing with Cypress:** This blog post (https://www.browserstack.com/guide/cypress-database-testing) walks you through setting up and testing a real database with Cypress.

These resources will give you a broader understanding and practical examples of the concepts you've learned in this chapter.

CHAPTER 8
Advanced Cypress Techniques

Introduction

This chapter will explore advanced Cypress techniques, such as creating custom commands, using videos and screenshots for debugging, and working with plugins. These techniques will help readers improve their test automation workflow and make their tests more efficient and maintainable.

Structure

In this chapter, we will discuss the following topics:

- Creating custom commands
- Using videos and screenshots for debugging
- Working with Cypress plugins
- Handling Authentication and Authorization
- Parallel Test Execution
- Cross-Browser Testing
- Network Stubbing and Mocking
- Visual Regression Testing

Cypress custom commands

Using custom commands is a powerful technique that aids in reducing the complexity of tests by encapsulating repetitive sequences of actions. Custom commands can make tests easier to read, write, and maintain. In this section, we'll delve deeper into the process of creating and leveraging custom commands in Cypress.

Before we begin, let's discuss the following reasons why we might need custom commands:

- **Reduced Redundancy:** Custom commands allow us to avoid repetition in our test code, keeping our tests DRY (Don't Repeat Yourself). If you find yourself writing identical sequences of actions in multiple tests, consider creating a custom command.
- **Improved Readability:** We make our test code more readable by bundling multiple actions or assertions into one command. A well-named custom command can immediately clarify what a test code does.
- **Easier Maintenance:** It's much easier to update a single custom command rather than multiple instances of the same code scattered throughout your tests when changes are required.

Creating a custom command

Custom commands in Cypress are defined in the `commands.js` file within the support folder of your Cypress project. Here is an example of how to define a simple custom command:

```
Cypress.Commands.add('login', (username, password) => {
  cy.visit('/login');
  cy.get('input[name="username"]').type(username);
  cy.get('input[name="password"]').type(password);
  cy.get('button[type="submit"]').click();
});
```

This `login` command encapsulates the actions necessary to log into our application. Instead of writing these steps every time we want to log in during a test, we can simply use the command `cy.login('myUsername', 'myPassword')`.

Using a custom command

To use a custom command, we simply call it like any other Cypress command, prefixed with `cy`. Using the `login` command we defined earlier, a test that uses this command might appear as follows:

```
describe('Dashboard Test', () => {
```

```
    it('displays user data after login', () => {
      cy.login('myUsername', 'myPassword');
      cy.visit('/dashboard');
      cy.contains('Welcome, myUsername');
    });
  });
```

Custom command overwrites

You can overwrite existing Cypress commands with your custom behavior. You use `Cypress.Commands.overwrite()` instead of `Cypress.Commands.add()`. This can be useful when you want to extend the functionality of an existing command. Here's an example:

```
Cypress.Commands.overwrite('visit', (originalFn, url, options) =>
{
  console.log(`Visiting: ${url}`);
  originalFn(url, options);
});
```

In this example, we've extended the `cy.visit()` command to log the URL being visited before navigating to it. The `originalFn` parameter refers to the original, built-in command we're overwriting.

Asynchronous custom commands

Custom commands can also be asynchronous and valuable when dealing with network requests, timeouts, or any operation that may not be completed immediately. To handle this, Cypress commands utilize Promises. Here is an example of an asynchronous custom command:

```
Cypress.Commands.add('createUser', (username, email) => {
  return new Cypress.Promise((resolve, reject) => {
    cy.request('POST', '/users', { username, email }).then((re-
sponse) => {
      if (response.status === 201) {
        resolve(response.body);
      } else {
        reject(`Failed to create user: ${response.body}`);
```

```
        }
      });
    });
  });
```

In this example, our `createUser` command makes a `POST` request to the `/users` endpoint of our application, creating a new user. The command returns a Promise, which resolves with the created user's data if the request is successful, or rejects with an error message if it fails.

This command can be used in the following manner:

```
cy.createUser('myUsername', 'myEmail').then((user) => {
  expect(user.username).to.equal('myUsername');
  expect(user.email).to.equal('myEmail');
});
```

Custom commands in Cypress offer an efficient way to streamline your tests, making them more readable and easier to maintain. They offer flexibility to meet your testing requirements, from simple actions to asynchronous network operations. By mastering custom commands, you can significantly enhance the power and effectiveness of your Cypress tests.

Chaining custom commands

Cypress's command chaining feature also extends to custom commands. Because custom commands are executed in the same run-loop as built-in Cypress commands, they can be chained together similarly. Here is an example:

```
Cypress.Commands.add('loginAndVisitDashboard', (username,
password) => {
  cy.login(username, password);
  cy.visit('/dashboard');
});
```

This `loginAndVisitDashboard` command chains together our earlier `login` command and the built-in `visit` command. Using this command, a test case could be as simple as follows:

```
it('Should display user dashboard after login', () => {
  cy.loginAndVisitDashboard('myUsername', 'myPassword');
```

```
  cy.contains('Welcome, myUsername');
});
```

Passing options to custom commands

Custom commands can also take an options object as an argument. This can be useful for handling optional parameters or flags in your commands. Here is an example:

```
Cypress.Commands.add('login', (username, password, options = {})
=> {
  cy.visit(options.loginUrl || '/login');
  cy.get('input[name="username"]').type(username);
  cy.get('input[name="password"]').type(password);
  cy.get('button[type="submit"]').click();
});
```

In this example, we've added an options parameter to our `login` command. The `loginUrl` option can be used to specify a custom login URL. If no `loginUrl` is provided, the default `'/login'` is used.

Custom commands with aliases

Custom commands can take advantage of Cypress's aliasing feature to store and retrieve data. For example, you might want to create a custom command that makes an HTTP request and then aliases the response for use in later tests:

```
Cypress.Commands.add('fetchUser', (userId) => {
  cy.request(`/users/${userId}`).as('user');
});
```

Later on in your tests, you can reference this alias using `cy.get()`:

```
cy.fetchUser(1);
cy.get('@user').its('body').should('have.property', 'username');
```

Validating custom commands

Finally, it's crucial to validate the functionality of your custom commands. Custom commands can (and should) be tested just like any other part of your application. Consider adding a test suite that explicitly targets your custom commands to ensure they function as expected.

Creating custom commands in Cypress allows you to abstract and encapsulate commonly used sequences of actions or assertions into reusable pieces of code. They can improve your test suite's readability, maintainability, and robustness. By thoughtfully organizing your custom commands, you can create a powerful testing DSL (Domain-Specific Language) specific to your application's needs.

Use cases for custom commands

Here are a few common use cases that illustrate why and when you might want to create a custom command:

- **Logging in:** If your tests require logging in before certain operations can be performed, you can create a custom command that performs the login operation instead of writing the login code in every test.
- **Form filling:** If your application has complex forms that need to be filled out in many different tests, you can create a custom command to fill the form.
- **Navigating through the app:** If a complex series of clicks or page visits need to be performed to get to a particular state in your app, these can be abstracted into a custom command.
- **Complex assertions:** If complex assertions are frequently used across your tests, these can be abstracted into a custom command.

Let's illustrate these with the following examples:

- **Logging in**

```
Cypress.Commands.add("login", (username, password) => {
    cy.visit('/login');
    cy.get('#username').type(username);
    cy.get('#password').type(password);
    cy.get('#login-button').click();
});

// Usage in test
cy.login('testuser', 'testpassword');
```

- **Form filling**

```
Cypress.Commands.add("fillForm", (name, email, password) => {
    cy.get('#name').type(name);
    cy.get('#email').type(email);
    cy.get('#password').type(password);
    cy.get('#confirmPassword').type(password);
});

// Usage in test
cy.fillForm('Test User', 'testuser@example.com', 'testpass-
word');
```

- **Navigating through the app**

```
Cypress.Commands.add("navigateTo", (menu) => {
    cy.get('#menu-button').click();
    cy.contains(menu).click();
});

// Usage in test
cy.navigateTo('Profile');
```

- **Complex assertions**

```
Cypress.Commands.add("assertUserCount", (count) => {
    cy.get('.user').should('have.length', count);
});

// Usage in test
cy.assertUserCount(5);
```

Overriding existing commands

Sometimes, you may want to change the behavior of an existing Cypress command. You can do this by creating a custom command with the same name as the existing command.

For example, let's say you want to change the behavior of the visit command so that it always waits for a particular element to be visible after the page load:

```
Cypress.Commands.overwrite("visit", (originalFn, url, options) =>
{
  originalFn(url, options);
  cy.get('#page-loaded-indicator', { timeout: 10000
}).should('be.visible');
});

// Usage in test
cy.visit('/profile');
```

This version of the visit command will wait for the `#page-loaded-indicator` element to be visible, with a timeout of 10 seconds. This could be useful if you always want to ensure a specific element is loaded before the test continues.

This feature should be used with caution as it could lead to confusion if the behavior of a standard Cypress command is drastically different from what's expected. However, sometimes, it can help make your tests more concise and easier to understand.

One exciting addition to this section on custom commands might be handling custom command errors and debugging. This would enhance the robustness of your testing suite and provide deeper insights into the possible issues that might occur during testing.

Handling errors in custom commands

Like the built-in Cypress commands, custom commands can also fail. They might fail because the element they're looking for doesn't exist, an assertion fails, a request times out, and many other reasons.

Here's a simple example of handling errors in custom commands:

```
Cypress.Commands.add('login', (username, password) => {
    cy.visit('/login')
        .get('#username').type(username).should('have.value',
username)
        .get('#password').type(password).should('have.value',
password)
```

```
            .get('#login-button').click()
            .wait('@loginCall').its('status').should('eq', 200);
    });
```

Here, `.should('have.value', username)` will fail if, after typing, the input field doesn't contain the expected username. Similarly, `.its('status').should('eq', 200);` will fail if the status of the `loginCall` is not `200`.

When a custom command fails, Cypress will automatically provide an error message with details about the failure. After any chained command, you can add custom error messages using .and('contain', 'Expected text').

Debugging custom commands

Debugging custom commands is similar to debugging any Cypress test. You can use `.debug()` to pause the execution of the command and open your browser's developer tools to inspect the state of your application at that point.

Here's an example:

```
    Cypress.Commands.add('login', (username, password) => {
        cy.visit('/login')
            .get('#username').type(username).debug()
            .get('#password').type(password)
            .get('#login-button').click()
            .wait('@loginCall').its('status').should('eq', 200);
    });
```

In this case, `.debug()` is chained after `.type(username)`, so the test execution will pause after typing the username.

Best practices for custom commands

To conclude this section, let's revisit some best practices for using custom commands in Cypress as follows:

- Keep your custom commands small and focused. If your custom command gets too complex, consider breaking it down into smaller commands.
- Avoid using custom commands to implement test logic. Custom commands should be used for actions that are repeated across multiple tests.

- Use meaningful names for your custom commands. The name should describe what the command does.
- Document your custom commands. This will help other team members understand what each command does and when to use it.
- Handle errors and exceptions in your custom commands. This will make your tests more robust and easier to debug.
- Test your custom commands. Even though custom commands are part of your tests, they're also code that can contain bugs. Make sure to test them as you would any other aspect of your codebase.

Cypress's custom commands are powerful tools for enhanced test reusability, maintainability, and efficiency, as they encapsulate repetitive test actions or assertions. It's crucial to ensure these commands are small, focused, and meaningfully named for clarity, and they should be appropriately handled for errors and debugged, contributing to robust and reliable tests. While custom commands provide significant advantages, it's important to remember that they should not be used to implement test logic. Like any other code, they need to be thoroughly tested and documented.

Using videos and screenshots for debugging

As a testing tool, Cypress does not merely serve as an executor of test scripts. It's a multi-faceted framework that simplifies debugging and makes issue diagnosis more straightforward and faster. In this chapter, we delve into two key features Cypress provides out of the box: screenshots and videos for debugging purposes.

Before proceeding with the advanced capabilities of Cypress, it's crucial to comprehend the essence of debugging. Debugging is the process of locating and fixing or bypassing bugs (errors) in computer program code or the engineering of a hardware device.

In testing, debugging is of utmost importance. This process enables us to find the cause of a failure or unexpected behavior and resolve it. Debugging tests differ slightly from debugging the application code, as our primary focus is to understand why a test failed rather than why the application did not work as expected.

Debugging with screenshots

Cypress offers an automatic screenshot-capturing feature, providing a visual trail of the actions performed during a test case. The screenshots taken can be perused to understand test failures or reference purposes.

Consider the following test case:

```
describe('Login Test', function() {
    it('Logs in to the system', function() {
        cy.visit('/login')                              // Navigate to the
login page
        cy.get('#username').type('testUser')            // Enter the
username
        cy.get('#password').type('testPassword')        // Enter the
password
        cy.get('#login').click()                        // Click on the
login button
        cy.url().should('include', '/dashboard')        // Assert that the
URL contains '/dashboard'
    })
})
```

If the preceding test fails, Cypress will automatically take a screenshot at the point of failure and save it into the `cypress/screenshots` directory by default.

You can also take screenshots manually in your test by using the `cy.screenshot()` command:

```
cy.screenshot('login-screen')  // captures screenshot of the
entire screen
```

You can capture a screenshot of a specific element too:

```
cy.get('#username').screenshot() // captures screenshot of username
input
```

You can crop a screenshot to a specific position and size:

```
 // screenshot will be clipped 20px from the top and left
// to the dimensions 400px x 300px
cy.screenshot({ clip: { x: 20, y: 20, width: 400, height: 300 }
})
```

Remember, screenshots are still images and might not give a complete picture of the system's state at the time of failure. It's also essential to rely on error messages, logs, and other resources.

Debugging with videos

While screenshots provide a snapshot of the state at a specific point in time, Cypress goes one step ahead and offers a feature to capture the whole testing process as a video. By default, Cypress records a video for every spec file when running `cypress run`.

These videos are invaluable when tests run in the Continuous Integration (CI) environment, where observing the tests in action is hard. The videos are stored in the `cypress/videos` directory by default.

To control the video recording, you can adjust the settings in your `cypress.config.js` configuration file:

```
{
    "video": true,
    "videoUploadOnPasses": false,
    "videosFolder": "cypress/videos",
    "videoCompression": false,
    "numVideoFrames": 30
}
```

- **`"video": true`** - Enables or disables video recording entirely.
- **`"videoUploadOnPasses": false`** - Tells Cypress not to process and upload the video if all tests pass.
- **`"videosFolder": "cypress/videos"`** - Specifies where to save the recorded video files.
- **`"videoCompression": false`** - Disables video compression to speed up processing at the cost of larger video files.
- **`"numVideoFrames": 30`** - Controls the frames per second of the recorded video.

If your specification files take a while to run, you may observe a pause between when one spec finishes and the next one begins during a Cypress run. This delay occurs as Cypress encodes the recorded video and potentially uploads it to the Cypress Cloud.

If you've noticed that your machine is encoding videos slowly, it may be worth adjusting the `videoCompression` configuration to improve the speed. This is particularly relevant if you use a virtual machine with fewer CPU cores. Here are some common situations where you may want to make this adjustment:

```
const { defineConfig } = require('cypress')


module.exports = defineConfig({
  videoCompression: 15,
})
```

If you use a lower value for video compression, the compression process will take less time, and the resulting video file size will be more significant.

During your Cypress test execution, there may be instances where you wish to exercise more control over the videos you preserve and send to the Cypress Cloud. The prudent management of video resources can economize storage space on your local machine and bypass the time required for the video's processing, compression, and subsequent upload to the Cypress Cloud.

One way to selectively manage your videos is using the `videoUploadOnPasses` configuration option. When set to false, this setting ensures videos are only processed if a test fails:

```
// In the cypress.json file
{
  "videoUploadOnPasses": false
}
```

Cypress provides the `after:spec` event listener for even more detailed control. This listener is triggered after each spec file completes its run. You can implement conditions within this listener to determine if a video should be deleted post-run. This allows for a custom, condition-based video management approach.

Here is an example of how to use `after:spec` to delete a video when no tests fail in that spec:

```
// In your config file
module.exports = (on, config) => {
  on('after:spec', (spec, results) => {
    if (results && results.video) {
      // Do we have failures for this spec?
```

```
          if (results.stats.failures === 0 && results.video) {
            // delete the video if the spec passed and there's a video
            return new Promise((resolve, reject) => {
              fs.unlink(results.video, (err) => {
                if (err) return reject(err)
                // video removed successfully
                resolve()
              })
            })
          }
        }
      })
    }
```

By wisely managing your test videos, you can optimize your usage of resources, speed up your test runs, and still maintain access to crucial debugging information when a test fails.

The following example demonstrates how to eliminate the recorded video for specs without retry attempts or failures when using Cypress's test retry functionality. This approach can help manage your resources more effectively by only keeping videos for tests that had issues during execution:

```
const { defineConfig } = require('cypress')
const fs = require('fs')

module.exports = defineConfig({
  // setupNodeEvents can be defined in either
  // the e2e or component configuration
  e2e: {
    setupNodeEvents(on, config) {
      on('after:spec', (spec, results) => {
        if (results && results.video) {
          // Are there any failures during the test attempts?
          const hasFailures = results.tests.some((test) =>
            test.attempts.some((attempt) => attempt.state ===
```

```
'failed')
          )
          if (!hasFailures) {
            // If the spec passed without any test retries, de-
lete the video
            fs.unlinkSync(results.video)
          }
        }
      })
    },
  },
})
```

In the preceding code, we're utilizing the `after:spec` event to examine the results of each test attempt. If no test has a state of '**`failed`**', it implies that the spec executed without issues, and, therefore, the associated video recording is deleted. This allows for effectively retaining only those videos that may aid in debugging problematic test cases.

Using screenshots and videos effectively

Screenshots and videos can both be beneficial for debugging, but they also serve different purposes:

Feature	**Use Case**
Screenshots	Useful for quickly checking a specific point in a test run, mainly when a particular error or failure point is known
Videos	Useful for viewing the entire flow of a test run, particularly beneficial in cases where tests are passing locally but failing on a CI server

Table 8.1: *Screenshots and Videos use cases*

These two features complement each other and provide a powerful means to debug tests effectively.

Here are some best practices for using screenshots and videos in Cypress:

- Only take screenshots when necessary to avoid cluttering your test results.

- Name your screenshots and videos in a way that makes it easy to identify the test scenario they relate to.
- Regularly clean up old screenshots and videos to conserve storage space.
- Use screenshots and videos as complementary debugging tools to your console logs and test results.
- Configure your pipeline to preserve these files as artifacts for each test run when running tests in a CI environment.

Following these guidelines, you can effectively utilize Cypress's screenshot and video features to debug your tests.

Working with Cypress plugins

Custom plugins are a powerful tool in Cypress that allow you to alter, enhance, or extend the internal behavior of Cypress. Under typical conditions, all your test code, application, and Cypress commands execute in the browser. However, Cypress also operates as a Node process that you can tap into using plugins, offering a unique ability to execute custom code during various stages of the Cypress lifecycle.

Let's create a simple plugin to log messages to the console. First, we must add a new task inside the exported function in the plugins file. Here is an example:

```
const { defineConfig } = require('cypress')


module.exports = defineConfig({
    e2e: {
     setupNodeEvents(on, config) => {
       on('task', {
         log(message) {
           console.log(message)
              return null
         },
       })
    }
  },
})
```

In this example, we've created a `log` task to print whatever message it receives to the console. The `return null` statement is necessary because Cypress expects the task function to return a value.

Use the **`cy.task()`** command to call this task from a test:

```
it('logs a message', () => {
  cy.task('log', 'This is a message from a test')
})
```

When this test runs, **`This is a message from a test`**, will be printed to the console in the terminal where you ran `cypress open` or `cypress run`, not the browser's console.

Configuration

Cypress allows you to change the resolved configuration and environment variables programmatically using plugins. This includes variables from the Cypress configuration file (`cypress.env.json`), the command line, or system environment variables. With this functionality, you can:

- Set up distinct environments with their respective configurations
- Change environment variables depending on the environment
- Use the built-in `fs` lib to read configuration files
- Modify the list of browsers used for testing
- Employ YAML for your configuration

Preprocessors

By default, Cypress handles ES2015+, TypeScript, and CoffeeScript, packaging it for the browser using webpack. The `file:preprocessor` event allows you to customize this process, enabling you to:

- Write your test code in ClojureScript
- Customize Babel settings to include your own plugins
- Customize options for compiling TypeScript
- Swap webpack for Browserify or another preference

Run lifecycle

The `before:run` and `after:run` events occur before and after a run, respectively.

You can utilize `before:run` for setting up reporting on a run or starting a timer for the run. On the other hand, `after:run` can be used to wrap up reporting set up in `before:run` or stop the timer initiated in `before:run`.

Spec lifecycle

Similar to the Run Lifecycle events, `before:spec` and `after:spec` run before and after a single spec, respectively. You can utilize these events for setting up reporting on a spec, starting a timer for the spec, wrapping up reporting set up in `before:spec`, or stopping the timer initiated in `before:spec`. Additionally, you can delete the video recorded for the spec using `after:spec`, preserving computational resources and time by not compressing and uploading the video. You may make this conditional based on the spec results, for instance, only deleting the video if the spec passes.

Browser launching

The `before:browser:launch` event can be utilized to modify the launch arguments for different browsers. This event can load a Chrome extension, enable or disable experimental Chrome features, or control which Chrome components load.

Screenshot handling

The `after:screenshot` event is triggered after a screenshot is taken and saved to disk. You can use this event to save details about the screenshot, rename the screenshot, or manipulate the screenshot image by resizing or cropping it.

cy.task

The task event is used in conjunction with the `cy.task()` command. It permits you to write arbitrary code in Node to accomplish tasks that can't be performed in the browser. This enables tasks like:

- Manipulating a database (seeding, reading, writing, and so on)
- Storing state in Node that you want to persist (since the driver refreshes completely on visits)
- Performing parallel tasks (like making multiple HTTP requests outside of Cypress)
- Running an external process (like spinning up a Webdriver instance of another browser like Safari or Puppeteer)

List of plugins

Cypress provides a curated list of plugins, both from the Cypress team and the community. These plugins can be installed via npm, allowing them to be versioned and updated separately without updating Cypress.

You can install any published plugin using npm:

```
npm install <plugin name> --save-dev
```

Add a plugin in Cypress to the `setupNodeEvents` function in the Cypress configuration (as of Cypress version 10.0.0). If you're using an older version of Cypress, you can add your plugin to the (now deprecated) plugins file.

Here's a sample of what this might look like in `cypress.config.js`:

```
const { defineConfig } = require('cypress')

module.exports = defineConfig({
  e2e: {
    setupNodeEvents(on, config) {
      on('<event>', (arg1, arg2) => {
        // plugin code here
      })
    },
  },
})
```

Crafting a plugin

The Plugins API empowers you to customize and enhance the behavior of Cypress. The `setupNodeEvents function` (or the deprecated plugins file function) receives two arguments: `on` and `config`. It can return a value immediately or return a Promise, which Cypress will wait to resolve. This facilitates performing asynchronous operations such as reading files from the filesystem.

When you return an object or resolve a Promise with an object, Cypress will incorporate this object into the config, letting you overwrite configuration or environment variables.

Following is an example of how you might use `setupNodeEvents` in `cypress.config.js`:

```
const { defineConfig } = require('cypress')

module.exports = defineConfig({
  e2e: {
    setupNodeEvents(on, config) {
      // Plugin configurations go here
    },
  },
})
```

The `on` function is used to register listeners to various Cypress events.

Registering to listen to an event might appear as follows:

```
const { defineConfig } = require('cypress')

module.exports = defineConfig({
  e2e: {
    setupNodeEvents(on, config) {
      on('<event>', (arg1, arg2) => {
        // Plugin operations here
      })
    },
  },
})
```

Each event documents its own argument signature. The `config` parameter is the resolved Cypress configuration for the current project. It includes all the values passed into the browser for your project. Some plugins might need these values to perform specific actions based on the configuration. If these values are altered programmatically, Cypress will utilize the new values.

The `config` object also includes extra values that are not part of the standard configuration. These values are read-only and cannot be modified from the plugins. These include the absolute path to the Cypress configuration file (`configFile`), the absolute path to the root of the project (`projectRoot`), and the version number of Cypress (`version`).

A list of available events includes:

- **`after:run`:** Triggered after the run is complete.
- **`after:screenshot`:** Triggered after a screenshot is taken.
- **`after:spec`:** Triggered after a spec is finished running.
- **`before:browser:launch`:** Triggered just before a browser is launched.
- **`before:run`:** Triggered before the run begins.
- **`before:spec`:** Triggered when a spec is about to be run.
- **`file:preprocessor`:** Triggered when a spec or spec-related file needs to be transpiled for the browser.
- **`task`:** Triggered in conjunction with the cy.task command.

The `setupNodeEvents` function (or deprecated plugins file function) is invoked when Cypress opens a project. It runs in a separate `child_process` that requires the Cypress configuration file. This code will be executed using the Node version that initiated Cypress.

When Cypress executes the `setupNodeEvents` function, it will execute with `process.cwd()` set to your project's path. You'll also be able to require any node module you have installed, including local files within your project.

Errors in your `setupNodeEvents` function won't crash Cypress. They will be caught and displayed in the console and within Cypress itself.

Any changes made to your Cypress configuration file will take effect immediately since Cypress automatically watches the file. You can thus update plugin code even while Cypress is running.

Custom plugin examples

Custom plugins in Cypress allow you to tailor the testing framework according to your specific needs, enabling more effective and efficient testing. By creating custom plugins, you can extend the core functionalities of Cypress and automate complex processes, which can significantly improve the quality of your tests and save time. For example, you might develop a custom plugin to set up a specific testing environment, generate dynamic test data, or manage test dependencies. As a result, custom plugins allow you to maximize the capabilities of Cypress and deliver more robust and reliable software. Let's explore several custom plugin examples, shedding light on how you can harness the full potential of Cypress in your unique testing context.

Interacting with a database

In some cases, you may want to connect to a database directly from a Cypress test. This could be useful for setting up test data or asserting that certain database operations were performed. As mentioned, plugins enable you to do just that since they run in the Node.js environment.

Assuming we're using an SQLite database and the `sqlite3` package is installed, we can add a new task to our plugins file to query the database:

```
const sqlite3 = require('sqlite3').verbose();
const { defineConfig } = require('cypress');

module.exports = defineConfig({
  e2e: {
    setupNodeEvents: (on, config) => {
      on('task', {
        queryDatabase(query) {
          let db = new sqlite3.Database('./test.db', sqlite3.
OPEN_READONLY);
          return new Promise((resolve, reject) => {
            db.all(query, (err, rows) => {
              if (err) {
                reject(err);
              } else {
                resolve(rows);
              }
            });
          });
        },
      });
    },
  },
});
```

With this task, you can make SQL queries directly from your tests:

```
it('queries the database', () => {
  cy.task('queryDatabase', 'SELECT * FROM users').then((rows) => {
    // rows is an array with the results of the query
  })
})
```

Plugin Events

Plugin events offer hooks into the internal Cypress mechanism, allowing developers to execute custom actions or modifications at specific stages of a test run. For example, you may use the `before:browser:launch` event to customize browser launch options. Here is an example:

```
const { defineConfig } = require('cypress')


module.exports = defineConfig({
  e2e: {
    setupNodeEvents(on, config) {
       on('before:browser:launch', (browser = {}, launchOptions)
=> {
         if (browser.name === 'chrome') {
          launchOptions.args.push('--start-fullscreen')
          return launchOptions
        }
      })
    },
  },
})
```

In the preceding example, Cypress will launch Chrome in full-screen mode.

Environment variables

Environment variables in Cypress can be manipulated within the plugins. This is beneficial when needing to dynamically adjust configurations based on specific conditions, such as different development, testing, and production environments. Here's how to do it:

```
const { defineConfig } = require('cypress')

module.exports = defineConfig({
  e2e: {
    setupNodeEvents(on, config) {
      config.env.customMessage = 'Hello from plugins file!'
      return config
    },
  },
})
```

In your test files, you can access this variable as follows:

```
Cypress.env('customMessage')
```

Browser launch API

Cypress's Browser Launch API allows even deeper control over how your browser is launched. This is extremely useful for adding extensions, opening developer tools, or enabling certain flags. Here's a snippet that shows how to add an extension to Chrome:

```
const { defineConfig } = require('cypress')

module.exports = defineConfig({
  e2e: {
    setupNodeEvents(on, config) {
      on('before:browser:launch', (browser = {}, launchOptions)
=> {
        if (browser.name === 'chrome') {
          launchOptions.extensions.push('/path/to/exten-
sion')
          return launchOptions
        }
      })
    },
  },
})
```

Custom Webpack preprocessor

If you're using Webpack in your project, Cypress allows you to create a custom preprocessor within the plugins file. This allows you to have full control over how your spec files are transpiled before they are loaded into the browser. Here's an example:

```
const { defineConfig } = require('cypress')
const webpack = require('@cypress/webpack-preprocessor')

module.exports = defineConfig({
  e2e: {
    setupNodeEvents(on, config) {
const options = {
        webpackOptions: require('../webpack.config'),
      }
      on('file:preprocessor', webpack(options))
   },
 },
})
```

In the preceding example, we set up Cypress to use our webpack configuration to preprocess the files before testing.

Existing Cypress plugin examples

Cypress has a rich ecosystem of plugins developed by both the Cypress team and the community. These plugins serve various purposes, from adding custom assertions to integrating with reporting tools.

cypress-cucumber-preprocessor

Cypress Cucumber Preprocessor enables you to write your Cypress tests using Gherkin syntax. This is extremely useful when practicing Behavior Driven Development (BDD) as it allows you to describe the behavior of your application in a language that's easy to understand.

```
npm install --save-dev cypress-cucumber-preprocessor
```

In your cypress.config.js:

```
const { defineConfig } = require('cypress')
const cucumber = require('cypress-cucumber-preprocessor').default

module.exports = defineConfig({
  e2e: {
    specPattern: "**/*.feature",
    setupNodeEvents(on, config) {
on('file:preprocessor', cucumber())
     },
   },
})
```

Create a new file: cypress/e2e/Login.feature:

```
Feature: Login

Scenario: Successful Login
  Given I visit the login page
  When I type in my credentials
  Then I see the dashboard page
```

You'll need to implement the step definitions in a JavaScript file with the same name as the feature file. For example, for the Login.feature, you'd create Login.js in cypress/e2e:

```
const { Given, When, Then } = require("cypress-cucumber-pre
processor/steps");

Given("I visit the login page", () => {
  cy.visit("/login");
});

When("I type in my credentials", () => {
  cy.get("input[name=username]").type("myUsername");
```

```
  cy.get("input[name=password]").type("myPassword");
  cy.get("button[type=submit]").click();
});

Then("I see the dashboard page", () => {
  cy.url().should("include", "/dashboard");
});
```

In the preceding example, each step in the Gherkin syntax maps to a function implemented using Cypress commands. The functions use Cypress commands to interact with the web application and verify its state.

cypress-axe

Cypress-axe integrates the axe-core accessibility testing library with Cypress.

```
npm install --save-dev cypress-axe
```

In your `commands.js` or `commands.ts` file, input next:

```
import "cypress-axe";
```

In your test:

```
it("Has no detectable accessibility violations on load", () => {
  cy.visit("/");
  cy.injectAxe();
  cy.checkA11y();
});
```

In the preceding test, `cy.injectAxe()` injects the `axe-core` runtime into the page under test. `cy.checkA11y()` checks the page for accessibility errors.

Cypress plugins offer a level of extensibility that's hard to match. They allow you to hook into various stages of the test lifecycle and perform otherwise impossible or complicated operations. By harnessing the power of plugins, you can make your tests more efficient, flexible, and robust.

Handling authentication and authorization

When it comes to developing web applications, authentication and authorization processes often present a challenging set of scenarios. These processes are integral to securing access to the application and ensuring user identities. In test automation, Cypress offers practical ways to deal with these aspects. This section delves into understanding how Cypress can handle authentication and authorization during test execution.

Authentication vs authorization

Before proceeding, let's distinguish between authentication and authorization. Authentication involves verifying the user's identity (that is, ensuring the user is who they claim to be), usually through credentials like a username and password. Authorization, conversely, pertains to the permissions granted to an authenticated user - what they can do and access within the application.

Parameter	Authentication	Authorization
Purpose	Verifies user's identity	Determines user's permissions
Purpose	Typically involves a username and password	Grants access based on user role/privileges

***Table 8.2**: Authentication vs. Authorization*

Approaches to testing authentication and authorization

There are two main approaches to test authentication and authorization in Cypress as follows:

- **Testing the UI:** This involves simulating user interactions with the UI, such as filling in details in a login form. Although this approach mirrors actual user behavior, it can slow down tests as each test case would require its login operation.
- **Programmatic Login:** This approach bypasses the UI to login the user programmatically before the tests run. This can significantly speed up the test execution as the login step doesn't need to be repeated for each test case.

Testing the UI

Testing the UI for authentication involves interacting with the application just as a user would. For example, consider the following Cypress code that tests a typical login scenario:

```
describe('Login Test', () => {
    it('Authenticates user with valid credentials', () => {
        cy.visit('https://your-application-url.com/login'); //
Replace with your application URL

        cy.get('input[name=username]').type('testUser');
        cy.get('input[name=password]').type('password123');

        cy.get('button[type=submit]').click();

        // Verify successful login
        cy.url().should('include', '/dashboard'); // Replace '/
dashboard' with a URL specific to your application
    });
});
```

In this code snippet, Cypress visits the login page, enters the credentials, clicks the submit button, and verifies whether the URL changes to the expected page (for example, a dashboard) after a successful login. Although this approach thoroughly tests the login functionality, repeatedly performing these steps can make the tests slower, especially when many test cases require authentication.

Programmatic login

Programmatic login is an effective alternative when numerous test cases require authentication. This method involves making a request to the server, storing the response (usually an authentication token), and applying this token to future requests to access protected resources.

Consider the following example:

```
Cypress.Commands.add('login', (username, password) => {
    cy.request({
```

```
            method: 'POST',
            url: 'https://your-application-url.com/api/login',
            body: {
                username: username,
                password: password,
            },
        })
        .its('body').then((body) => {
            window.localStorage.setItem('authToken', body.token);
        });
    });
    // Use the login command in your test
    describe('Dashboard Test', () => {
        beforeEach(() => {
            cy.login('adminUser', 'adminPassword');
     });

        it('Admin should be able to access the dashboard', () => {
            cy.visit('https://your-application-url.com/dashboard');
            // Assert that the dashboard is accessible to the admin
    user
        });
    });
```

The command `cy.login` sends a POST request to the login API with the username and password as the request body. It then stores the received token into `localStorage`. The `beforeEach` hook ensures the login process completes before each test case.

In the test case, the admin user visits the dashboard. The test then verifies if the dashboard is accessible, providing an assertion accordingly.

Handling authorization

While authentication verifies the identity of a user, authorization determines what an authenticated user can do within the application. It is essential to test if various user roles are granted the appropriate permissions and denied access where necessary.

Here's an example of how you can use Cypress to test different levels of access for an admin user and a guest user:

```
describe('Role-based Authorization Test', () => {
    it('Admin user should have access to Admin Dashboard', () => {
        cy.login('adminUser', 'adminPassword');
 cy.visit('https://your-application-url.com/admin-dashboard');
        // Assert that the admin user can access the admin dashboard
    });

    it('Guest user should not have access to Admin Dashboard', () => {
        cy.login('guestUser', 'guestPassword');
        cy.visit('https://your-application-url.com/admin-dashboard');
        // Assert that the guest user is unable to access the admin
dashboard and
    the appropriate error message is displayed
    });
});
```

In this example, the admin user is expected to have access to the admin dashboard. In contrast, the guest user should be denied access, ideally receiving an error message or being redirected.

Testing API authorization

Testing authorization isn't limited to UI interactions. You can verify authorization at the API level, ensuring that APIs respond appropriately to different user roles. Here's an example of how to test API authorization with Cypress:

```
describe('API Authorization Test', () => {
    it('API should respond with status 200 for admin user', () => {
        cy.login('adminUser', 'adminPassword');
        cy.request({
            method: 'GET',
```

```
            url: 'https://your-application-url.com/api/admin-end-
point',
            headers: {
                'Authorization': 'Bearer ' + window.localStorage.
getItem('authToken')
            }
        }).then((response) => {
            expect(response.status).to.eq(200);
        });
    });

    it('API should respond with status 403 for guest user', () =>
{
        cy.login('guestUser', 'guestPassword');
        cy.request({
            method: 'GET',
            url: 'https://your-application-url.com/api/admin-end-
point',
            headers: {
                'Authorization': 'Bearer ' + window.localStorage.
getItem('authToken')
            },
            failOnStatusCode: false // !This is important because
a 403 response will cause the test to fail
        }).then((response) => {
            expect(response.status).to.eq(403);
        });
    });
});
```

The admin user is expected to receive a `200` status code when making a GET request to an admin-only API endpoint. On the other hand, the guest user should receive a `403` status code (forbidden), indicating they don't have the necessary permissions.

Authentication by visiting a different domain with cy.origin()

The advent of web applications has brought about the integration of third-party services for user authentication. This often means redirecting to a different domain to authenticate users before returning to the original application. In earlier versions of Cypress, tests were restricted to visiting domains of the same origin, necessitating programmatic login for authenticating users via third-party services.

However, the release of Cypress v12.0.0 introduced a key improvement, lifting the restriction of single-origin domain visits within a test. With this update, Cypress tests can now handle redirections to different domains, allowing the convenient authentication of users via third-party providers like **Auth0** through the user interface.

Here's a basic example of how you can take advantage of this feature to authenticate a user via a third-party provider:

```
describe('Third-Party Authentication Test', () => {
    it('Authenticates user with third-party provider', () => {
        // Gather necessary login information
        const user = {
            username: 'testUser',
            password: 'password123'
        };

        // Run commands in secondary origin, passing in
serializable values
        cy.origin('https://third-party-provider.com', { args: {
user } }, ({ user }) => {
            // Inside callback baseUrl is the third-party
provider
            cy.visit('/login');
            // Commands are executed in secondary origin
            cy.get('input[name=username]').type(user.username);
            cy.get('input[name=password]').type(user.password);
            cy.get('button[type=submit]').click();
```

```
                // Confirm successful login
                cy.get('.success').should('exist');
            });

            // Redirect back to primary domain
            cy.visit('https://your-application-url.com/dashboard');
    // Replace with your application URL

            // Continue running commands on primary origin
            cy.get('h1').contains('Welcome, testUser');
        });
    });
```

This test uses **`cy.origin()`** to visit the third-party provider's domain, allowing Cypress to run commands on this secondary origin. During this process, necessary information like user credentials can be passed in via the args option. Inside the `cy.origin()` callback function, the **`baseUrl`** is automatically set to the secondary origin, allowing Cypress commands to be executed there.

After successful login at the secondary origin, the test returns to the primary origin to confirm that the user is indeed authenticated. To achieve this, `cy.visit()` redirects back to the primary domain where the rest of the commands are executed.

The introduction of `cy.origin()` in Cypress v12.0.0 provides an easier way to authenticate users via third-party domains in your end-to-end tests. By enabling tests to visit multiple domains of different origins, Cypress allows for more realistic testing scenarios, ultimately enhancing the robustness of your test suite.

Programmatic login using Auth0 authentication

Auth0 is a powerful, versatile, and easy-to-implement platform for managing user identities and providing secure access to your applications. Its wide range of features and options provides developers with the tools they need to build secure, user-friendly applications.

The following segment provides a custom command to automate login with

Auth0, utilizing the `/oauth/token` endpoint. It subsequently sets an item in `localStorage` containing the authenticated user's details, which the application code can leverage to confirm authentication during testing.

The custom command `loginByAuth0Api` orchestrates the following operations:

- Makes a request to the `/oauth/token` endpoint to initiate the automated login.
- Sets the `'auth0Cypress'` item in `localStorage` with the access token, **id_token**, and user profile.

```
// cypress/support/commands.js
Cypress.Commands.add(
  'loginByAuth0Api',
  (username: string, password: string) => {
    cy.log(`Authenticating as ${username}`)
    const client_id = Cypress.env('auth0_client_id')
    const client_secret = Cypress.env('auth0_client_secret')
    const audience = Cypress.env('auth0_audience')
    const scope = Cypress.env('auth0_scope')

    cy.request({
      method: 'POST',
      url: `https://${Cypress.env('auth0_domain')}/oauth/token`,
      body: {
        grant_type: 'password',
        username,
        password,
        audience,
        scope,
        client_id,
        client_secret,
      },
    }).then(({ body }) => {
      const claims = jwt.decode(body.id_token)
      const {
```

```
      nickname,
      name,
      picture,
      updated_at,
      email,
      email_verified,
      sub,
      exp,
    } = claims
    const item = {
      body: {
        ...body,
        decodedToken: {
          claims,
          user: {
            nickname,
            name,
            picture,
            updated_at,
            email,
            email_verified,
            sub,
          },
          audience,
          client_id,
        },
      },
      expiresAt: exp,
    }
    window.localStorage.setItem('auth0Cypress', JSON.
stringify(item))
    cy.visit('/')
  })
```

```
    }
  )
```

Once your **Auth0** application is correctly configured via the **Auth0** Developer console, the required environment variables are set, and the **loginByAuth0Api** command is operational, you can automate the **Auth0** authentication during testing. The following segment illustrates a test that logs in a user via **Auth0**, completes the onboarding process, and logs out:

```
describe('Auth0', function () {
  beforeEach(function () {
    cy.task('db:seed')
    cy.loginByAuth0Api(
      Cypress.env('auth0_username'),
      Cypress.env('auth0_password')
    )
  })

  it('shows onboarding', function () {
    cy.contains('Get Started').should('be.visible')
  })
})
```

The `'loginByAuth0Api'` custom command allows programmatic login via the `/oauth/token` endpoint in Auth0 and sets up a `localStorage` item to verify user authentication during testing. This command works by executing a POST request to the Auth0 domain, where it decodes the user's token and stores the user's credentials in `localStorage` as `'auth0Cypress'`. This approach allows for automated **Auth0** authentication during application testing. An example test was also shared, demonstrating the process of logging in a user via Auth0, executing the onboarding process, and finally logging out.

Parallel test execution

Parallel test execution refers to the practice of running multiple test cases simultaneously to reduce the overall test execution time. It is an integral part of effective and efficient test automation as it not only fast-tracks testing but also increases the accuracy of the process.

Cypress provides built-in support for parallel test execution, taking full advantage of its Dashboard Service, which smartly distributes tests across multiple machines to minimize overall test execution time. When running in parallel, each machine running a spec file independently stores its test results, and then the Cypress Cloud aggregates those results.

While Cypress Cloud provides out-of-the-box parallelization, there are other ways to achieve this. You can also use plugins or your Continuous Integration/ Continuous Deployment (CI/CD) tool of choice to run tests in parallel. It's important to note that the underlying principle remains the same: tests are divided and executed across multiple machines or processes simultaneously.

The effectiveness of parallel test execution depends on the number of test files and their distribution. Cypress splits tests based on the test files, meaning having a good number of test files can lead to better parallelization.

Moreover, the balance of the test files also matters. If one test file is significantly larger than others, it will become a bottleneck, elongating the overall execution time. Therefore, it's essential to structure and balance your tests across spec files effectively.

Scenario	**Execution Time (Single Machine)**	**Execution Time (Parallel, 10 machines)**
Scenario A (Each spec file takes 1 min)	10 minutes	1 minute
Scenario B (One spec file takes 10 min, others take 1 min each)	19 minutes	10 minutes

***Table 8.3**: Benefits of test parallelization*

Using CI/CD tools for parallelization

If you prefer not to use the Cypress Dashboard, many CI/CD tools also provide parallelization functionality. For example, GitHub Actions, Jenkins, and CircleCI all provide ways to split your test suite across multiple machines or processes.

Here's an example using GitHub Actions:

```
name: End-to-End Tests
on: [push]
jobs:
  test:
```

```
    runs-on: ubuntu-latest
    strategy:
      fail-fast: false
      matrix:
        containers: [1, 2, 3, 4]
    steps:
      - name: Checkout
        uses: actions/checkout@v2
      - name: Cypress Run
        uses: cypress-io/github-action@v2
        with:
          record: true
          parallel: true
        env:
          CYPRESS_RECORD_KEY: ${{ secrets.CYPRESS_RECORD_KEY }}
```

In this setup, the `matrix` strategy creates four copies of the same job, which are then run in parallel.

Parallelization beyond the Dashboard: plugins

If you prefer more control over your testing processes, several plugins can help manage test distribution, including cypress-parallel and cypress-split. These tools split your spec files into chunks, which can run concurrently.

cypress-parallel

Plugins like cypress-parallel can add a layer of customization to your parallel testing process, providing you control over the number of threads and specific tests to be executed concurrently. cypress-parallel divides the test suite based on a generated weights file and executes them in parallel according to the thread number specified.

Installation

First, to use cypress-parallel, you need to install it in your project. Run the following command at the root directory of your project:

```
npm i cypress-parallel
```

Execution

Once the plugin is installed, you can execute your tests in parallel. The execution command contains three main parts as follows:

- **`-s <npm script>`:** This flag is followed by the npm script to be run. In this case, cypress:run is the npm script in your `package.json` file.
- **`-t <number of threads>`:** This flag is followed by the number of threads to be run in parallel.
- **`-d <spec file path>`:** This flag is followed by the path of the spec files to be run.

For instance:

```
npx cypress-parallel -s cypress:run -t 3 -d "cypress/e2e/
dropdown-examples/*.js"
```

The preceding command will create a `parallel-weights.json` file, and the spec files will be divided and executed in parallel according to this file and the thread number provided.

Adjusting the thread number based on your machine's hardware capacity is essential to prevent overloading and ensure optimal performance. For instance, if your machine has eight cores, you should limit your threads to 7 to reserve one for the operating system and other processes.

cypress-split

Another plugin that you can leverage for running your Cypress tests in parallel, particularly in Continuous Integration (CI) builds, is cypress-split. This plugin enables you to run specific tests across multiple containers or distribute them amongst various agents.

Installation

Begin by adding cypress-split as a development dependency to your project and include it in your Cypress configuration file. Here's how you can install the plugin:

If you're using npm, run the following command:

```
npm i -D cypress-split
```

Configuration

Now, you can incorporate the plugin into your Cypress configuration. To do so, update your `cypress.config.js` file to call the cypress-split plugin from your Cypress config object's `setupNodeEvents` method:

```
// cypress.config.js
const { defineConfig } = require('cypress')
const cypressSplit = require('cypress-split')  // Import
cypress-split

module.exports = defineConfig({
  e2e: {
    setupNodeEvents(on, config) {
      cypressSplit(on, config) // Invoke cypress-split
      return config  // IMPORTANT: return the config object
    },
  },
})
```

Running tests in CI

With the plugin configured, you can now update your CI scripts to run the tests in parallel. This will involve running several containers and starting Cypress with the `--env split=true` parameter.

Example for GitLab CI:

In your `.gitlab-ci.yml` file:

```
stages:
  - build
  - test

install:
  image: cypress/base:16.14.2-slim
  stage: build
  script:
    - npm ci
```

```
test:
  image: cypress/base:16.14.2-slim
  stage: test
  parallel: 3
  script:
    - npx cypress run --env split=true
```

Here, all specs will be split into three groups automatically.

Example for CircleCI:

In your **config.yml** file:

```
parallelism: 3
command: npx cypress run --env split=true
```

Example for GitHub Actions:

In your workflow file:

```
# run 3 copies of the current job in parallel
strategy:
  fail-fast: false
  matrix:
    containers: [1, 2, 3]
steps:
  - name: Run split Cypress tests
    uses: cypress-io/github-action@v5
    # pass the machine index and the total number
    env:
      SPLIT: ${{ strategy.job-total }}
      SPLIT_INDEX: ${{ strategy.job-index }}
```

Note that for GitHub Actions, we need to pass the `SPLIT` and `SPLIT_INDEX` numbers from the strategy context for the plugin to grab.

This flexibility offered by cypress-split allows you to orchestrate your tests in a way that best suits your CI/CD pipeline, ensuring efficient utilization of resources and faster test execution.

Remember, parallelization is a powerful tool that can significantly reduce your test execution time when used effectively. However, care must be taken to manage your system resources for optimal performance appropriately.

Cross-browser testing

As the web continues to evolve, developers are challenged to ensure that their applications function seamlessly across a multitude of web browsers. Each browser has unique quirks and behaviors, which may influence how your application behaves for the end-user. Hence, Cross-Browser Testing becomes a crucial aspect of any robust testing strategy.

Cypress provides extensive support for Cross-Browser Testing, allowing you to execute your tests across multiple browsers and ensuring that your application delivers a consistent user experience, irrespective of the browser in use.

Cypress out-of-the-box supports Chrome, Firefox, Edge, and Electron, with experimental support for other Chromium-based browsers like Opera and Brave. Recently, Cypress has extended its support to include WebKit, the engine behind Safari, paving the way for comprehensive cross-browser testing.

Running tests in a specific browser

To execute your tests in a specific browser, use the `--browser` flag followed by the name of the desired browser. The command syntax is as follows:

```
npx cypress run --browser <browser-name>
```

For example, to run your tests in Firefox, you would use:

```
npx cypress run --browser firefox
```

Running tests in all supported browsers

Cypress does not have a built-in feature to run tests across all supported browsers simultaneously. However, it can be easily achieved by writing a simple script in your `package.json` file. Here's an example:

```
"scripts": {
  "test:chrome": "cypress run --browser chrome",
  "test:firefox": "cypress run --browser firefox",
  "test:edge": "cypress run --browser edge",
```

```
  "test:all": "npm run test:chrome && npm run test:firefox && npm run
test:edge"
}
```

You can run tests across all supported browsers with the command:

```
npm run test:all
```

Electron browser: an integral part of Cypress

Electron, a unique offering in the list of browsers supported by Cypress, is a version of Chromium that comes integrated with the Electron framework. A significant advantage of the Electron browser is its seamless integration into Cypress; there's no separate installation needed.

While Cypress, by default, runs tests headlessly (without a UI) using the CLI command `cypress run`, Electron can also be launched in a headed mode using:

```
cypress run --headed
```

Given its built-in nature, Electron is typically the default browser for Continuous Integration (CI) runs. If you encounter failures in CI, running tests locally using the `--headed` option with Electron can help in debugging.

Chrome browsers

Chrome and its different flavors are detected and supported by Cypress, provided they are above version 64.

Standard Chrome:

```
cypress run --browser chrome
```

Chromium:

```
cypress run --browser chromium
```

Chrome Beta:

```
cypress run --browser chrome:beta
```

Chrome Canary:

```
cypress run --browser chrome:canary
```

Firefox browsers

Firefox and its editions are supported seamlessly by Cypress.

Standard Firefox:

```
cypress run --browser firefox
```

Firefox Developer/Nightly Edition:

```
cypress run --browser firefox:dev
cypress run --browser firefox:nightly
```

To integrate these commands into CI, ensure the required Firefox version is installed or opt for the recommended docker images.

Managing test flakiness across different browsers

While executing your tests across multiple browsers, you might encounter instances where a test passes in one browser but fails in another. This phenomenon, known as *test flakiness*, can occur due to differences in how browsers handle JavaScript execution, CSS rendering, and other factors.

To mitigate test flakiness, Cypress recommends the following best practices:

- **Create Idempotent Tests:** An idempotent test is one that produces the same results regardless of how many times it's executed. This ensures your test assertions remain consistent across different browsers.
- **Avoid Conditional Testing:** This is where you create different paths in your tests based on the browser being used. Such practices can lead to unnecessarily complex tests that are difficult to maintain.
- **Utilize Cypress Retry-ability:** Cypress automatically retries failing assertions until they pass or time out. This feature can help manage test flakiness due to temporary discrepancies in different browsers.

Comparing browser behaviors

Cypress does not provide a built-in tool to compare behaviors across different browsers. However, you can use the `cy.log()` command to log events or behaviors during your test execution, which can then be used to compare and analyze behaviors across different browsers.

For instance:

```
cy.visit('/login')
cy.get('button').click().then(() => {
  cy.log('Clicked on the login button')
})
```

WebKit (experimental)

Cypress has made strides in supporting WebKit, which powers the Safari browser. However, this support remains experimental. The following steps should be performed to use it:

- Enable the feature in your configuration:

  ```
  {
    "experimentalWebKitSupport": true
  }
  ```

- Install the required dependencies:

  ```
  npm install --save-dev playwright-webkit@1.34
  ```

- Now, run tests using the following:

  ```
  cypress run --browser webkit
  ```

With Cypress's cross-browser testing capabilities, you can effectively handle the diverse range of user browser environments. Leveraging the broad range of browser support Cypress provides assures you of a solid and resilient web application delivery.

Network stubbing and mocking

In any web application, communicating with a server via network requests such as HTTP or HTTPS is a common occurrence. To enhance the reliability and speed of your tests, Cypress provides a robust feature set for controlling and validating these communications. We'll delve into network stubbing and mocking in Cypress, which allows you to simulate server responses and behavior, ensuring your tests are faster and not dependent on server state or behavior.

Let's start by understanding what stubbing and mocking are. Stubbing can be thought of as a way to force a function to return a specific value. Regarding network requests, this means we are forcing the response of a server request to be what we specify in the test. On the other hand, mocking involves simulating the behavior of real objects in a controlled way, which in the case of network requests, consists in creating a dummy server or response.

Using the cy.intercept() command

In Cypress, the `cy.intercept()` command is your best friend regarding network stubbing. It enables you to manage the behavior of network requests. Let's examine how we can use `cy.intercept()` to stub a GET request:

```
cy.intercept('GET', '/todos', { fixture: 'todos.json' })
```

In the preceding code snippet, we're instructing Cypress to intercept all HTTP GET requests that go to the `'/todos'` URL. Instead of fetching data from the server, the response is supplied from the **todos.json** fixture file.

Intercepting responses and asserting with cy.wait()

Cypress can also intercept a response and do more than just stubbing the response. We can inspect the response and make assertions based on its content. Let's see how to do this:

```
cy.intercept('GET', '/todos').as('getTodos')
cy.visit('/')
cy.wait('@getTodos').its('response.body').should('have.length', 3)
```

In this example, we're naming the intercepted route with `as('getTodos')`. Then, we use `cy.wait('@getTodos')` to wait for the request's response. Once the response is there, we make an assertion to check if the body of the response contains three items.

POST request stubbing

Cypress can also intercept and stub **POST** requests, simulating the behavior of server data being updated. Here's an example:

```
cy.intercept('POST', '/todos', {
  statusCode: 201,
  body: { id: 1, name: 'Stubbed todo', completed: false },
}).as('newTodo')


cy.get('.new-todo').type('Stubbed todo{enter}')
cy.wait('@newTodo')
cy.get('.todo-list li').should('have.length', 1).and('contain',
'Stubbed todo')
```

In this code, we're simulating the creation of a new **todo**. After typing in the name of the new todo and pressing *enter*, we wait for the `'newTodo'` POST request to complete. Finally, we assert that the new todo appears in the list.

Wildcards and glob patterns

Cypress also supports using wildcards and glob patterns in the `cy.intercept()` command, making it easier to match multiple URLs. Here's an example:

```
cy.intercept('GET', '/todos/*')
cy.intercept('GET', '/todos/**')
```

The first command will match routes such as `'/todos/1'`, `'/todos/2'`, and so on, while the second command will match any route under `'/todos'`, even routes like `'/todos/1/details'`, `'/todos/2/items'`, and more.

Visual regression testing

The appearance of your web application is just as important as its functionality. Your users expect your website to look visually consistent each time they use it. Inconsistencies or visual bugs may diminish your users' trust in your application. Visual Regression Testing is a crucial strategy to ensure that your web application remains visually consistent and that any visual changes are intentional.

With Cypress, it's possible to perform Visual Regression Testing by comparing screenshots taken over different periods or versions. We will explore how to perform Visual Regression Testing with Cypress using the `cypress-image-snapshot` and `cypress-visual-regression` plugins.

Setting up cypress-image-snapshot plugin

The first step is to add the `cypress-image-snapshot` plugin to your project. This plugin extends Cypress's functionality to capture snapshots and compare them. Add the plugin using the following commands:

```
# Using npm
npm install --save-dev cypress-image-snapshot


# Using yarn
yarn add -D cypress-image-snapshot
```

After installing the plugin, we need to add it to the commands and plugins files:

```
// Add this to commands.js
import { addMatchImageSnapshotCommand } from 'cypress-image-snap-
shot/command'
addMatchImageSnapshotCommand()


// Add this to cypress.config.js
const { addMatchImageSnapshotPlugin } = require('cypress-im-
age-snapshot/plugin')
module.exports = (on, config) => {
  addMatchImageSnapshotPlugin(on, config)
}
```

Now, we have a new command available in Cypress called `cy.matchImageSnapshot()`. This command takes a screenshot of the current state of the DOM and compares it to a previous snapshot.

Creating your first visual test

Let's create a simple test that validates the visual appearance of a page:

```
Describe('Visual Regression Test', () => {
  it('should display the homepage correctly', () => {
    cy.visit('/')
    cy.matchImageSnapshot()
  })
})
```

In this test, we visit the homepage. Then, we use `cy.matchImageSnapshot()` to take a screenshot of the page. When this test runs for the first time, it will create a baseline homepage image. Subsequent test runs will capture and compare a new image with the baseline image. If there are significant differences, the test will fail.

Dealing with dynamic content

In real-world applications, you may have elements on your page that change dynamically, such as dates, times, or randomized content. These dynamic elements can cause your visual regression tests to fail even if there are no significant visual changes.

To handle dynamic content, we can use the power of Cypress to interact with the DOM before taking a snapshot. We can modify the dynamic content to a fixed value or hide it entirely. Here's an example:

```
it('should display the homepage correctly', () => {
  cy.visit('/')
  cy.get('.date-display').invoke('text', '2023-07-01') // Fix the
date value
  cy.get('.random-banner').should('not.exist') // Remove a dynamic
banner
  cy.matchImageSnapshot()
})
```

In this test, we first visit the homepage. We then fix the date value and remove a dynamic banner before taking a snapshot.

Image comparison strategies

The `cypress-image-snapshot` plugin uses the `pixelmatch` library under the hood to compare images. It has various comparison strategies, such as pixel matching and perceptual diffing. Depending on your needs, you may need to configure the plugin to use a different comparison strategy.

The plugin can be configured by passing an options object to the `addMatchImageSnapshotCommand` function or directly to the `cy.matchImageSnapshot()` command:

```
// Setting options for the command
addMatchImageSnapshotCommand({
  failureThreshold: 0.03, // threshold for entire image
  failureThresholdType: 'percent', // percent of image or number of pixels
  customDiffConfig: { threshold: 0.1 }, // threshold for each pixel
  capture: 'viewport', // capture viewport in screenshot
  blackout: ['.date-display'] // blackout the date display element in snapshot
})
```

Here are some of the options described in *Table* 8.4:

Option	Description
`failureThreshold`	The threshold for pixel differences that will trigger a test failure
`failureThresholdType`	The type of thresholding to apply: `'pixel'` or `'percent'`
`customDiffConfig`	Custom config for `pixelmatch`
`capture`	`'viewport'` or `'fullPage'` to capture the full page
`blackout`	An array of selectors to blackout in the snapshot

Table 8.4: *Configurable options for cypress-image-snapshot plugin*

Setting up cypress-visual-regression

First, you need to install the `cypress-visual-regression` plugin into your project:

```
# Using npm
npm install --save-dev cypress-visual-regression


# Using yarn
yarn add -D cypress-visual-regression
```

Once installed, add the plugin to your `commands.js` file:

```
// Add this to commands.js
import compareSnapshotCommand from 'cypress-visual-regression/
dist/command';
compareSnapshotCommand();
```

Add the following config to your `cypress.config.js` file:

```
const { defineConfig } = require("cypress");
const getCompareSnapshotsPlugin = require('cypress-visual-regres-
sion/dist/plugin');

module.exports = defineConfig({
  screenshotsFolder: './cypress/snapshots/actual',
  trashAssetsBeforeRuns: true,
  video: false,
  e2e: {
    setupNodeEvents(on, config) {
      getCompareSnapshotsPlugin(on, config);
    },
  },
});
```

With the setup complete, you can access two new Cypress commands: `cy.compareSnapshot()` and `cy.initSnapshot()`.

Basic usage of cypress-visual-regression

Let's create a simple visual regression test:

```
describe('Visual Regression Test', () => {
  beforeEach(() => {
    cy.initSnapshot();
  });

  it('should display the homepage correctly', () => {
    cy.visit('/')
    cy.compareSnapshot('homepage');
  });
});
```

In this test, `cy.initSnapshot()` is called at the start of each test case to initialize the snapshot. Then, we navigate to the homepage and take a snapshot with `cy.compareSnapshot()`, providing `'homepage'` as the snapshot name.

Dealing with dynamic content

Similar to using `cypress-image-snapshot`, handling dynamic content requires either setting a static value or entirely hiding dynamic elements to avoid test inconsistencies. Here's an example:

```
it('should display the homepage correctly', () => {
  cy.visit('/')
  cy.get('.date-display').invoke('text', '2023-07-01') // Fix the date value
  cy.get('.random-banner').should('not.exist') // Remove a dynamic banner
  cy.compareSnapshot('homepage')
});
```

Customizing cypress-visual-regression

The `cypress-visual-regression` plugin is highly configurable, with the `compareSnapshotCommand()` function accepting an optional configuration object. You can find a few key options you may want to adjust in *Table* 8.5.

Option	Description
`capture`	`'viewport'` or `'fullPage'`. Determines if the full page or only the viewport should be captured
`clip`	`{ x: number, y: number, width: number, height: number }`. Captures a specific portion of the page
`scale`	`boolean`. Scales down the image before comparison to reduce the comparison time
`threshold`	`number`. The threshold percentage difference to trigger a failure

Table 8.5: *Configurable options for cypress-visual-regression plugin*

For example:

```
compareSnapshotCommand({
  scale: false,
  capture: 'viewport',
  clip: { x: 0, y: 0, width: 1280, height: 720 },
  threshold: 0.1
});
```

By incorporating the `cypress-visual-regression` plugin into your testing suite, you gain the ability to verify the visual consistency of your web application quickly and accurately. This bolsters the overall effectiveness of your testing efforts and gives you even more confidence in your deployments.

Conclusion

This chapter delves into advanced Cypress techniques that elevate the test automation workflow. Readers will learn how to create custom commands, allowing for reusable and expressive test code. The chapter also covers utilizing videos and screenshots as debugging aids to identify and resolve issues effectively. Additionally, it explores working with Cypress plugins to extend the functionality and enhance testing capabilities. The chapter delves into handling authentication and authorization, ensuring seamless testing of secure areas. It also covers parallel test execution and cross-browser testing, enabling faster and broader test coverage. Lastly, network stubbing, mocking, and visual regression testing are explored to ensure comprehensive and reliable testing. By applying these advanced techniques, readers will be able to improve the efficiency, maintainability, and effectiveness of their Cypress test suites.

The upcoming chapter will focus on Cypress Cloud and its advanced features, including Smart Orchestration and Flaky Test Management. Readers will be introduced to Cypress Cloud and understand how it can enhance their test automation process. The chapter explores Smart Orchestration, which optimizes test runs by intelligently distributing tests across multiple machines. It also covers managing flaky tests and providing strategies to handle and mitigate the impact of unstable tests. Additionally, readers will learn about Cypress Analytics, which offers valuable insights into test suite performance and reliability. By leveraging these features, readers can optimize their test automation workflow and improve their Cypress tests' overall efficiency and reliability.

Further Reading

Here are recommended resources for further reading, references, and links related to this chapter on advanced Cypress techniques.

1. **Cypress plugins:** The Cypress Plugins documentation (https://docs.cypress.io/plugins) offers guidance on creating and utilizing Cypress plugins to extend the functionality of Cypress. It covers plugin development, configuration, and integration into Cypress test suites.

2. **Cypress recipes:** The Cypress Recipes section of the official Cypress documentation (https://docs.cypress.io/examples/examples/recipes.html) provides a variety of advanced examples and techniques to enhance Cypress test automation. It covers topics like handling file uploads, interacting with iframes, and more.

3. **Cypress Network Stubbing and Spying:** The Cypress documentation on network stubbing and spying (https://docs.cypress.io/guides/guides/network-requests) provides insights into stubbing and spying on network requests in Cypress tests. It covers intercepting and manipulating network requests to simulate scenarios and test APIs' interactions.

4. **cypress-visual-regression plugin:** The official GitHub repository of the plugin (https://github.com/cypress-visual-regression/cypress-visual-regression).

5. **Parallel test execution with Cypress:** The official blog of Gleb Bahmutov (https://glebbahmutov.com/blog/cypress-parallel-free/).

These resources will give you a deeper understanding of advanced Cypress techniques, offer practical examples, and guide you in leveraging custom commands, plugins, screenshots, videos, network stubbing, parallelization, and more to enhance your Cypress test automation workflow.

Chapter 9

Cypress Cloud, Smart Orchestration, and Flaky Test Management

Introduction

In this chapter, readers will learn about Cypress Cloud and its features, such as Smart Orchestration and Flaky Test Management. We will also introduce them to Cypress Analytics, which can provide valuable insights into their test suite's performance and reliability. This chapter will also help readers leverage these advanced features to optimize their test automation process.

Structure

In this chapter, we will discuss the following topics:

- Introduction to Cypress Cloud
- Smart Orchestration in Cypress
- Managing flaky tests
- Leveraging Cypress Analytics

Introduction to Cypress Cloud

As we traverse the sphere of advanced test management, we need to observe a comprehensive, enterprise-ready solution known as Cypress Cloud. This robust service, a companion to the open-source Cypress app, is designed to augment your end-to-end testing by providing an integrated, scalable, and streamlined environment for running, managing, and observing your tests in real time. The objective of this chapter is to comprehensively introduce Cypress Cloud, laying the foundation for understanding its advanced features and functionalities.

Understanding Cypress Cloud

Cypress Cloud is an ancillary service offered by Cypress, designed to provide an integrated, hassle-free environment for running, managing, and monitoring your test suites. It takes your testing suite to a new level by enabling powerful functionalities like parallelization, advanced analytics, CI/CD integration, and flaky test management.

To access the power of Cypress Cloud, you first need to create a Cypress account and incorporate the Cypress test runner into your project.

1. Navigate to the Cypress Cloud to sign up (https://cloud.cypress.io/signup)
2. Choose one of the three options to sign up: using a Google account, GitHub, or using email. Then you need to follow the Cypress Cloud sign-up wizard.
3. Make sure to follow the instructions provided by Cypress to set up your project correctly.
4. Update your **`Cypress config file`** by adding `projectId`.

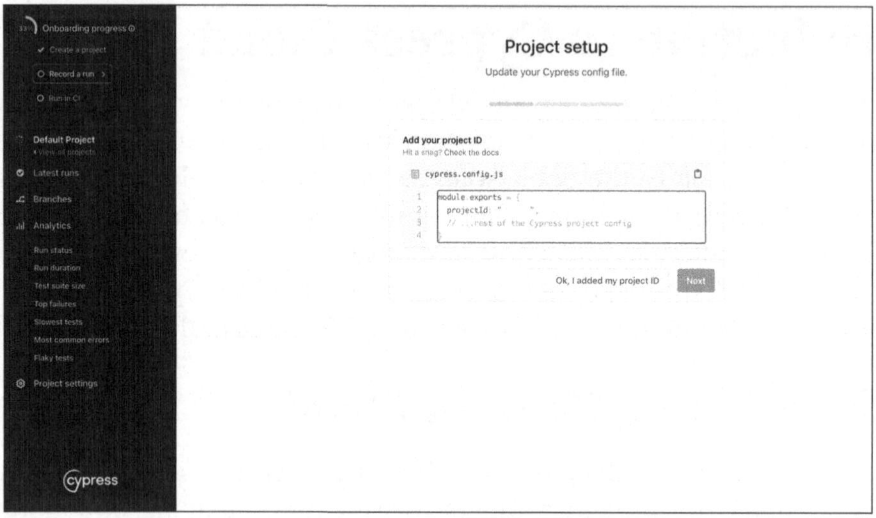

Figure 9.1: *Update your Cypress config file*

Take a look at this example to see what your **cypress.config.js** should look like.

```
import { defineConfig } from “cypress”;


export default defineConfig({
  e2e: {
    setupNodeEvents(on, config) {
      // implement node event listeners here
    },
  },
  projectId: “YOUR_PROJECT_ID”
});
```

After finishing the sign up Cypress will display your project Record Key. You don’t need to remember or store it. You can find this key Project Settings.

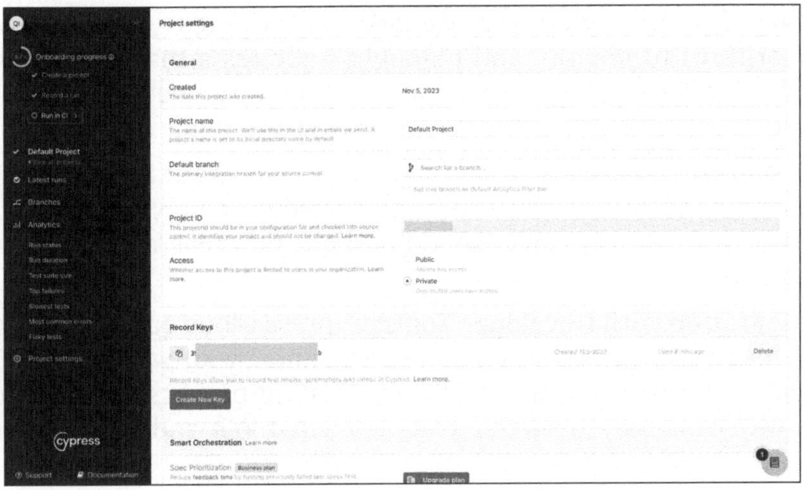

Figure 9.2: Cypress Cloud – Project Settings

Once set up, you can start recording your tests on the Cypress Dashboard by using the command:

```
npx cypress run --record --key YOUR_PROJECT_RECORD_KEY
```

In this command, the `--record` flag instructs Cypress to capture detailed records of test runs, while the `--key` provides your specific project record key, found within the Cypress Dashboard.

Key features of Cypress Cloud

The key features of Cypress Cloud are as follows:

- **Dashboard Service:** The Cypress Dashboard is a service that gives you access to recorded test results, including videos and screenshots of failed tests, performance data, etc. It provides a user-friendly interface for managing and analyzing your tests.
- **Smart Orchestration:** This feature is particularly beneficial for extensive test suites, as it allows Cypress Cloud to balance the testing load across multiple machines automatically. Through intelligent orchestration, test run times are drastically reduced, saving time and financial resources.
- **CI/CD Integration:** Cypress Cloud is designed to co-exist seamlessly with popular Continuous Integration/Continuous Deployment (CI/CD) platforms, including but not limited to Jenkins, CircleCI, Travis CI, and GitHub Actions. This integration aids in establishing an uninterrupted flow from testing to deployment.

- **Flaky Test Detection and Management:** Cypress Cloud uses complex algorithms to identify and highlight flaky tests that show inconsistent behavior. This feature aids in quickly isolating and addressing issues that could otherwise compromise the reliability of your test suite.
- **Advanced Analytics:** Comprehensive and intuitive analytics are a cornerstone of Cypress Cloud. It provides valuable insights into your test suite's performance, shedding light on areas needing attention or improvement.
- **Integration with Developer Tools:** Cypress Cloud can be integrated with various developer tools, further streamlining your workflow. This feature enables a smoother, more efficient testing process, where information flows seamlessly between your chosen tools and the Cypress Cloud platform.
- **Customizable Configurations & Enterprise SSO:** Cypress Cloud allows you to configure its features to best suit your enterprise's needs, including enabling Single Sign-On (SSO). This feature enhances both convenience and security, especially in large organizations.
- **In-app CI Runs and Test Health Overview:** Directly from the Cypress app, you can view CI runs and get an overview of your test health. This feature eliminates the need to switch between multiple platforms, enhancing productivity.

Detailed test recording and optimized management

Whenever you execute your tests with the `--record` flag, Cypress captures and uploads the results to the Dashboard. This collection of data is comprehensive, comprising screenshots and video recordings that can be pivotal in diagnosing why a test may have failed, especially in intricate CI environments.

Consider, for instance, a test that consistently passes in a local environment but fails within a CI context. With Cypress Cloud, you can access a video of the failing test, providing a step-by-step replay of the circumstances leading up to the failure. This feature can significantly expedite the debugging process, especially in cases with complex or unclear causes.

Smart Orchestration in Cypress

As we continue to explore the breadth of functionalities Cypress Cloud offers, we encounter a sophisticated feature known as Smart Orchestration. This feature is created to smartly distribute the workload of your test suite to numerous machines, which helps to handle the challenging computational demands of comprehensive testing scenarios.

Introduction to Smart Orchestration

Smart Orchestration is a groundbreaking strategy to simultaneously manage and run test cases across various machines. This methodology aims to balance the workload optimally, significantly decreasing the overall time required for test execution. By balancing the load of test cases efficiently, Smart Orchestration ensures rapid, cost-effective, and optimized testing procedures.

Cypress Cloud provides four distinct features as part of its Smart Orchestration strategy as follows:

- Parallelization
- Load Balancing
- Spec Prioritization
- Run Cancellation

Let's delve deeper into each of these features.

Parallelization

For projects with numerous tests, executing them sequentially on a single machine can consume substantial time. Parallelization is a lifesaver in such scenarios, allowing you to run multiple test spec files concurrently across several CI machines. This simultaneous execution dramatically speeds up the test process, saving time and costs when running tests in a Continuous Integration (CI) environment.

Cypress allows the execution of recorded tests in parallel across multiple machines. While parallel tests could technically run on a single machine, it's not recommended due to the hefty resources required to execute your tests efficiently.

Cypress uses a file-based parallelization strategy. As a result, your tests need to be divided across different files to leverage parallelization effectively.

Consider a scenario where you have 200 test files, each taking about 1 minute to execute. If you were to run these tests sequentially on one machine, it would take approximately 200 minutes. However, Cypress can distribute these 200 tests across ten machines with parallelization. Each machine runs only 20 tests, reducing the test execution time to just 20 minutes.

The process of enabling parallelization is straightforward. After setting up multiple machines within your CI environment (as per your CI provider's documentation), you can pass the `--parallel` key to the `cypress run` command to parallelize your recorded tests:

```
cypress run --record --key=abc123 --parallel
```

Load Balancing

Load Balancing optimizes the distribution of test spec files across the available CI resources. Cypress intelligently balances the test load based on data collected from previous runs, ensuring the fastest possible execution of your spec files.

Table 9.1 shows a simplified example of how load balancing might occur with three machines and six test spec files. In this case, the specs have been distributed based on their estimated run duration, leading to a balanced workload across the available machines:

Machine	Specs Assigned	Estimated Run Time (minutes)
1	Spec 1, Spec 4	20
2	Spec 2, Spec 5	19
3	Spec 3, Spec 6	20

Table 9.1: *Load balancing example*

Spec Prioritization

Spec Prioritization is another essential feature of Smart Orchestration that allows quicker verification that the latest changes have fixed a build by prioritizing the specs that failed in the previous Cypress run. This feature is particularly beneficial in speeding up the debugging process and reducing the time taken to troubleshoot failures and deploy fixes.

Let's consider a scenario. Suppose you have a test suite consisting of Spec A, B, C, D, and E, and Spec D fails during a run. In the next run, Cypress will prioritize Spec D. The order of execution will appear as follows:

- Spec D (failed in the last run)
- Spec A
- Spec B

- Spec C
- Spec E

This order ensures that if the same error persists, it gets detected early in the test process, saving valuable debugging time.

Run Cancellation

Run Cancellation is another feature designed to make the most efficient use of your resources. With this feature, you can specify a threshold for the number of test failures allowed in a given test run. Once this threshold is exceeded, Cypress will automatically halt the test run, conserving computational power and saving time that would have otherwise been spent running an already-failed test suite.

Run Cancellation is introduced as a key component of Smart Orchestration in the Cypress Cloud suite, debuting in version 12.6.0. It provides an invaluable command line interface (CLI) flag, namely `--auto-cancel-after-failures`, which allows users to dictate the number of acceptable test failures before initiating the cancellation process. This configuration flexibility provides granular control over Auto Cancellation, enabling a unique configuration for each test run.

The concept of Run Cancellation is particularly beneficial in several scenarios as follows:

- **Development Environments:** If you are working in a development environment where rapid feedback is necessary, setting a lower threshold for the `--auto-cancel-after-failures` flag will fail the test suite earlier, providing faster feedback.
- **Important Branches:** In some branches of your project, letting the entire test suite run might be critical, regardless of the number of failures. In such scenarios, you can disable Auto Cancellation by specifying `false` for the value of `--auto-cancel-after-failures` flag value.
- **Case-by-case Overrides:** You might encounter situations where the project value for the threshold needs to be overridden. In such cases, specifying a value for the `--auto-cancel-after-failures` flag will precede the project setting in Cypress Cloud.

In cases where you don't determine a value for the `--auto-cancel-after-failures` flag, Cypress will default to the value specified in the project settings.

Here's how you can set a numeric value for the `--auto-cancel-after-failures` flag:

```
npx cypress run --record --key <<your_record_key>> --auto-cancel-af-
ter-failures 1
```

The `1` after `--auto-cancel-after-failures` specifies that the test run should be canceled after the first failure.

Alternatively, you can disable Auto Cancellation for the run by setting `false`:

```
npx cypress run --record --key <<your_record_key>> --auto-cancel-af-
ter-failures false
```

The configuration flexibility provided by the `--auto-cancel-after-failures` flag allows you to tune your test runs to your unique requirements. By defining the acceptable number of test failures or disabling Run Cancellation entirely, you can optimize your CI resources, control CI costs, and manage testing time effectively.

In essence, Run Cancellation contributes to an efficient and cost-effective testing process. Coupled with the other features of Smart Orchestration, it forms an integral part of a high-performing, intelligent test automation suite.

Managing flaky tests

Flaky tests, in the context of software testing, refer to those tests that exhibit passing and failing results with the same code. They are infamous for their unpredictability and the challenges they pose in terms of debugging and maintaining software quality. Cypress, known for its robust testing mechanisms, provides built-in functionalities to handle and manage such flaky tests.

Tests may become flaky for many reasons, including network instability, concurrency issues, test order dependencies, or insufficient waits for rendering or asynchronous operations. These tests tend to fail or pass unexpectedly when rerun over time without any code modifications. They can be problematic for maintaining the reliability of your test suite and can lead to wasted time and resources when attempting to identify the cause of the issue.

Network instability

Flaky tests can often occur due to network instability or delayed API responses.

Consider the following test, which checks if a specific item is present on the page. This item is fetched via an API call:

```
it('displays the item', () => {
  cy.visit('/items')
  cy.get('.item').should('contain', 'My Special Item')
```

```
})
```

The preceding test might fail if the API response is slower than usual, causing the item to not yet be present in the DOM when the test is executed.

Solution: Cypress provides an automatic retry-ability feature for its commands. Here, the `cy.get()` command will automatically retry until the element is found in the DOM or the command times out (the default timeout is 4 seconds). This helps to ensure the element is loaded before the assertion is made:

```
it('displays the item', () => {
  cy.visit('/items')
  cy.get('.item', { timeout: 10000 }).should('contain', 'My Spe-
cial Item') // increase the timeout to 10 seconds
})
```

Concurrency issues

Concurrency issues can often lead to flaky tests. For example, two tests attempting to access and manipulate the same resource concurrently can lead to unpredictable test outcomes.

Consider a test scenario where two test cases are attempting to update the same user profile:

```
it('test1: update user profile', () => {
  // ...code to update profile
})

it('test2: update user profile', () => {
  // ...code to update profile
})
```

Solution: One way to avoid this is by ensuring your tests can run in isolation and are not dependent on a shared state. If this is impossible, you can utilize mechanisms such as locks to ensure resources are not accessed concurrently.

Test order dependency

Flaky tests can occur when they depend on the order in which they're run.

For example, consider two tests where the first test creates an item, and the second test deletes the item:

```
it('creates an item', () => {
  // ...code to create an item
})

it('deletes an item', () => {
  // ...code to delete the item created by the first test
})
```

If these tests are run in the wrong order or in isolation, the second test will fail because it's trying to delete an item that doesn't exist.

Solution: Tests should be atomic, capable of running in any order and in isolation. Refactor the tests to ensure they set up and clean up their own data.

Insufficient wait for rendering or asynchronous operations

Tests may become flaky if they don't properly wait for rendering or asynchronous operations to complete. For example:

```
it('submits a form', () => {
  cy.visit('/form')
  cy.get('input[name="email"]').type('test@email.com')
  cy.get('input[name="password"]').type('password123')
  cy.get('button').click()
  cy.get('.success-message').should('be.visible')
})
```

In the preceding test, the form submission might be asynchronous and might not be complete before the test checks for the success message, causing the test to fail intermittently.

Solution: In Cypress, you can use `.should()` function that will automatically re-run until the assertion passes or it times out:

```
it('submits a form', () => {
```

```
  cy.visit('/form')
  cy.get('input[name="email"]').type('test@email.com')
  cy.get('input[name="password"]').type('password123')
  cy.get('button').click()
  cy.get('.success-message', { timeout: 10000 }).should('be.
visible')
})
```

In the updated test, Cypress will wait up to 10 seconds for the success message to appear before failing the test.

It's important to note that while automatic retries can help combat flakiness, they are not a silver bullet. Sometimes, flaky tests are symptomatic of deeper issues, such as race conditions in the application code, and these should be addressed directly for the most robust solution.

With its advanced capabilities, Cypress offers several tools and strategies to handle flaky tests, thereby enhancing the reliability of your test suite and increasing confidence in your application's functionality. Let's explore some techniques and practices for managing flaky tests in Cypress.

Test retry ability

Introduced in version 5.0, Cypress provides a 'test retries' feature that can automatically retry failed tests. By leveraging this feature, you can allow Cypress to automatically retry failing tests several times before marking them as failed. Test retries are an excellent way to handle intermittent test failures caused by flaky tests.

You can enable test retries in your configuration (`cypress.json`) by setting the retries option:

```
{
  "retries": {
    "runMode": 2,
    "openMode": 0
  }
}
```

In the preceding configuration, `runMode` allows you to define the number of test retries when running `cypress run`, while `openMode` lets you set the number of retries in `cypress open`. In this case, Cypress will retry tests twice when running in 'run mode' and will not retry tests in 'open mode'. You can adjust these values as per your project's requirements.

Use of `cy.should()` assertion for automatic retrying

Cypress commands are built to automatically retry and ensure that elements exist in the DOM and are actionable before executing actions or assertions on them. Using Cypress's `cy.should()` function in combination with its built-in automatic waiting mechanism can help manage flaky tests effectively. For example:

```
// Example usage of `cy.should()`
cy.get('.my-element').should('be.visible');
```

In the aforementioned example, the `cy.get()` command will automatically retry until the element with class `'my-element'` becomes visible. If the element does not become visible within the default timeout period (4 seconds), the test will fail.

Flaky test management in Cypress Cloud

The fundamental premise of Flaky Test Management is that by enabling test retries, Cypress Cloud can detect, flag, and track flaky tests from your recorded Cypress test runs in your CI/CD pipeline. In other words, a test is labeled as flaky when it can succeed and fail during multiple retry attempts without any alterations to the code. These flaky tests can be troublesome and may disrupt the CI/CD pipeline, highlighting the importance of managing flaky test effectively.

Please note that Flaky test management features are not included in the free tier of Cypress Cloud. These capabilities are available only in the paid plans, which provide advanced test analytics and additional tools to identify, monitor, and handle flaky tests.

Test retries and flake detection

The essential mechanism enabling the detection of flaky tests in Cypress Cloud is the automatically retry capability of Cypress. Therefore, enabling test retries is necessary to take advantage of any flaky test management feature.

When a test is retried, and the subsequent attempts yield different results (for example, fail then pass), Cypress Cloud identifies it as a flaky test. These Flaky tests are tracked and flagged, helping teams in maintaining the robustness of their test suite and the reliability of their CI/CD pipeline.

Here is an example of a Cypress test with retries enabled:

```
it('flaky test', { retries: 2 }, () => {
  // ...flaky test code
})
```

In this test, Cypress will automatically retry the test two times if it fails initially, potentially mitigating the effect of flaky tests.

Flagging flaky tests

Test runs containing flaky tests will be flagged indicating the number of flaky tests on the Cypress Cloud's "Latest runs" page. In addition, you can filter Flaky test runs by using the "Flaky" filter within this page. A test case will be considered flaky if it fails across multiple test run attempts triggered by test retrying.

Flaky test analytics

The flaky tests analytics page offers a comprehensive view of the flakiness status within your project. It displays a plot explaining the number of flaky tests over time, flakiness level of the entire project, and the number of flake tests grouped based on their severity. Furthermore, it provides a log of all flaky test cases that can be filtered and ordered by severity.

These analytics can help you understand the state of flakiness in your tests and can guide you toward which tests to prioritize for debugging. High flakiness levels might indicate deeper issues in your application or tests and could signal that you must investigate further.

Flake severity

Flake severity is determined by the frequency of flake or the flake rate of a given test. Tests that flake more often are assigned a higher severity level. This level can help you prioritize which tests to investigate and fix first.

By clicking on a test case on the analytics page, you can view the historical log of the latest flaky runs, the most common errors across the runs, the related test case changelog, and the plot depicting the failure and flaky rates over time.

Flake alerting

Cypress Cloud can provide alerts via GitHub and Slack integrations to further assist with staying on top of flake occurrences. By enabling these integrations, you can receive immediate notifications when a flaky test is detected, keeping your team informed and ready to take action.

For example, once GitHub flake alerting is enabled, GitHub PR comments will present the number of flaky tests associated to the PR within the test summary. It will also include a "Flakiness" section that highlights the specific tests that flaked. Similarly, with Slack alerts, Cypress Cloud will send Slack messages whenever it identifies flaky tests.

This way, the whole team stays informed about the state of the tests, and can swiftly respond to any emerging issues, keeping the test suite and the application in a healthy state.

By diligently managing flaky tests, you can maintain a robust and reliable test suite that genuinely aids your development process and ensures the quality of your application.

Leveraging Cypress Analytics

With an effective test suite, you have a robust line of defense against bugs, but it continues beyond there. Understanding your test suite's performance over time can be as important as the test themselves. In Cypress, this is where Cypress Analytics steps in.

Cypress Analytics provides insights into your test suite's behavior over time, displaying key metrics and trends to help you make informed decisions about your tests. It offers comprehensive insights into your tests' performance, including their execution time, pass rate, and failure rate. This information can help you understand whether your tests are improving over time or if there are areas that require attention.

Accessing Cypress Analytics

To access Cypress Analytics, navigate to your Cypress Dashboard. On the left-side menu, click on the `Analytics` option. Here, you will find a range of data about your tests. The main dashboard displays information on all of your test suites together, and you can view data for individual suites by clicking on them.

Key metrics in Cypress Analytics

In Cypress Analytics, several metrics are essential to pay attention to. Here is a brief explanation of each as follows:

- **Run Status:** The status of a run is one of the most immediate and crucial pieces of information about your test suite.

***Figure 9.3**: Cypress Cloud – Run Status*

- **Run Duration:** This is the total time your tests take to run. Ideally, you want this to be as low as possible to reduce the time it takes to get feedback on your code.

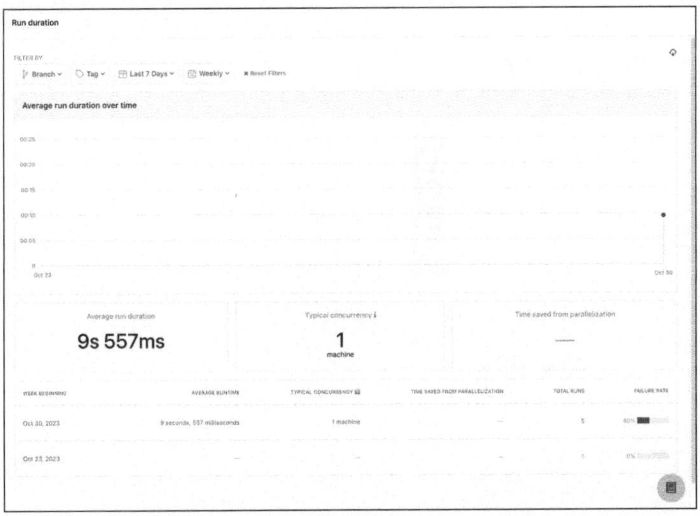

***Figure 9.4**: Cypress Cloud – Run Duration*

- **Pass Rate:** This is the percentage of tests passing each run. A high pass rate usually indicates that your code is functioning as expected.
- **Fail Rate:** This is the percentage of failed tests in each run. A high fail rate might indicate issues in your code or your tests.
- **Test Suite Size:** The size of your test suite is an essential metric for understanding the complexity of your testing process.

***Figure 9.5**: Cypress Cloud – Test Suite Size*

- **Top Failures:** Understanding your top failures can help you prioritize which tests to fix first.

***Figure 9.6**: Cypress Cloud – Top Failures*

- **Slowest Tests:** Identifying your slowest tests can help you optimize your test suite for speed.

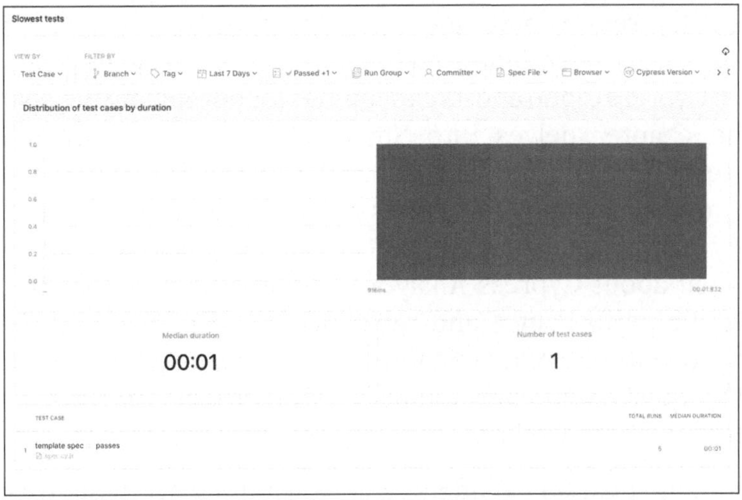

***Figure* 9.7**: *Cypress Cloud – Slowest Test*

Cypress Analytics is a powerful tool that can providc invaluable insights into your test suite. Using this tool effectively improves your tests, making them faster, more reliable, and, ultimately, more valuable to your team.

Combining Analytics with Other Cypress Features

Cypress Analytics becomes even more powerful when combined with other features offered by Cypress, such as Flaky Test Management. Flaky tests are marked in your analytics, making the process of identifying and addressing these troublesome tests easy.

Similarly, Smart Orchestration features can also be effectively combined with Cypress Analytics. For instance, by comparing the run time of different spec files in your analytics, you can balance your test suite across multiple machines effectively, reducing the total run time.

In conclusion, Cypress Analytics, coupled with the other advanced features of Cypress, provides a comprehensive toolkit to help you optimize your test automation process. This data-driven approach to test management keeps you informed about your test suite's performance and empowers you to take the necessary steps to ensure your tests provide the utmost value.

Conclusion

We explored Cypress Cloud and its advanced features, including Smart Orchestration, Flaky Test Management, and Cypress Analytics. Readers are introduced to Cypress Cloud and its capabilities for optimizing the test automation process. The chapter delves into Smart Orchestration, which intelligently distributes tests across multiple machines for faster and more efficient test runs. It also covers managing flaky tests and provides strategies and techniques to effectively handle and mitigate the impact of unstable tests. Additionally, readers learned about Cypress Analytics, a powerful tool that offers valuable insights into the performance and reliability of their test suite. By leveraging these advanced features, readers can enhance their test automation workflow, improve test stability, and gain valuable metrics to ensure their Cypress tests' overall efficiency and reliability.

In the upcoming chapter, readers will learn how to seamlessly integrate Cypress with popular version control systems like GitHub and GitLab, allowing for efficient collaboration and automated testing. The chapter covers the use of Git hooks to automate testing processes, enabling developers to run tests automatically on specific events. Additionally, readers will explore how to implement Behavior-Driven Development (BDD) with Cucumber and Cypress, fostering a more collaborative and user-centric approach to test automation. By the end of the next chapter, readers will be equipped with the knowledge and skills to streamline their testing workflows, collaborate effectively with their teams, and implement BDD practices for more robust and maintainable tests.

Further Reading

To expand readers' knowledge on the topics discussed in this chapter, it is suggested to explore the following additional resources:

- **Cypress Cloud Documentation:** The official Cypress documentation on Cypress Cloud (https://docs.cypress.io/guides/cloud/introduction) provides detailed information on Cypress Cloud and its features. It covers Smart Orchestration, Flaky Test Management, and Cypress Analytics, offering insights into effectively leveraging these advanced features.
- **Cypress Real World App on GitHub:** The Cypress Real World App repository on GitHub (https://github.com/cypress-io/cypress-realworld-app) includes examples and practical implementations of using Cypress Cloud features, such as Smart Orchestration and Flaky

Test Management. Exploring this repository can provide real-world use cases for optimizing test automation with Cypress Cloud.

These resources will give you a broader understanding and practical examples of the concepts you've learned in this chapter.

CHAPTER 10
Integrating with GitHub, GitLab, and Cucumber

Introduction

This chapter will explain how to integrate Cypress with popular version control systems like GitHub and GitLab and use Git Hooks for automated testing. It will also cover implementing Behavior-Driven Development (BDD) using Cucumber with Cypress, enabling a more collaborative approach to test automation.

Structure

In this chapter, we will discuss the following topics:

- Version control with GitHub and GitLab
- Using Git Hooks for automated testing
- Implementing BDD with Cucumber and Cypress

Version control with GitHub and GitLab

In modern software development, using version control systems is not a matter of choice but a necessity. GitHub and GitLab are two of the most popular version control platforms today. This section explores how you can integrate Cypress with these platforms to enhance your test automation processes.

Version control is an essential aspect of software development that assists developers in managing changes to source code over time. It keeps track of modifications made to the codebase and helps resolve conflicts when several team members work concurrently on the same project. Let's delve deeper into understanding version control systems and their significance.

Types of version control systems

Version control systems can be categorized into three primary types:

- **Local Version Control Systems:** The simplest form of VCS, local version control systems involve storing copies of project files in another directory, often with timestamp comments. However, this approach can be error-prone; it's easy to accidentally write to the wrong file or forget where you stored a particular version of a file.
- **Centralized Version Control Systems (CVCS):** CVCS, such as SVN, provide a central server that stores all versions of a project's files. Developers can then check out files they wish to change from the main place. This setup can offer several advantages, including increased visibility of collaborators' activities and centralized control over access to project files.
- **Distributed Version Control Systems (DVCS):** Unlike CVCS, where the central server is the single point of failure, DVCS, such as Git, allows multiple replicas of the entire repository, including its history, to exist on different users' systems. This means that even if one server dies, any client repositories can be copied back to replace it.

Importance of version control

- **Collaboration:** Without VCS, working together on a project would involve constant file swapping with the risk of overwriting someone else's work. A VCS like Git allows everyone to operate freely in their local environment, merging their changes with the shared repository only when ready.
- **Recoverability:** Version control systems keep a history of changes, enabling developers to revert to a previous version if something goes wrong. This history also serves as an audit trail, allowing you to trace changes back to their source.
- **Tracking Changes:** Each commit to the repository is tagged with an author and timestamp, meaning you can understand who made which changes and when.
- **Branching and Merging:** With a VCS, you can create separate branches to isolate changes for specific features or issues. Once the feature or

fix is tested and approved, you can merge these changes into the main codebase.

Version control with Git

Git is the most widely used version control system today. It is a distributed version control system, meaning that every user has a complete copy of the project, including all changes history. Git is also open-source and free to use.

The fundamental concepts of Git include the following:

- **Repository:** This is a directory where Git has been initiated to start version controlling your files.
- **Commit:** This is a snapshot of your files at a given point in time. Every commit has a unique ID (a SHA-1 hash) that lets you track your changes.
- **Branch:** This is a line of development. The default branch in Git is called master. You can create other branches to work on new features or fixes.
- **Checkout:** This is the act of switching between different versions of a target entity.
- **Push:** Pushing refers to sending your committed changes to a remote repository such as GitHub or GitLab.
- **Pull:** Pulling refers to fetching changes from a remote repository and merging them into your local one.

Git is known for its speed, data integrity, and support for distributed non-linear workflows. Integrating Git with Cypress testing can significantly streamline your test management and project workflow.

GitHub

GitHub is a web-based platform used for version control, which is vital in large projects where multiple software developers are working. GitHub simplifies the process of collaborating with peers and minimizes the chances of both teams simultaneously working on the same part of a project and making conflicting changes. This platform uses Git, a distributed version control system, which means the complete codebase and history reside on every developer's local machine, leading to easy branching and merging.

Setting up projects on GitHub

Here's a simple step-by-step guide to setting up your projects on GitHub:

1. **Create a GitHub account:** The first step is to create a GitHub account if you haven't already. Visit the GitHub website and sign up.
2. **Create a new repository:** After logging into your account, you can create a new repository by clicking on the '+' icon in the upper right corner of your GitHub homepage. Then click on "New Repository." You'll be asked to name your repository and provide a description. For your repository to be accessible to the public, make sure to keep it public. Finally, click on "Create Repository."
3. **Add project files to the repository:** Now, you can add your project files to this repository. You have the option to either create new files or upload existing files.

Integrating Cypress with GitHub

When combined with GitHub, Cypress can bring immense automation and efficiency to your testing workflow. You can add your Cypress tests to any project in GitHub. Here's how you can achieve this:

1. **Set up Cypress in your project:** First, you need to set up Cypress in your local project. You can do this by installing Cypress via `npm`. Navigate to your project directory in the terminal and type:

   ```
   npm install cypress --save-dev
   ```

   This will add Cypress to your `devDependencies` in your project's `package.json`.
2. **Create Cypress tests:** After setting up Cypress, you can create Cypress tests in the `cypress/e2e` directory.
3. **Push your project to GitHub:** Once you've created your tests, you can add all your project files (including Cypress tests) to your GitHub repository. Initialize the local directory as a Git repository:

   ```
   git init
   ```

   Add all the files in the local repository staging area:

   ```
   git add .
   ```

   Commit the files:

   ```
   git commit -m "First commit"
   ```

Copy the remote repository URL provided by GitHub when you created the new repository and add it to your local repository:

```
git remote add origin <remote repository URL>
```

Finally, push the changes in your local repository to GitHub:

```
git push origin main
```

Collaboration on GitHub

One of the significant advantages of GitHub is the ease with which developers can collaborate on projects. Collaboration typically occurs as follows:

- **Forking a repository:** A developer can create a copy of a repository to their account and make changes without affecting the original project.
- **Pull requests:** Once the developer is ready to share their changes, they can open a pull request. This alerts the original repository maintainers that someone has proposed modifications. The maintainers can review the changes and merge them into the repository or suggest improvements.
- **Branching:** Developers can create branches in a repository, allowing them to isolate their changes until they're ready to share them with the rest of the team.

By integrating Cypress with GitHub, you can achieve a streamlined, efficient, and collaborative approach to automated testing.

GitLab

Like GitHub, GitLab is also a web-based DevOps lifecycle tool that provides a Git repository manager. It offers features like wiki, issue-tracking, CI/CD pipelines, and more, enabling teams to collaborate effectively, manage and track work, and automate software development and delivery processes.

Setting up projects on GitLab

To set up your projects on GitLab, follow these steps:

1. **Create a GitLab account:** First, if you still need to get a GitLab account, navigate to the GitLab website to sign up.
2. **Create a new project:** After you've logged into your account, you can create a new project by clicking on the 'New project' button on your GitLab homepage. You'll need to name your project and provide a description.

You can also decide whether the repository should be public (accessible to everyone) or private (accessible only to selected individuals). Click 'Create project' when you're done.

3. **Add project files to the project:** Now, you can add your project files to the new project. You can create new files directly in GitLab or push existing files from your local machine using Git.

Integrating Cypress with GitLab

The integration of Cypress with GitLab can supercharge your testing workflow by incorporating automated end-to-end tests into your CI/CD pipeline. Here's how you can add Cypress to your project in GitLab:

1. **Set up Cypress in your project:** Start by setting up Cypress in your local project, similar to how you would for any local development. You can install Cypress via `npm` by navigating to your project directory in the terminal and entering:

   ```
   npm install cypress --save-dev
   ```

   This adds Cypress to your `devDependencies` in your `package.json`.

2. **Create Cypress Tests:** Once you've set up Cypress, create your test files in the cypress/e2e directory.

3. **Push your project to GitLab:** With your Cypress tests created, you can now push all your project files to your GitLab project. Assuming you have Git installed on your local machine, initialize the local directory as a Git repository:

   ```
   git init
   ```

   Add all the new files in the local repository to the staging area:

   ```
   git add .
   ```

   Commit the files:

   ```
   git commit -m "First commit"
   ```

   Copy the remote repository URL provided by GitLab and add it to your local repository:

   ```
   git remote add origin <remote repository URL>
   ```

Finally, push the changes from your local repository to GitLab:

```
git push -u origin main
```

Collaboration on GitLab

GitLab fosters team collaboration via several features:

- **Merge requests:** Similar to GitHub's pull requests, merge requests in GitLab allow developers to propose changes to the codebase. The team can review these proposed changes, discuss them, and finally approve and merge them.
- **Issue tracking:** GitLab's issue tracking feature allows teams to track bugs and feature requests, assign work, and manage project milestones.
- **CI/CD pipelines:** GitLab's built-in continuous integration (CI) and continuous delivery/deployment (CD) capabilities enable teams to automate their testing and deployment process, increasing efficiency and reducing manual errors.

Integrating Cypress with GitLab allows for a more automated, reliable, and collaborative testing process, making it easier for teams to build and deploy high-quality software.

Using Git Hooks for automated testing

Git hooks are scripts that Git executes before or after events such as `commit`, `push`, etc. These hooks are a built-in feature of Git, designed to trigger actions at specific points in the development workflow. The hooks reside in the `.git/hooks` directory of every Git repository.

Git hooks are extremely useful because they automate tasks during your development process. For example, they can enforce a commit message format, run tests before committing your code, or even push updates to a live test server after each commit.

Let's take a look at the six Git hooks that are mainly used:

- **pre-commit:** This hook is invoked before the `commit` process. It is typically used to perform checks on the snapshot that's about to be committed, such as enforcing coding style guidelines, checking for syntax errors, or running tests. If this script exits non-zero, Git aborts the commit process, offering an opportunity to fix the issues and commit again.
- **prepare-commit-msg:** This hook is invoked after receiving the commit message and before the message editor is fired up, but after the default

message is created. It allows you to edit the default message before the commit author sees it. This hook can be used to modify the message to create a standardized commit message format.

- **commit-msg:** The `commit-msg` hook takes one parameter (the path to a temporary file containing the commit message) and is invoked after the message editor has been closed before the commit is made. If this hook exits non-zero, Git aborts the `commit` process, meaning it can be used to validate the project state or commit message before allowing a commit to go through. For example, you could use it to check that your commit message follows a specified pattern or prevent committing if certain files have been updated.
- **post-commit:** The `post-commit` hook is invoked immediately after a commit is made. Unlike the `pre-commit` and `commit-msg` hooks, its exit status does not affect the commit. This hook can't alter the outcome of the `git commit` operation. Instead, it performs actions that don't modify the commit, such as notifying a continuous integration server, updating an issue tracking system, or sending an email notification.
- **post-checkout:** The `post-checkout` hook works similarly to the `post-commit` hook, but it is called whenever you successfully check out a reference with `git checkout`. This can be useful for regenerating files your build system doesn't take care of, auto-loading new post-checkout dependencies, or notifying tools about the change in the working directory context.
- **pre-rebase:** The `pre-rebase` hook runs before the rebase process begins, and, much like the `pre-commit` hook, it can halt the process by returning a non-zero exit status. You can use this hook to disallow rebasing of specific branches. It's also useful for checking whether your code adheres to the project's standards (similar to the `pre-commit` hook) before changes are re-applied.

In summary, Git hooks play a crucial role in the automated workflow by triggering actions at specific points in the development cycle. They allow developers to enforce policies, validate commit messages, and even integrate with other tools. They help make the development process smoother and more efficient, contributing significantly to code quality and reliability.

Setting up Git Hooks with Husky

While you can directly write scripts in the `.git/hooks` directory, it is not version-controlled, making sharing these hooks across the team challenging. This is where Husky comes in. Husky is a tool that makes setting up Git hooks easy and allows them to be version-controlled.

To set up Husky in your project, install it as a development dependency by running the following:

```
npm install husky --save-dev
```

Then you need to set up Husky Hooks. Husky hooks are defined in your `package.json` file. Let's set up a `pre-push` hook to run our Cypress tests before the code is pushed to the remote repository:

```
{
  "husky": {
    "hooks": {
      "pre-push": "npm run test"
    }
  }
}
```

In the preceding configuration, `npm run test` is the command to run your tests, which should be defined in your scripts section of `package.json` like so:

```
"scripts": {
  "test": "cypress run"
}
```

Now, every time you try to push your changes, Cypress will run your test suite. If any test fails, the push is aborted.

Using Git Hooks for automated testing

With Husky set up, we can now use Git hooks to automate our Cypress testing. Consider an example where we want to ensure no failing tests are pushed to the remote repository. For this, we can use the `pre-push` hook.

```
{
  "husky": {
    "hooks": {
      "pre-push": "npm run test"
    }
  },
  "scripts": {
```

```
    "test": "cypress run"
  }
}
```

With this configuration, Cypress will automatically run your entire test suite before every git push. If any test fails, the push is aborted, preventing the propagation of failing tests to the remote repository.

Caveats and considerations

While automated testing with Git hooks can significantly enhance your testing workflow, there are a few considerations to keep in mind:

- **Time:** End-to-end tests can take a long time to run, which could make the commit or push process slower. Consider this trade-off before deciding to run the entire test suite on every commit or push.
- **Scope:** You might not need to test the entire application for every minor change. In such cases, consider structuring your tests so that you can select which ones to run based on the scope of the changes.

Despite these considerations, the ability to automatically run tests before commits or pushes can dramatically improve the reliability of your codebase and catch issues earlier in the development cycle.

Git Hooks examples

Git hooks are extremely beneficial for automated testing, allowing you to incorporate tests seamlessly into your workflow. They can run unit tests, integration tests, or any other type of test automatically, right before or after certain Git operations.

Here's a rundown of how Git hooks can facilitate automated testing:

Scenario 1: Running tests before each commit with the `pre-commit` Hook

The `pre-commit` hook is invoked before a commit is made. We can leverage this hook to run our test suite. The commit will be aborted if any test fails, ensuring that only code that passes all tests is committed to the repository. This prevents faulty code from being added to the codebase.

```
#!/bin/bash
npm test
if [ $? -ne 0 ]; then
```

```
 echo "Tests failed! Aborting commit."
 exit 1
fi
```

When placed in .git/hooks/pre-commit and made executable, this script will run your tests using npm test (you can replace this with your own test command) each time you attempt to commit. If the tests fail (signified by a non-zero exit code), the script outputs a message and exits with `1`, aborting the commit.

Scenario 2: Running tests after each commit with the `post-commit` Hook

The `post-commit` hook runs immediately after a commit. Although it can't prevent the commit, it's still useful for running tests to give developers immediate feedback.

```
#!/bin/bash
npm test
```

In the preceding script, the commit has already been made, even if the tests fail. However, you'll be immediately alerted if your commit has a problem.

Scenario 3: Running tests after a successful checkout with the `post-checkout` Hook

If your application's dependencies or configuration changes based on the branch (such as environment variables), it may be useful to automatically run tests after switching branches with git checkout. This is where the `post-checkout` hook comes in handy.

```
#!/bin/bash
npm install
npm test
```

This script will install any dependencies required for the branch you've checked out and then run your test suite.

Scenario 4: Running tests before rebase with the `pre-rebase` Hook

In some workflows, especially ones that maintain a linear commit history, you might want to run tests before a rebase operation to ensure your changes are still valid on top of the updated base branch.

```
#!/bin/bash
npm test
if [ $? -ne 0 ]; then
 echo "Tests failed! Aborting rebase."
 exit 1
fi
```

This hook will run your tests before starting the rebase. If any tests fail, the rebase will be aborted.

Running specific Cypress tests with Git Hooks

While running the entire test suite before each commit can be beneficial, sometimes you might want to run only a subset of your tests, for example, only the tests related to the files being committed. This can significantly speed up the pre-commit testing process. You can use a tool like `lint-staged` along with Husky to accomplish this. Here's a sample configuration in your `package.json`:

```
{
  "husky": {
    "hooks": {
      "pre-commit": "lint-staged"
    }
  },
  "lint-staged": {
    "*.js": "cypress run --spec cypress/integration/related-tests.spec.js"
  }
}
```

With this configuration, only the tests in `related-tests.spec.js` will run before a commit is made.

Using `pre-push` Hook for integration tests

While `pre-commit` hooks are excellent for unit tests or smaller sets of tests, you may want to run a more extensive set of tests, like integration tests, which can take longer. In this case, a `pre-push` hook can be more suitable. This hook runs just before you push your changes to the remote repository. Here's how you can set it up:

```
"husky": {
  "hooks": {
    "pre-push": "npm run test:integration"
  }
},
"scripts": {
  "test:integration": "cypress run --spec cypress/integration/**/*.spec.
js"
}
```

With this setup, your integration tests will run automatically before you push your changes to the remote repository.

`post-merge` Hook for regression tests

A `post-merge` hook is invoked after a successful `git pull` or `git merge` operation. You can use this hook to run regression tests to ensure the newly merged changes have not caused any regressions.

```
"husky": {
  "hooks": {
    "post-merge": "npm run test:regression"
  }
},
"scripts": {
  "test:regression": "cypress run --spec cypress/regression/**/*.spec.
js"
}
```

This way, you can be assured that any merged changes are not causing unexpected regressions in other parts of your application.

By strategically placing Cypress tests in your Git workflow, you can create a robust and efficient system that ensures high-quality code while providing quick feedback to developers. Choosing the hooks that make the most sense for your team and project is essential, as the optimal setup can vary based on your specific needs.

Implementing BDD with Cucumber and Cypress

Behavior-Driven Development (BDD) is a software development approach that emphasizes collaboration among developers, quality assurance engineers, and non-technical or business participants in a software project. It encourages teams to use conversation and concrete examples to formalize a shared understanding of how the application should behave.

BDD is primarily facilitated through a simple, domain-specific scripting language. One famous example is Gherkin. Gherkin uses a simple, natural language syntax to describe business requirements and scenarios through Given-When-Then steps.

For instance, a BDD scenario for a user login functionality might be:

```
Feature: User login
  Scenario: Successful login
    Given a user has an active account
    When the user inputs correct username and password
    Then the user is redirected to their dashboard
```

In BDD, these scenarios are called "specifications" and can be directly translated into automated tests. The Given-When-Then format corresponds directly to the "arrange, act, assert" structure found in most test cases, making it easy to transition from specifications to code.

BDD has numerous benefits, including:

- **Improved collaboration:** BDD helps to ensure that everyone involved in the project (developers, testers, business analysts, product owners, etc.) have the same understanding of what needs to be achieved. This shared understanding helps to ensure clarity and understanding that can lead to bugs and rework.
- **Focus on business value:** BDD encourages teams to focus on delivering features that provide business value. Because BDD scenarios are written from the user's perspective, they help the team to keep the user's needs at the forefront of their development efforts.
- **Living documentation:** Because the BDD scenarios are written in plain language and stored alongside your code, they can serve as up-to-date documentation. New team members can read the scenarios to understand what the system does without reading the code.

- **Facilitates test-driven development (TDD):** BDD scenarios can be written before the feature is implemented, providing clear acceptance criteria for the feature. Developers can then use these scenarios to guide their development, a practice known as Test-Driven Development (TDD).

Setting up Cypress and Cucumber

Cucumber is an open-source software tool that supports Behavior-Driven Development (BDD). It allows you to write software requirements in a business-readable and domain-specific language. The Gherkin language defines This readable format, a simple set of grammar rules that makes plain text structured enough for Cucumber to understand.

The primary objective of Cucumber is to allow non-technical stakeholders to engage more directly in defining software behavior by writing or reviewing behavior scenarios. These scenarios are both the specifications and the acceptance tests for the software.

A typical Cucumber test script written in the Gherkin language might look like this:

```
Feature: Search functionality on the homepage
  Scenario: User can search for a product
    Given the user is on the homepage
    When they enter "Running Shoes" into the search bar
    And they click the "SEARCH" button
    Then they should see a list of products related to "Running Shoes"
```

Each line here is an instruction for the test. **"Given"** specifies the initial context, **"When"** describes the action taken, and **"Then"** details the expected outcome.

Here are some key benefits of using Cucumber in a BDD framework:

- **Improved communication and collaboration:** Because Cucumber test scenarios are written in plain language, they can be read and understood by anyone on the team, including non-technical stakeholders. This improves communication and collaboration across the team.
- **Living documentation:** The Cucumber test suite, written in Gherkin language, serves as up-to-date system documentation. This can be a valuable resource for developers, testers, business analysts, and even manual testers.

- **Facilitates test-driven development (TDD):** Cucumber tests can be written before the code is developed, serving as a guide during development. This practice aligns well with the Test-Driven Development (TDD) approach.
- **Provides a basis for regression testing:** Cucumber tests are automated, meaning they can be re-run quickly and at any time. This makes them a valuable tool for regression testing to ensure new changes don't break existing functionality.

When integrated with a testing framework like Cypress, Cucumber becomes an even more powerful tool, allowing you to implement BDD principles in your end-to-end testing.

Setting up Cucumber with Cypress

To use Cucumber with Cypress, you need to install the `cypress-cucumber-preprocessor` package. It allows you to write your Cypress tests in Gherkin syntax and automatically generates the necessary boilerplate code.

Install the package with **`npm`**:

```
npm i @badeball/cypress-cucumber-preprocessor
```

In addition to setting up the preprocessor, the plugin documentation advises the installation of the `esbuild` bundler, developed by Gleb Bahmutov. This integration will significantly enhance the speed of your runs. Install it using the following **`npm`** command:

```
npm i @bahmutov/cypress-esbuild-preprocessor
```

Upon successfully installing the necessary packages, it's time to configure Cypress to use these plugins. The final configuration at your `cypress.config.js` file should somewhat resemble the following example:

```
const {defineConfig} = require("cypress");

const createBundler = require("@bahmutov/cypress-esbuild-preprocessor");

const addCucumberPreprocessorPlugin = require("@badeball/cypress-cucum-
ber-preprocessor").addCucumberPreprocessorPlugin;

const createEsbuildPlugin = require("@badeball/cypress-cucumber-prepro-
cessor/esbuild").createEsbuildPlugin;


module.exports = defineConfig({
  e2e: {
```

```
    async setupNodeEvents(on, config) {
       const bundler = createBundler({
plugins: [createEsbuildPlugin(config)]
       });
      on("file:preprocessor", bundler);
        await addCucumberPreprocessorPlugin(on, config);
      return config;
    },
    specPattern: "**/*.feature",
  },
});
```

In this configuration:

- We import the necessary modules for configuring Cypress, bundling with `esbuild`, and adding the Cucumber preprocessor plugin.
- We define the configuration for Cypress with `defineConfig`.
- We specify that any file with a `.feature` extension is a spec file.
- In the `setupNodeEvents` function, we add the Cucumber preprocessor plugin to Cypress and set up the `esbuild` bundler as a file preprocessor.
- `on("file:preprocessor", ...)` is where we instruct Cypress to use `esbuild` for bundling whenever a file needs preprocessing.
- Finally, the modified configuration is returned and will be used by Cypress for the testing process.

Drafting test scenarios and actions

For initiating, we should construct a simple test scenario in Gherkin syntax. Create a new file titled `cypress/e2e/login.feature` and fill it with the following content:

```
Feature: Login


Scenario: Successful Login
  Given I open the login page
  When I type in valid credentials
  Then I should be redirected to the dashboard page
```

Each scenario represents a different path through the feature. The `Given` step sets up the context, the `When` step describes the action, and the `Then` step specifies the expected outcome.

Now you need to implement the step definitions for this feature file. For each step in the scenario, you'll write a corresponding function in Cypress. Create a new directory that matches the `.feature` file name in `cypress/e2e` and add a new file named `login.js`:

```
import { Given, When, Then } from '@badeball/cypress-cucumber-prepro
cessor'


Given('I open the login page', () => {
  cy.visit('/login')
})


When('I type in valid credentials', () => {
  cy.get('#username').type('testuser')
  cy.get('#password').type('password')
  cy.get('#login-button').click()
})


Then('I should be redirected to the dashboard page', () => {
  cy.url().should('include', '/dashboard')
})
```

We're using the Given, When, and Then functions provided by `@badeball/cypress-cucumber-preprocessor` to implement our step definitions. Each function takes a string that matches a step in the `.feature` file and a callback function that executes the step using Cypress commands.

Incorporating parameters into step definitions

Step definitions have the capacity to accept parameters, facilitating you to establish more flexible and reusable test scenarios. Let's modify our previous step definition file so that we can input a board name of our preference to our test:

```
import { When, Then, Given } from "@badeball/cypress-cucumber-prepro
cessor";
```

```
Given("I open the login page", () => {
  cy.visit("/");
});

When('I type in {string} and {string}', (username, password) => {
  cy.get('#username').type(`${username}`)
  cy.get('#password').type(`${password}`)
  cy.get('#login-button').click()
})

Then('I should be redirected to the dashboard page', () => {
  cy.url().should('include', '/dashboard')
})
```

The parameters are automatically sent to the corresponding step definition functions as arguments. Pay attention to the `{string}` in the step definition. This will check whether we are passing the appropriate type into our step.

We will now generate a scenario in our `cypress/e2e/login.feature` file that accepts the `username` and `password` as parameters. It will look somewhat like this:

```
Feature: Login

Scenario: Successful Login
  Given I open the login page
  When I type in 'myLogin' and 'myPassword'
  Then I should be redirected to the dashboard page
```

Data-driven testing

Another crucial concept in cucumber that you should be aware of is data tables. A Data table in Gherkin syntax allows you to transmit a data table to a step, simplifying the management of multiple data sets in your test scenarios. This is particularly beneficial for data-driven testing, where you aspire to test the same scenario with different sets of input data.

Data tables are defined in the Examples section of your `.feature` file. Let's continue with our previous file:

```
Feature: Login functionality

  Scenario: Successful Login with diff types of users
    Given I open the login page
    When I type in "<username>"and "<password>"
    Then I should be redirected to the dashboard page

  Examples:
      | username | password  |
      | user1    | password1 |
      | user2    | password2 |
```

With `Examples` steps defined, you'll run your test multiple times, transferring different data with every step. Notice how we generate variables `username` and `password` and wrap them in < > to be passed as parameters into our step definitions.

Processing array of data

These data tables can also be utilized to feed data into a single step, as demonstrated in the following example:

```
Feature: Creating cards functionality

  Scenario: Create multiple cards
    Given I am in board detail
    When I create cards with names
    | Milk | Bread | Butter | Jam |
    Then 4 cards are visible
```

However, the step must be capable of digesting the data table. This is how you can make it work:

```
When("I create cards with names", (table: DataTable) => {
  cy.get('[data-cy="new-card"]')
```

```
    .click()

  table.raw()[0].forEach(item => {

    cy.get('[data-cy="new-card-input"]')
      .type(`${item}{enter}`)

  })
});
```

The `table.raw()[0]` function will return the first line ([0]) of the table as an array. Inside the step definition, we are looping over this array to create items in the list.

Grouping tests

Apart from the Given, When, Then and keywords, alternative methods exist for organizing numerous tests in one `.feature` file. Our test hitherto has revolved around creating a new board and a new list, but let's tweak our test a little and develop one test that solely creates another board and places it before our existing test:

Path: `cypress/e2e/digital_organizer.feature`

```
Feature: Digital Organizer Functionality

  Scenario: Launching a digital organizer
    Given I am on an empty home page
    When I input "<organizerName>" and confirm
    Then I should be navigated to the organizer details

  Scenario: Generating a <listName> list within a digital organizer
    Given I am on an empty home page
    When I input "<organizerName>" and confirm
    And Develop a list titled "<listName>"
    Then I should be navigated to the organizer details
```

```
  Examples:
    | organizerName | listName |
    | Vacation Planner | Attractions |
    | Wedding Planner | Guest List |
```

In a similar fashion to the `describe()`, `context()`, and `it()` blocks in Mocha, we can further group our tests and arrange them into logical collections. The `Feature` keyword acts as a `describe()` block and provides a top-level grouping.

Within a Feature's scope, you can incorporate a `Rule` block, which divides your scenarios into subgroups.

As different scenarios are tested, a Background step can be added, functioning similarly to a `beforeEach()` hook in Mocha and executing a sequence of steps prior to each scenario. We can abstract our `Given` and `When` steps from our existing `.feature` file and make our test tidier.

Coupled with a `Rule` keyword, our test might resemble the following:

Path: `cypress/e2e/digital_organizer.feature`

```
Feature: Digital Organizer Functionality

  Rule: Positive paths

  Background: Empty digital organizer page
    Given I am on an empty home page

  Scenario: Launching a digital organizer
    When I input “new organizer” and confirm
    Then I should be navigated to the organizer details

  Scenario: Generating a <listName> list within a digital organizer
    When I input “<organizerName>” and confirm
    And Develop a list titled “<listName>”
    Then I should be navigated to the organizer details

  Examples:
```

```
| organizerName | listName |
| Vacation Planner | Attractions |
| Wedding Planner | Guest List |
```

Implementing hooks

Despite the ability to add a Background, it's still possible to define Before and After steps, which function like `beforeEach()` and `afterEach()` hooks in Mocha. These will not cause your tests to fail as they are run within your tests.

Before and After steps are part of your step definition file, meaning there is no need to include them in the .feature file.

Path: `cypress/e2e/digital_organizer.js`

```
import { When, Then, Given, Before } from "@badeball/cypress-cucumber
-preprocessor";


Before(() => {
  // reset the application
  cy.request('POST', '/api/reset')
})
Given("I am on an empty home page", () => {
  cy.visit("/");
});
When("I input {string} and confirm", (organizerName) => {
  cy.get("[data-cy=first-organizer]").type(`${organizerName}{enter}`);
});
When("Develop a list titled {string}", (listName) => {
  cy.get('[data-cy="add-list-input"]').type(`${listName}{enter}`);
});
Then("I should be navigated to the organizer details", () => {
  cy.location("pathname").should('match', /\/organizer\/\d/);
});
```

Test labelling

Labels are a robust feature in the Cucumber syntax that facilitates scenario categorization and filtering. Labels can be utilized to execute specific scenarios or exclude scenarios from the test run.

To append labels to your scenarios, simply prefix the scenario or feature with an `@` symbol followed by the label name. For instance, let's affix a `@regression` label to the successful login scenario in the `cypress/e2e/digital_organizer.feature` file:

Path: `cypress/e2e/digital_organizer.feature`

```
Feature: Digital Organizer Functionality

  Rule: Positive paths

  Background: Empty digital organizer page
    Given I am on an empty home page

  @sanity
  Scenario: Launching a digital organizer
    When I input "new organizer" and confirm
    Then I should be navigated to the organizer details

  Scenario: Generating a <listName> list within a digital organizer
    When I input "<organizerName>" and confirm
    And Develop a list titled "<listName>"
    Then I should be navigated to the organizer details

  Examples:
    | organizerName | listName |
    | Vacation Planner | Attractions |
    | Wedding Planner | Guest List |
```

To execute tests with a specific label, use the following command:

```
npx cypress run --env tags="@sanity"
```

This will exclude tests that do not contain the `@sanity` label.

Additionally, all tests with a particular label can be run, or the not keyword can be passed to run all labels except the specified one.

```
npx cypress run --env tags="not @sanity"
```

There also exists a method of running all tests that contain either one of the labels:

npx cypress run --env tags="@sanity or @regression"

With BDD, Cucumber, and Cypress, you can write readable tests that can be understood by all stakeholders, ensuring that everyone understands the application's behavior and requirements. You can write scenarios covering both the happy path and edge cases, ensuring your application behaves correctly in various situations. This also promotes collaboration between developers, QA engineers, and business stakeholders, leading to better communication and, ultimately, better software.

Comparison: Traditional testing vs BDD with Cucumber and Cypress

Here's a table that compares traditional testing with BDD using Cucumber and Cypress:

	Traditional Testing	**BDD with Cucumber and Cypress**
Readability	Tests are often written in programming languages, making them less accessible to non-technical stakeholders.	Tests are written in Gherkin, a natural language that's easy for everyone to understand.
Collaboration	Developers and QA engineers often work in isolation.	BDD promotes collaboration between developers, QA engineers, and business stakeholders.
Coverage	It can be difficult to ensure that all edge cases are covered.	BDD encourages you to think through various scenarios, ensuring thorough coverage.
Maintenance	Code-centric tests can be more brittle and harder to maintain.	BDD tests focus on behavior, which tends to be more stable.

Table 10.1: *Traditional testing vs BDD*

By implementing BDD with Cucumber and Cypress, you can enhance the effectiveness and efficiency of your testing process, ensure higher-quality software, and improve collaboration within your team.

Conclusion

We explored the seamless integration of Cypress with popular version control systems like GitHub and GitLab, providing efficient collaboration and automated testing workflows. The chapter covers using Git hooks to automate testing processes, enabling developers to run tests automatically on specific events, such as code commits or merges. Additionally, readers explored the implementation of Behavior-Driven Development (BDD) with Cucumber and Cypress, fostering a more collaborative and user-centric approach to test automation. By combining these techniques, readers will be empowered to enhance their testing workflows, facilitate effective teamwork, and create maintainable tests that align with the application's behavior. This chapter equips readers with the knowledge and skills to optimize their test automation process and ensure seamless integration with their version control systems.

In the upcoming chapter, readers will gain insights into Continuous Integration and Continuous Deployment (CI/CD) principles and how to seamlessly integrate Cypress into their CI/CD pipelines. The chapter explores the use of Docker to incorporate Cypress tests into containerized environments, allowing for consistent and reproducible testing. It also covers building Jenkins pipelines with Cypress, providing step-by-step instructions on automating test execution within Jenkins CI/CD workflows. Additionally, readers will be introduced to other CI/CD tools that can be employed with Cypress, offering a range of options to suit their specific project requirements. By the end of this chapter, readers will be equipped with the knowledge and techniques to incorporate Cypress effectively into their CI/CD processes, enabling efficient and reliable automated testing within their development pipelines.

Further reading

To expand readers' knowledge on the topics discussed in this chapter, I suggest exploring these additional resources:

1. **Cypress GitHub Integration Guide:** The official Cypress documentation on GitHub integration (https://docs.cypress.io/guides/dashboard/github-integration) provides detailed instructions on integrating Cypress

with GitHub. It covers setting up GitHub Actions to automate Cypress test runs within your GitHub repositories.

2. **Cypress GitLab Integration Guide:** The official Cypress documentation on GitLab integration (https://docs.cypress.io/guides/dashboard/gitlab-integration) offers guidance on integrating Cypress with GitLab. It explains how to configure GitLab CI/CD pipelines to run Cypress tests as part of your GitLab workflow.

3. **Cypress with Cucumber:** This blog post (https://filiphric.com/cucumber-in-cypress-a-step-by-step-guide) demonstrates how to implement BDD with Cucumber and Cypress. It provides examples and best practices for writing Cucumber feature files and integrating them with Cypress tests.

4. **Cypress with Git Hooks:** This blog post on Medium (https://ankittrehan2000.medium.com/automated-end-to-end-testing-with-cypress-and-husky-pre-commit-hooks-edd5385c027b) provides a step-by-step guide on using Git hooks to trigger Cypress tests before a commit is made. It includes code examples and explanations to help you implement Git hooks effectively.

These resources will give you a broader understanding and practical examples of the concepts you've learned in this chapter.

CHAPTER 11

Continuous Integration and Continuous Deployment (CI/CD)

Introduction

In this chapter, readers will learn about the principles of CI/CD and how to integrate Cypress into their CI/CD pipelines using tools like Docker and Jenkins. The chapter will also cover other CI/CD tools Cypress can use, providing readers with various options based on their project requirements.

Structure

In this chapter, we will discuss the following topics:

- Overview of CI/CD
- Integrating Cypress with Docker
- Building Jenkins Pipelines with Cypress
- Other CI/CD tools for Cypress

Overview of CI/CD

Continuous Integration and Continuous Deployment (CI/CD) is a method that involves automating the various stages of software delivery, right from integration, and testing, to deployment. The strategy aims to identify and fix issues promptly, improve software quality, and reduce the time it takes to validate and release new updates.

There are two critical components of this strategy:

- **Continuous integration (CI):** Continuous integration involves merging all developers' working copies to a shared mainline several times daily. This helps to ensure that code changes made by individual developers don't conflict with one another. Post the integration, automated build and test processes are run to validate the changes.
- **Continuous deployment (CD):** Continuous deployment is the automatic deployment of integrated changes to the staging or production environment after passing the build and test stages.

Components of CI/CD

To effectively implement CI/CD, it is essential to understand its core components. These foundational elements collectively ensure smooth automation of the software delivery process.

- **Version control system (VCS)**: A Version Control System (VCS) is a tool that helps manage changes to source code over time. VCS keeps track of every modification to the code in a special kind of database, allowing developers to revisit older versions of the code or examine the changes over time. It can help resolve conflicts when multiple developers work on the same codebase. Popular version control systems include Git, Subversion, and Mercurial. We discovered this CI component in one of the previous chapters of this book.
- **Build system:** A build system takes the source code and converts it into a runnable state. The build process can include compilation, linking, packaging, copying of files, generation of resources, etc. Examples of build tools include Gradle, Maven, Ant for Java, and MSBuild for .NET.

  In the context of software development, build tools are special applications designed to automate the process of converting source code files into standalone software artifact(s) that can be run on a computer or the process of packaging source code into executable form. This process involves compiling the source code, linking it with libraries, and packaging it into an executable format.

In modern web development, build tools have evolved to incorporate several tasks such as linting (checking for common errors in code), minification (compressing the code to be smaller in size), concatenation (combining multiple files into one), transpiling (converting newer code syntax into older versions for compatibility), running tests, and more.

Some of the more widely used build tools in JavaScript environments include:

- **Webpack:** Webpack is an open-source JavaScript module bundler. It takes modules with dependencies and generates static assets representing those modules. Webpack can handle JavaScript and any front-end resources, such as styles like CSS. It also offers a dev server with Hot Module Replacement (HMR) for development purposes and can split the output bundle for better caching.

  Example of a basic Webpack configuration file (`webpack.config.js`):

```
module.exports = {
  entry: './src/index.js', // the entry point of your application
  output: {
    filename: 'bundle.js', // the output bundled file
    path: path.resolve(__dirname, 'dist'), // where to output the bundle
  },
  module: {
    rules: [
      {
        test: /\.css$/, // regex to match CSS files
        use: ['style-loader', 'css-loader'], // loaders to handle CSS files
      },
    ],
  },
};
```

- **Rollup:** Rollup is a module bundler for JavaScript that compiles small pieces of code into larger, more complex code suitable for browsers and the transition between server and client-side scripts. It uses the new standardized format for code modules included in the ES6 revision of JavaScript. This allows developers to write code that can be shared between client and server.

  A basic Rollup configuration file (`rollup.config.js`):

```
export default {
  input: 'src/main.js', // the entry point of your application
  output: {
    file: 'bundle.js', // the output bundled file
    format: 'cjs', // the format of the output bundle
  },
  plugins: [
    resolve(), // allows you to load third-party modules in
node_modules
    commonjs(), // converts CommonJS modules to ES6
  ],
};
```

- **Parcel:** Parcel is a web application bundler that offers blazing-fast performance utilizing multicore processing and requires zero configuration. It is particularly suitable for simple applications where you want to start coding without spending time setting up the build process.

  Here's how you can use Parcel to build your app without any configuration:

```
npx parcel build src/index.html
```

  These tools enable efficient project builds, incorporating different libraries and frameworks, handling assets and styles, and optimizing for production. The choice of build tool often depends on the project's specific requirements and the development team's preference.

- **Automated testing:** Automated testing is the practice of running automated tests against the integrated codebase to ensure the code works as expected. Automated tests can range from unit tests (which test individual units of code like functions or methods), component tests, integration tests (which test the integration between different parts of the system), to end-to-end tests (which test the system as a whole).

Automated testing is essential in a CI/CD pipeline for several reasons:

- **Faster feedback:** Automated tests provide immediate feedback on the impact of the changes, allowing developers to address issues as soon as they are introduced.
- **Increased efficiency:** Automated tests eliminate the manual testing effort, freeing up the developer's time to focus on writing code.
- **Reduced business costs:** Finding and fixing bugs in the development stage is much cheaper than doing so in production.
- **Improved quality:** Automated tests increase the overall quality of the software by catching bugs that might have been missed during manual testing.

Automated testing is an integral part of Continuous Integration. Its primary purpose is to automatically validate the code's correctness, improving software quality and developer productivity.

- **Continuous integration server:** Continuous integration (CI) servers automate the process of integrating code changes from multiple contributors into a single software project. This practice is a vital part of modern software development workflows. They regularly build the software, run tests, and help developers to detect issues early.

  CI servers typically provide feedback about the health of your code base, and many can be configured to email developers when the build breaks. Some of them also have a feature to automatically deploy your application to a staging environment or production.

  Let's delve into details about some popular CI servers:

  - **Jenkins:** Jenkins is an open-source CI/CD server that allows developers to automate the different stages of their delivery pipeline. The main reason behind Jenkins' popularity is its huge plugin ecosystem. It offers over 1,000 plugins, so it integrates with almost all DevOps tools, from Docker to Puppet.

    Here is a basic "Hello World" Jenkins Pipeline script:

```
pipeline {
    agent any

    stages {
```

```
            stage('Build') {
                steps {
                    echo 'Building..'
                }
            }
            stage('Test') {
                steps {
                    echo 'Testing..'
                }
            }
            stage('Deploy') {
                steps {
                    echo 'Deploying....'
                }
            }
        }
    }
```

- **Travis CI:** Travis CI is a hosted CI service used to build and test software projects hosted on GitHub. It provides various paid plans for private projects and a free plan for open source. Travis CI can run tests in different runtime environments and different versions of languages. `.travis.yml` file is needed at the root of your repository to start building your project with Travis CI.

  A basic `.travis.yml` file for a Node.js project might look like this:

  ```
  language: node_js
  node_js:
    - "node"
    - "lts/*"
  script: npm run test
  ```

- **CircleCI:** CircleCI is a CI/CD service that supports rapid software development and publishing. It can be configured to deploy code to various environments, including AWS CodeDeploy, AWS EC2 Container Service (ECS), AWS S3, Google Kubernetes Engine (GKE),

Microsoft Azure, and Heroku. Other features include parallelism to speed up jobs and workflows to orchestrate jobs.

A simple configuration of CircleCI in `.circleci/config.yml` file:

```
version: 2.1
jobs:
  build:
    docker:
      - image: circleci/node:18.16.0
    steps:
      - checkout
      - run: npm install
      - run: npm test
```

- **GitHub actions:** GitHub actions make it easy to automate all your software workflows, now with world-class CI/CD. You can build, test, and deploy your code right from GitHub. Make code reviews, branch management, and issue triaging work the way you want. It is tightly integrated with the GitHub ecosystem and provides a YAML-based workflow configuration.

  A simple GitHub actions workflow in `.github/workflows/main.yml` file:

```
name: Node.js CI
on: [push, pull_request]
jobs:
  build:
    runs-on: ubuntu-latest
    steps:
    - uses: actions/checkout@v2
    - name: Use Node.js
      uses: actions/setup-node@v2
      with:
        node-version: '16'
    - run: npm ci
    - run: npm test
```

Each of these CI servers has strengths and weaknesses, and the choice often depends on your specific requirements. Regardless of your choice, using a CI server is essential to implement Continuous Integration and Continuous Delivery practices.

Configuration management tools

Configuration management (CM) tools help manage software and hardware resources, ensure software product integrity, reproducibility, and traceability. They ensure that all systems perform as expected when changes are made.

Let's take a deeper dive into some of the most popular Configuration Management tools:

Ansible

Ansible is an open-source software provisioning, configuration management, and application-deployment tool that provides significant productivity gains to various automation challenges. It's simple, agentless, and powerful, focusing on security and reliability.

A simple Ansible playbook to install Nginx might look like this:

```
---
- hosts: web_servers
  tasks:
    - name: Install Nginx
      apt:
        pkg: nginx
        state: present
```

In the preceding playbook, `hosts` specifies where we want to run these `tasks`. The tasks section is a list of tasks to be executed. Each task is given a descriptive name and uses a module like `apt` or `yum` to process a package.

Puppet

Puppet is an open-source software configuration management tool that includes its declarative language to describe system configuration. It's produced by Puppet, founded by Luke Kanies in 2005. Puppet follows a client-server model where one machine controls many.

Here is a basic Puppet manifest that ensures NTP (Network Time Protocol) is installed:

```
package { 'ntp':
  ensure => installed,
}
```

In this Puppet code, `package` is the resource type, `'ntp'` is the title, and `ensure => installed` is the resource attribute which states that the NTP package should be installed.

Chef

Chef is a powerful automation platform that provides a way to define infrastructure as code. It is designed to manage server applications and utilities, and its primary function is to streamline the task of configuring and maintaining a company's servers.

Here is a simple Chef recipe to install Apache:

```
package 'httpd' do
  action :install
end

service 'httpd' do
  action [ :enable, :start ]
end
```

In the preceding code, `package 'httpd'` tells Chef to manage a package, and `action :install` tells it to install the package. Similarly, `service 'httpd'` handles a service, and `action [ :enable, :start ]` tells Chef to enable the service at startup and start the service.

Terraform

Terraform, a tool created by HashiCorp, is used to define and provide data center infrastructure using a declarative configuration language. It's cloud-agnostic and allows a single configuration to manage multiple providers and even handle cross-cloud dependencies.

A basic example of using Terraform to manage AWS resources:

```
provider "aws" {
  region = "us-west-2"
}


resource "aws_instance" "example" {
  ami           = "ami-0c94855ba95c574c8"
  instance_type = "t2.micro"


  tags = {
    Name = "example-instance"
  }
}
```

This code sets up an AWS provider and an AWS instance resource, all within the `us-west-2` region.

Docker

Docker is an open-source platform that automates application deployment, scaling, and management. It does this by using containerization, a lightweight form of virtualization. Docker allows you to package an application with all of its dependencies into a standardized unit for software development and distribution.

Docker containers are lightweight because they use the host operating system, unlike a virtual machine requiring its own operating system. This means you can have more Docker containers running on the same hardware than if you were using virtual machines, increasing your environment's efficiency.

A crucial element of Docker is a Dockerfile. Dockerfile is a text document that contains all the commands a user could call on the command line to assemble an image. Docker can build images automatically by reading the instructions from a Docker file.

Here's a simple Dockerfile that installs Node.js and your application into an image:

```
# Use an official Node.js runtime as a parent image
```

```
FROM node:14

# Set the working directory in the container
WORKDIR /usr/src/app

# Copy package.json and package-lock.json to the working directory
COPY package*.json ./

# Install any needed packages specified in package.json
RUN npm install

# Bundle app source
COPY . .

# Make port 8080 available to the world outside this container
EXPOSE 8080

# Define the command to run your app
CMD [ "npm", "start" ]
```

To build your Docker image, you would use the following command:

```
docker build -t my-nodejs-app .
```

And to run your Docker image:

```
docker run -p 8080:8080 -d my-nodejs-app
```

In a CI/CD context, Docker helps maintain consistency across multiple development, staging, and production environments. Docker containers ensure that the same software, with the same version and configuration, is used throughout the entire pipeline, from development to production.

Docker plays nicely with many popular continuous integration services, and it's often a vital component of a robust CI/CD pipeline. The following sections discuss how Docker integrates with Cypress and other CI/CD tools.

All these tools can be used in conjunction with one another to create a well-automated infrastructure setup and maintain configuration consistency across large-scale infrastructures. Your selection among these tools depends on your specific use case, the scale of your infrastructure, and the environment in which you work.

Monitoring and logging

In CI/CD, monitoring tools are crucial to ensure the application runs smoothly and catches real-time issues as changes are continuously integrated and deployed. These tools can monitor various aspects of the system, such as resource usage, performance metrics, and system health.

- **Prometheus:** This open-source monitoring system collects metrics from monitored targets by scraping metrics HTTP endpoints on these targets. Prometheus's main features are its multi-dimensional data model and powerful query language, allowing for high dimensionality and flexibility in time series data.
- **Grafana:** Often combined with Prometheus, Grafana is an open-source analytics and interactive visualization platform. It supports various backends, including Prometheus, and provides charts, graphs, and alerts for the web when connected to supported data sources.
- **New Relic:** A software analytics product that delivers real-time and trending data about your web or non-web application's performance and the level of satisfaction among users. It helps track errors, logs, network requests, and usage patterns.
- **Datadog:** A monitoring service for cloud-scale applications, providing monitoring of servers, databases, tools, services, and apps and providing a unified view across the entire stack.

While monitoring tools help keep an eye on the system's state, logging tools are used to record events or messages from the application, the system, or user events. They provide detailed insight into the system's behavior and are extremely useful for debugging.

- **ELK Stack:** This is an acronym for a collection of three open-source products: Elasticsearch, Logstash, and Kibana. Elasticsearch is a search and analytics engine, Logstash is a server-side data processing pipeline that simultaneously ingests data from multiple sources, and Kibana lets users visualize data with charts and graphs in Elasticsearch.

- **Graylog:** A free and open-source powerful centralized log management platform based on Elasticsearch and MongoDB. It provides real-time insights into what is happening in your IT environment.
- **Splunk:** It captures, indexes, and correlates real-time data in a searchable repository from which it can generate graphs, reports, alerts, dashboards, and visualizations.
- **Fluentd:** An open-source data collector that unifies the data collection and consumption for better use and understanding of data.

Each of these tools has its strengths and weaknesses and should be chosen based on the project's requirements. In a CI/CD pipeline context, these tools provide visibility into the system as changes are continuously integrated and deployed, helping to catch and fix issues quickly.

Deployment strategies

There are different strategies for deploying changes, including blue-green deployments, canary releases, and rolling updates. These strategies help minimize downtime during deployments and provide mechanisms for quick rollback if something goes wrong.

Blue-Green deployment

In Blue-Green Deployment, two environments (Blue and Green) are created to run the application. At any given time, only one environment is live.

The Blue environment runs the current application version, while the Green environment is idle. When a new application version is ready for release, it is deployed to the sedentary Green environment. Any final testing can be conducted in this environment before it is made live.

Once you are satisfied with the new version in the Green environment, you can switch the router so all incoming requests now go to the Green environment. The Blue environment is currently idle.

The main advantage of this method is the ability to roll back quickly - if something goes wrong, you switch the router back to the Blue environment.

Canary deployment

Named after the "canary in a coal mine" concept, Canary Deployment is a pattern where a new software version is gradually rolled out to a small subset of users before being rolled out to the entire infrastructure. The idea is to test the new version on a small part of the audience to make sure everything works as expected.

Once the software is verified to be stable, it's rolled out to the rest of the user base. If an issue is detected during the rollout, it's easier to roll back and limit the impact on users.

A/B testing

A/B testing is similar to Canary Deployment, but instead of just testing the new version for stability or any apparent issues, the different versions are evaluated based on specific metrics or goals.

For instance, suppose you're testing a new feature on an eCommerce site. You might roll out the feature to half of your users (group A) while the other half (group B) continues to use the current version without the new feature. You can then compare metrics like time spent on site, purchases made, or any other key performance indicators to inform your decision about whether to roll out the new feature to all users.

Rolling deployment

Rolling Deployment is a strategy that incrementally deploys a new version to all instances or servers of an application. Each instance is taken out of service, upgraded, and returned to service one after the other. This method ensures that the application remains available to users during the deployment process.

The main disadvantage is the temporary inconsistency, as some users will access the new version while others are still on the older version.

Each deployment strategy has pros and cons, and the decision on which one to use will depend on the specifics of your project, your team, and the nature of the application being developed. But by understanding these strategies, you can make a more informed decision about delivering updates and new features to your users and integrating the strategy into your CI/CD pipeline.

While the CI/CD process might seem daunting, remember that its purpose is to help your team deliver quality software faster and more reliably. The ultimate goal is to ensure that every software release you make is reliable, efficient, and free from regression bugs.

The following table outlines the CI/CD pipeline's crucial aspects and corresponding tools:

Aspect	**Tools**
Version Control System	Git, SVN
Build Tools	webpack, Rollup, Parcel
Testing and QA	Cypress, Jest, Mocha
CI Servers	Jenkins, GitLab CI, Travis CI, CircleCI
Configuration Management	Puppet, Chef, Ansible, Docker
Monitoring and Logging	Logstash, Grafana, Prometheus
Deployment Strategies	Kubernetes, Docker Swarm

Table 11.1: *CI/CD aspects and corresponding tools*

CI/CD Workflow with Cypress

Here's how Cypress fits into a typical CI/CD workflow:

1. Developers write code and commit changes to a version control system (like Git).
2. The CI/CD server (Jenkins, CircleCI, TravisCI, and so on) picks up the committed changes and starts a new build.
3. As part of the build process, the CI/CD server runs Cypress tests to verify the application's functionality.
4. If the tests pass, the build is considered successful, and the changes can be deployed to the staging environment.
5. If the tests fail, the build is considered unsuccessful, and the team is notified to fix the issues.
6. Once the issues are fixed, the process starts again from step 1.

Benefits of CI/CD with Cypress:

- **Increased Confidence:** By running tests on every commit, you can be confident that you're not breaking any existing functionality with your changes.
- **Faster Feedback:** The sooner you run tests, the sooner you can catch and fix bugs. This can significantly speed up your development cycle.

- **Reduced Risk:** By testing and deploying more minor changes more frequently, you can reduce the risk associated with big deployments.

In the following sections, let's see how to integrate Cypress into CI/CD pipelines using tools like Docker and Jenkins. We will also cover other CI/CD tools that Cypress can use, providing you with various options based on your project requirements.

Integrating Cypress with Docker

Docker is an open-source platform that automates application deployment, scaling, and management through containerization. It encapsulates software into packages known as containers, ensuring that the software runs seamlessly in any environment.

In this section of the book, we'll discuss how to integrate Cypress with Docker to achieve a more streamlined, reliable, and efficient testing and deployment process.

Before we delve into the integration process, we must understand why we want to combine Cypress with Docker. In the context of Continuous Integration and Continuous Deployment (CI/CD), the rationale can be summarized in the following points:

- **Environment Consistency:** Docker allows us to create a consistent environment for running tests, independent of the machine and its configuration. This eliminates the classic "it works on my machine" problem, as the environment is consistent across development, testing, and production.
- **Parallelization and Scaling:** With Docker, you can scale your testing efforts by running multiple Cypress tests in parallel. Docker's containerization capability lets you execute numerous isolated tests concurrently, reducing the total testing time.
- **Simplicity and Speed:** Docker can speed up the setup and execution of tests. A Docker image with the test environment pre-configured can be launched and ready to run tests in seconds.

To demonstrate how to set up Cypress in a Docker container, we'll use a Docker image provided by Cypress. It includes all the necessary dependencies to run Cypress.

First, ensure you have Docker installed on your machine. If not, you can download and install it from the official Docker website.

Let's start by creating a Dockerfile, which serves as a set of instructions for Docker to build an image. In the root directory of your project, create a file named `Dockerfile` and add the following lines:

```
FROM cypress/base:14.17.0
WORKDIR /app
RUN npm install
COPY . /app
RUN $(npm bin)/cypress verify
CMD ["npm", "test"]
```

In this Dockerfile:

- **`FROM cypress/base:14.17.0`** - fetches the Docker image provided by Cypress with Node.js version 14.17.0. The latest Docker image can be found in this GitHub repo (https://github.com/cypress-io/cypress-docker-images)
- **`WORKDIR /app`** - sets the working directory in the Docker container to `/app`.
- **`COPY . /app`** - copies all files from the current directory on your local machine to the `/app` directory in the Docker container.
- **`RUN npm install`** - installs the node modules needed for the project.
- **`RUN $(npm bin)/cypress`** - verify verifies that Cypress is installed correctly.
- **`CMD ["npm", "test"]`** - is the command that will be executed when the Docker container is run.

Next, build the Docker image using the following command:

```
docker build -t cypress-docker .
```

This command tells Docker to build an image using the `Dockerfile` in the current directory (`.`) and tag it (`-t`) as `cypress-docker`.

To run your Cypress tests in a Docker container, use the following command:

```
docker run -it cypress-docker
```

The `-it` flag tells Docker to run the container in interactive mode, and `cypress-docker` is the name of the image we just built.

Running tests in a Docker Container

By setting the Dockerfile `CMD` to `npm test`, Docker runs this command when the container is started, and your tests are executed inside the Docker container. To modify your tests or the test command, change the test script in your `package.json`.

Tips for using Cypress with Docker

- **Use `.dockerignore` file:** Similar to `.gitignore`, a `.dockerignore` file can prevent unwanted files or directories from being copied into the Docker image, making the build process faster and the final image size smaller.
- **Cleaning up:** Docker containers and images can take up a significant amount of disk space. Be sure to clean up unused or dangling images periodically, stopped containers, and build a cache.
- **Debugging:** If your tests fail when running in a Docker container but pass locally, you can start the container in interactive mode (`-it` flag) and manually run the tests to debug.
- **Memory:** Docker containers have limits for the amount of memory they can use. If your tests use a lot of memory, you may need to increase the limit in your Docker settings.

Integrating Cypress with Docker in your CI/CD pipeline provides a reliable, efficient, and scalable solution for end-to-end testing. Docker ensures that tests run in a consistent environment, while Cypress offers a rich set of testing features. This combination can significantly enhance the quality assurance process in your CI/CD pipeline.

The preceding information gives a good overview of integrating Cypress with Docker for end-to-end testing in a consistent environment. However, there are a couple of things we could still touch on for a more complete picture:

1. Multi-stage builds

A Docker multi-stage build is a method of organizing your Dockerfile to streamline your image-building process and reduce the size of the final Docker image. Essentially, a multi-stage build consists of multiple build stages where each stage starts with a new, fresh image. The artifacts from a previous stage can be selectively copied into the next one, reducing the image size as unnecessary files and dependencies are left behind.

In the context of Cypress, multi-stage builds can be used to separate the building of the application and the running of tests into different stages.

Here's an example Dockerfile:

```
# Stage 1 - Build
FROM node:14 as builder

WORKDIR /app

COPY package*.json ./
RUN npm install

COPY . .
RUN npm run build

# Stage 2 - Test
FROM cypress/included:12.17.0

WORKDIR /app

COPY --from=builder /app/build ./build
COPY cypress ./cypress
COPY cypress.json .

RUN npx cypress run
```

In this Dockerfile, we have two stages: the build stage and the test stage. In the build stage, we install our dependencies and build our application. In the test stage, we run our Cypress tests against the built application.

2. Docker Compose

Docker Compose is a tool for defining and running multi-container Docker applications. With Docker Compose, you can manage your application and its dependencies through a single file. This can be particularly useful for running Cypress tests as it allows you to set up your application and test environment as separate services.

Here's an example `docker-compose.yml` file for running Cypress tests:

```
version: '3'

services:
  web:
    build: .
    command: npm start
    ports:
      - '3000:3000'

  cypress:
    image: 'cypress/included:12.17.0'
    depends_on:
      - web
    environment:
      - CYPRESS_baseUrl=http://web:3000
    volumes:
      - .:/e2e
    working_dir: /e2e
    command: 'npx cypress run'
```

In this `docker-compose.yml`, we define two services: `web` for our application and `cypress` for our tests. We use the `depends_on` keyword to ensure the `web` service is started before the `cypress` service. We also set the `CYPRESS_baseUrl` environment variable to the URL of the `web` service.

3. Cypress configuration

When running Cypress in Docker, some configurations might need to be adjusted. For example, by default, Cypress records videos of your test runs. However, running Cypress in Docker can sometimes cause problems with video recording due to the additional requirements for the necessary libraries. To disable video recording, you can set the `video` configuration option to `false` in your `cypress.config.js` file:

```
{
  "video": false
```

```
}
```

If you still wish to record videos, you need to ensure that the necessary dependencies are installed in your Docker image. This can be achieved by extending the Cypress Docker image and adding the required libraries.

4. Integration with CI/CD tools

Running Cypress tests in a Docker container can be incorporated as a step in your CI/CD pipelines. In Jenkins, you can use the Docker Pipeline plugin to define your Docker-based pipeline:

```
node {
    stage('Test') {
        docker.image('cypress/included:12.17.0').inside {
            sh 'npm install'
            sh 'npx cypress run'
        }
    }
}
```

In GitLab CI/CD, you can specify a Docker image for each job in your pipeline:

```
test:
  image: cypress/included:12.17.0
  script:
    - npm install
    - npx cypress run
```

5. Running Cypress tests on different browsers

Cypress supports running tests on different browsers. To run Cypress tests on a specific browser in Docker, you can pass the `--browser` flag to the `cypress run` command:

```
npx cypress run --browser firefox
```

You can find Docker images in this GitHub repository: https://github.com/cypress-io/cypress-docker-images

However, running browsers like Firefox and Chrome in Docker requires some additional setup due to the dependencies required for these browsers. Cypress provides Docker images with different browsers and Node.js versions pre-installed to accommodate these requirements.

When using Cypress Docker images, it's crucial to select the appropriate tag. If no tag is specified, Docker defaults to using the `latest` tag (e.g., `cypress/included:latest`). However, it's advisable to use a specific tag to prevent breaking changes when new images are released, mainly when they include new major versions of Node.js or Cypress.

Here are some examples of specific tags and what they represent:

- **`cypress/base:18.16.0`**: This image includes Node.js version 18.16.0 only.
- **`cypress/browsers:node-18.16.0-chrome-114.0.5735.133-1-ff-114.0.2-edge-114.0.1823.51-1`**: This image includes Node.js version 18.16.0, Chrome version 114.0.5735.133-1, Firefox version 114.0.2, and Edge version 114.0.1823.51-1.
- **`cypress/included:12.17.1`**: This image includes Cypress version 12.17.1 and everything required to run it.

Once a Docker image with a specific version tag (other than `latest`) is published to the Cypress Docker Hub, it's frozen, meaning it will not receive any updates or changes. When a new version of an image is published, a copy with the `latest` tag is also published, so the image selected with the `latest` tag (or selected by default if no tag is specified) will change over time. To use a stable, unchanging version, specify an explicit version, like `cypress/base:18.16.0`.

Building Jenkins Pipelines with Cypress

Jenkins is an open-source automation server and Continuous Integration (CI) tool. It provides developers with a robust platform for integration through the automation of various development tasks, including building, testing, and deploying software.

One of the most powerful features of Jenkins is the Pipeline, a suite of plugins that supports implementing and integrating continuous delivery pipelines into Jenkins. In this sub-chapter, we'll explore how you can incorporate Cypress into your Jenkins pipeline for continuous integration and continuous deployment.

Before delving into the specifics of building Jenkins pipelines with Cypress, it's crucial to understand why these two tools work well together for CI/CD.

Firstly, Jenkins is a highly flexible tool. It has numerous plugins that extend its functionality, making it suitable for various projects. In our case, combining the Git plugin, Docker plugin, and Pipeline plugin will allow us to fetch our code, run our Cypress tests inside a Docker container, and define our entire CI/CD pipeline as code.

Secondly, Cypress provides a simple setup, clear syntax, and an interactive test runner, which makes writing and running tests a breeze. Furthermore, its ability to mock and stub network requests, directly control the browser's behavior, and automatically wait for commands and assertions before moving on makes it an excellent tool for end-to-end testing.

Creating a Jenkins Pipeline

To create a Jenkins Pipeline, you'll need to write a script that defines the pipeline's stages and steps. This script is often called a `Jenkinsfile` and is typically committed to your repository's root directory. The script is written in a language called Groovy, although the steps can include any scripts or shell commands that you would typically run in a terminal.

Let's see how to build a simple Jenkins pipeline for a project that uses Cypress for end-to-end testing:

```
pipeline {
    agent any

    stages {
        stage('Checkout') {
            steps {
                git 'https://github.com/username/repository.git'
            }
        }

        stage('Build') {
            steps {
                sh 'npm install'
```

```
                sh 'npm run build'
            }
        }

        stage('Test') {
            steps {
                sh 'npm run test'
            }
        }

        stage('Deploy') {
            steps {
                echo 'Deploying....'
                // Your deployment steps here
            }
        }
    }
}
```

Here's a breakdown of the stages in this Pipeline:

- **Checkout Stage:** This is where the source code is retrieved from the version control system. In this case, it's using `git` to clone the repository from the specified URL `https://github.com/username/repository.git.`
- **Build Stage:** This stage is for compiling the code, resolving dependencies, and performing preliminary testing. The commands `npm install`, and `npm run build` suggest that it's a Node.js project.
- **Test Stage:** Here, the script is set to run tests on the built code using `npm run test`. This step would typically involve running automated tests to ensure the code changes do not break any existing functionality.
- **Deploy Stage:** The final stage in this script is for deployment. In this stage, you would put commands that push the built code to a server or execute a script that deploys the application to a production environment. The details of the deployment process are not included in the snippet you have provided, just a placeholder comment.

The Jenkins Pipeline allows for defining the entire build/test/deploy pipeline as code, which can be versioned and treated like any other code file. This is part of the *Infrastructure as Code* philosophy, aiming to reduce errors and make the process repeatable and more manageable.

The script mentioned above will work for the Linux-based operating systems. In case you need to build the same script for Windows, we need to replace `sh` with `bat`

Here's an example of how you might adjust the script for a Windows environment:

```
pipeline {
    agent any

    stages {
        stage('Checkout') {
            steps {
                git 'https://github.com/username/repository.git'
            }
        }

        stage('Build') {
            steps {
                bat 'npm install'
                bat 'npm run build'
            }
        }

        stage('Test') {
            steps {
                bat 'npm run test'
            }
        }

        stage('Deploy') {
            steps {
                echo 'Deploying....'
```

```
                // Your deployment steps here
                // Use 'bat' or 'powershell' for Windows command execution
            }
        }
    }
}
```

Before running this pipeline, make sure that Node.js and npm are installed on the Jenkins agent running on Windows, and that the path to their executables is included in the system's PATH environment variable.

Running Cypress tests in Docker

While the preceding pipeline works well for a basic setup, it assumes that Jenkins has Node.js and Cypress installed. A more flexible and reliable approach is to run the tests inside a Docker container, ensuring the tests run in the same environment across all pipeline stages.

First, you'll need to have a `Dockerfile` in your repository that defines how to build your application and run the tests. As we discussed previously, you can use the Cypress Docker image (cypress/included) in a multi-stage build.

Next, update the `Jenkinsfile` to use Docker. You can use the `docker.image` function to define the Docker image and the `inside` function to run steps inside the Docker container:

```
pipeline {
    agent any

    stages {
        stage('Checkout') {
            steps {
                git 'https://github.com/username/repository.git'
            }
        }

        stage('Build and Test') {
```

```
            steps {
                script {
                    docker.image('node:14').inside {
                        sh 'npm install'
                        sh 'npm run build'
                        sh 'npm test'
                    }
                }
            }
        }

        stage('Deploy') {
            steps {
                echo 'Deploying....'
                // Your deployment steps here
            }
        }
    }
}
```

Here, we combined the Build and Test stages into a single stage that runs inside a Docker container. We used the official Node.js Docker image (`node:14`), but you could also use an image that contains your application and the Cypress tests.

Reporting with Cypress and Jenkins

Getting immediate feedback on test results is crucial in a CI/CD pipeline. Thankfully, Jenkins and Cypress can be configured to provide detailed reports about the test execution.

Firstly, you'll need to configure Cypress to generate JUnit reports, a popular XML format for recording test results that Jenkins can understand. You can use the `cypress-multi-reporters` plugin and `mocha-junit-reporter` to do this:

```
npm install cypress-multi-reporters mocha-junit-reporter --save-dev
```

Next, add the following configuration to your `cypress.config.js` file:

```
const { defineConfig } = require('cypress')

module.exports = defineConfig({
  reporter: 'cypress-multi-reporters',
  reporterOptions: {
    configFile: 'reporterOpts.json',
  },
})
```

And create a `reporterOpts.json` file:

```
{
    "reporterEnabled": "mocha-junit-reporter",
    "mochaJunitReporterReporterOptions": {
        "mochaFile": "cypress/results/results-[hash].xml",
        "toConsole": false
    }
}
```

Cypress will generate a JUnit report for each spec file with this configuration.

Finally, you need to update the Jenkinsfile to archive the JUnit reports. You can use the `junit` step in the Post stage, which is executed after all stages:

```
pipeline {
    agent any

    stages {
        // Your stages here
    }

    post {
        always {
```

```
            junit 'cypress/results/*.xml'
        }
    }
}
```

With this setup, Jenkins will provide a detailed report of the test results, including the number of tests that passed, failed, and skipped, along with the time it took to run them.

By integrating Jenkins and Cypress, developers can automate the end-to-end testing of their web applications and achieve a robust CI/CD pipeline. This process ensures that any changes to the codebase are automatically tested, resulting in quicker detection and resolution of bugs, improved code quality, and faster development cycles.

Other CI/CD tools for Cypress

Apart from Docker and Jenkins, you can integrate several other CI/CD tools with Cypress to streamline your application's testing and deployment process. This section will focus on some of these tools, specifically Travis CI, GitLab CI/CD, and GitHub Actions.

Travis CI

Travis CI is a popular continuous integration service to build and test software projects hosted on GitHub. It's highly flexible and can run Cypress tests as part of your CI/CD pipeline.

Before you start, ensure that you have the necessary dependencies:

- A project hosted on GitHub.
- Cypress is installed in your project.
- A Travis CI account is linked to your GitHub account.

Create a `.travis.yml` file in the root of your project. This file tells Travis CI what to do when you push a commit or pull request. Here's an example of a basic `.travis.yml` file for a Cypress project:

```
language: node_js
node_js:
  - '16'
```

```
cache:
  directories:
    - ~/.npm
    - ~/.cache
install:
  - npm ci
script:
  - npx cypress run
```

This file tells Travis CI to use Node.js v16 and to cache the `~/.npm` and `~/.cache` directories. This caching can significantly speed up your build times.

Next, the install directive tells Travis CI to install your project's dependencies using `npm ci`. This command is similar to `npm install`, but it's faster and more reliable for CI environments.

Finally, the script directive tells Travis CI to run your Cypress tests using the `npx cypress run` command.

GitLab CI/CD

GitLab is a web-based DevOps lifecycle tool that provides a Git-repository manager providing wiki, issue-tracking, and continuous integration/continuous deployment (CI/CD) pipeline features. With GitLab CI/CD, you can set up your pipeline to automatically build, test, and deploy your applications.

Before proceeding, you'll need:

- A project hosted on GitLab.
- Cypress is installed in your project.
- Docker installed (as we'll be using Cypress's Docker images).

To integrate Cypress with GitLab CI/CD, you will need to create a `.gitlab-ci.yml` file in the root of your project. GitLab uses this file to understand the structure of your pipeline and the tasks it needs to run.

Here's an example of a basic `.gitlab-ci.yml` file for a Cypress project:

```
image: cypress/base:18.16.0

stages:
```

```
  - build
  - test

install_dependencies:
  stage: build
  script:
    - npm ci

cypress_run:
  stage: test
  script:
    - npx cypress run
```

In this configuration, the `image` directive specifies the Docker image that GitLab CI/CD will use to run your jobs. The `stages` directive defines the stages of your pipeline. Each stage consists of a set of jobs that are executed in parallel. If all jobs in a stage pass, the pipeline proceeds to the next stage. In this case, there are two stages: `build` and `test`.

The `install_dependencies` job belongs to the `build` stage. Its `script` directive specifies that GitLab CI/CD should run `npm ci` to install your project's dependencies.

The `cypress_run` job belongs to the `test` stage. Its `script` directive specifies that GitLab CI/CD should run `npx cypress run` to execute your Cypress tests.

Parallelization

You can run your tests in parallel to reduce the total testing time. Cypress supports parallelization out of the box but requires the use of the Cypress Cloud, which is a paid service. To enable parallelization in GitLab CI/CD, you'd need to split your tests across multiple jobs and configure each job to run a different set of tests.

```
image: cypress/base:18.16.0

stages:
  - build
  - test
```

```
install_dependencies:
  stage: build
  script:
    - npm ci

cypress_run:
  stage: test
  script:
    - npx cypress run --spec "cypress/integration/test1.js"
  parallel:
    matrix:
      - SPEC: ["test1.js"]
cypress_run_2:
  stage: test
  script:
    - npx cypress run --spec "cypress/integration/test2.js"
  parallel:
    matrix:
      - SPEC: ["test2.js"]
```

In this example, we have two jobs under the `test` stage: `cypress_run` and `cypress_run_2`. Both jobs are configured to run in parallel.

The `script` directive for each job specifies the command to run the Cypress tests for a specific test file. The `--spec` flag is used to determine which test file to run.

The `parallel` directive with `matrix` strategy defines a multi-dimensional array of variables, creating a separate pipeline for each combination of variables.

Each job will run in a separate Docker container and will test a different part of your application, effectively reducing your total testing time.

This is a basic example, and there are many ways to split your tests for parallelization. How you split your tests depends mainly on the structure of your tests and the requirements of your application.

Running on merge requests

To automatically run your Cypress tests when a merge request is created or updated, you can use GitLab CI/CD's pipeline events:

```
cypress_run:
  stage: test
  script:
    - npx cypress run
  only:
    - merge_requests
```

With this configuration, the `cypress_run` job will only run when triggering a merge request event.

GitHub actions

GitHub actions is a CI/CD service provided by GitHub. It lets you automate, customize, and execute your software development workflows in your repository.

Ensure you have the following:

- A project hosted on GitHub with Cypress installed as a dependency.
- A basic understanding of GitHub Actions (refer to the GitHub Actions documentation if needed).

In your GitHub repository, create a directory named `.github/workflows`. In this directory, create a new file for your Cypress workflow. The name can be anything you like, but it must end with `.yml` or `.yaml`.

An example Cypress workflow file, `cypress.yml` might look like this:

```
name: End-to-end tests
on: [push, pull_request]
jobs:
  cypress-run:
    runs-on: ubuntu-latest
    steps:
      - name: Checkout repository
        uses: actions/checkout@v2
```

```
    - name: Setup Node.js
      uses: actions/setup-node@v2
      with:
        node-version: 16
    - name: Install dependencies
      run: npm ci
    - name: Run Cypress tests
      run: npx cypress run
```

- `name`: This is the name of your workflow, it will be displayed in the GitHub Actions UI.
- `on`: This specifies the events that will trigger the workflow. It's set to trigger whenever a push or a pull request event occurs.
- `jobs`: Jobs are a set of steps that execute on the same runner.
- `runs-on`: This specifies the type of machine to run the job on. Here, we're using the latest version of Ubuntu.
- `steps`: Steps are individual tasks that can run commands in a job. A job sequence is made up of one or more steps.
- `Checkout repository`: This step uses the `actions/checkout` action to check out your repository's code.
- `Setup Node.js`: This step uses the `actions/setup-node` action to set up the desired Node.js environment.
- `Install dependencies`: This step installs the project dependencies. It uses `npm ci`, which is faster and more suited for CI environments.
- `Run Cypress tests`: This step runs the Cypress tests using the `npx cypress run` command.

Comparing CI/CD tools

When choosing a CI/CD tool, several factors come into play, such as ease of setup, integration with version control systems, support for Docker, and cost. Here is a comparative table to help you choose:

CI/CD Tools	Ease of Setup	Integration with GitHub	Docker Support	Cost
Jenkins	Medium	Yes (via plugin)	Yes	Free (Self-hosted)

Travis CI	Easy	Yes	Yes	Free for public repos; Paid plans for private repos
GitLab CI/ CD	Easy	Yes	Yes	Free for public and private repos (with limitations)
GitHub Actions	Easy	Yes	Yes	Free for public repos; Paid plans for private repos

***Table 11.2**: Comparing CI/CD tools*

Integrating Cypress with CI/CD tools can significantly enhance your project's testing and deployment workflows. Whether you choose to use Jenkins, Travis CI, GitLab CI/CD, or GitHub Actions largely depend on your specific needs and the complexity of your project. Nonetheless, all of these tools provide excellent support for Cypress, and you can use them to achieve a robust CI/CD pipeline.

Conclusion

We delved into the world of Continuous Integration and Continuous Deployment (CI/CD) with Cypress, providing readers with a comprehensive understanding of these principles and how to integrate Cypress into their CI/CD pipelines seamlessly. The chapter begins with an overview of CI/CD, explaining its significance in streamlining development processes and ensuring reliable deployments. Readers will learn how to integrate Cypress with Docker, enabling consistent and isolated testing environments and leveraging Jenkins to build robust CI/CD pipelines that automate Cypress test execution. Additionally, the chapter explores other CI/CD tools that can be employed with Cypress, offering readers a range of options to tailor their CI/CD workflows based on their specific project requirements. By the end of this chapter, readers will have the knowledge and techniques to integrate Cypress effectively into their CI/CD processes, ensuring seamless and efficient automated testing and deployment within their development pipelines.

In the upcoming chapter, readers will gain insights into various reporting techniques and tools available for Cypress. The chapter covers the built-in reporting capabilities of Cypress, providing insights into ho11111w to view and interpret test results directly within the Cypress Test Runner. Additionally, readers will explore third-party reporting tools and plugins that offer enhanced reporting features and visualization options. The chapter also delves into generating custom reports tailored to specific project requirements, enabling readers to present test results in a more personalized and informative manner. By the end of this chapter, readers will have a clear understanding of different reporting options and how to effectively analyze test results to gain valuable insights and make improvements in their test automation process.

Further reading

To expand readers' knowledge on the topics discussed in this chapter, I suggest exploring these additional resources:

1. **Cypress CI/CD Integration Guide:** The official Cypress documentation on CI/CD integration (https://docs.cypress.io/guides/continuous-integration/introduction) provides comprehensive information on integrating Cypress with various CI/CD tools. It covers setting up CI/CD pipelines, parallel test execution, and other best practices for efficient test automation.

2. **Docker with Cypress:** This tutorial on the Lambdatest blog (https://www.lambdatest.com/learning-hub/cypress-docker) demonstrates how to use Docker with Cypress to create consistent testing environments. It includes practical examples and explains the benefits of containerizing Cypress tests.

3. **Cypress with Jenkins:** This guide on the Lambdatest.com blog (https://www.lambdatest.com/blog/jenkins-and-cypress-tutorial/) provides step-by-step instructions on integrating Cypress with Jenkins. It covers setting up Jenkins pipelines for automated test execution.

4. **Travis CI with Cypress:** This tutorial (https://offering.solutions/blog/articles/2018/06/01/running-cypress-tests-in-an-angular-project-with-travis-ci/) explains how to set up Cypress tests on Travis CI in parallel for faster test execution. It includes a practical example of Travis CI configuration.

These resources will give you a broader understanding and practical examples of the concepts you've learned in this chapter.

CHAPTER 12

Reporting and Test Results

Introduction

This chapter will discuss different reporting techniques and tools available for Cypress. It will cover built-in Cypress reporting, third-party reporting tools and plugins, and generating custom reports. By the end of this chapter, readers will clearly understand how to present and analyze their test results effectively.

Structure

In this chapter, we will discuss the following topics:

- Overview of reporting techniques
- Built-in Cypress reporting
- Third-party reporting tools and plugins
- Generating custom reports
- Analyzing test results for insights and improvements

Overview of reporting techniques

Effective reporting is crucial in software testing. It provides insights into the software's functionality, quality, and performance, allowing stakeholders to make informed decisions. Several reporting techniques are available when working with Cypress, from built-in reports to third-party tools and custom reports. This chapter offers an overview of these techniques, helping you select the most suitable for your project.

Reporting in testing is about creating understandable and clear reports of the results of your tests. It's not enough to execute the tests - the results need to be communicated effectively to all relevant stakeholders. This communication is achieved through reports summarizing the testing activities and their results.

The key reasons why reporting is essential include:

- **Tracking test progress:** Reports provide an overview of the testing progress over time. This allows teams to track how many tests have been executed, how many have passed or failed, and how these metrics change as the project evolves.
- **Identifying issues:** Detailed reports can help identify issues in the software. They provide valuable information about the failures, such as what tests failed, where they failed, and the error messages, enabling teams to diagnose and fix issues quickly.
- **Improving test effectiveness:** By analyzing the test reports, teams can identify areas of improvement in their tests, leading to better test effectiveness and coverage.

Different types of reports

Different types of reports can be generated depending on the needs of the project and the stakeholders. Here are a few common ones:

- **Test summary report:** This high-level report provides an overview of the test execution. It typically includes the total number of tests executed, the number of passed and failed tests, and the overall pass rate.
- **Test detailed report:** This report provides detailed information about each test executed. It includes the test description, test steps, expected and actual results, and the pass/fail status. When a test fails, the report should also include error messages or screenshots to help with troubleshooting.
- **Test trend report:** This report shows the trends in testing over time. It can help identify patterns, such as recurring failures or areas of the application that are prone to bugs.
- **Coverage report:** This report provides information about the code coverage of the tests. It shows what parts of the application code were executed during the tests, helping to identify areas of the code that are not tested.

Reporting formats

Test reports can be generated in various formats. The chosen format largely depends on the target audience and on how they prefer to consume the information. Some of the common reporting formats include:

- **HTML:** HTML reports are web-based reports that can be viewed in a browser. They are interactive and can include charts, tables, and other graphical data representations. They are often used to present the results to non-technical stakeholders.
- **JSON:** JSON reports are helpful in integrating with other tools or for further processing. They are machine-readable and can be used to feed data into dashboards or other reporting tools.
- **JUnit XML:** JUnit XML is a standard reporting format used by many CI/CD tools. If you're running your tests in a CI/CD pipeline, generating a JUnit XML report can allow the CI/CD tool to parse the results and display them in its interface.
- **Console:** Console reports are text-based reports displayed in the terminal. They are helpful during development for quickly checking the results of the tests.

HTML report example

HTML reports are a popular choice for their readability and interactivity. They are commonly generated by tools such as Mochawesome, which we covered in previous chapters. Here's a snippet of how a Mochawesome HTML report may look:

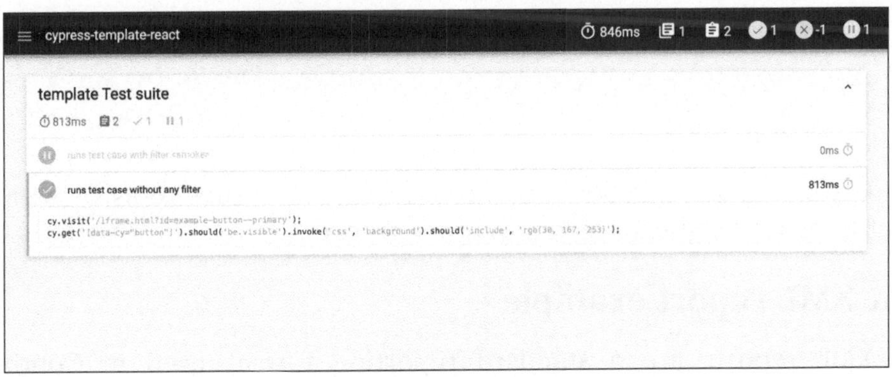

***Figure 12.1**: Mochawesome HTML report example*

You can interact with this report, drilling down into the details of individual tests and suites. This feature is handy when dealing with a large number of test cases.

JSON report example

JSON reports contain the raw data about the test results and can be used for further data analysis. Here's a truncated example of what a JSON report might look like:

```
{
  "stats": {
    "suites": 10,
    "tests": 30,
    "passes": 20,
    "pending": 5,
    "failures": 5,
    "start": "2023-07-29T07:30:26.000Z",
    "end": "2023-07-29T07:40:26.000Z",
    "duration": 600000,
    "testsRegistered": 30,
    "passPercent": 66.67,
    "pendingPercent": 16.67,
    "other": 0,
    "hasOther": false,
    "skipped": 0,
    "hasSkipped": false
  },
  ...
}
```

Each part of the JSON report can be processed by other tools or scripts to extract valuable insights or feed into other reports.

JUnit XML report example

JUnit XML reports are a standard reporting format used in Continuous Integration/Continuous Deployment (CI/CD) pipelines. Many CI/CD tools are capable of reading JUnit XML format and displaying the results in their interface. Here's a simplified example:

```
<testsuite name="Cypress" tests="50" failures="5" skipped="10"
time="35">
  <testcase classname="Login" name="should authenticate user with valid
credentials" time="1">
    <failure message="expected 'Welcome' to equal 'Hello'">Assertion
Error: expected 'Welcome' to equal 'Hello'</failure>
  </testcase>
  <testcase classname="Dashboard" name="should display user data
correctly" time="2"/>
  <testcase classname="Settings" name="should save changes" time="1">
    <skipped/>
  </testcase>
  ...
</testsuite>
```

Console report example

Console reports are often the simplest type of report, outputting the results directly to the terminal. This is what you see when you run your tests in the Cypress Test Runner:

```
 Running:  example_spec.js                              (1 of 1)


  Example spec
    √ checks the behavior of a single element (1349ms)
    √ checks the behavior of multiple elements (234ms)
    √ interacts with a form (590ms)


  3 passing (3s)


  (Results)
```

```
┌──────────────────────────────┐
| Tests:        3              |
| Passing:      3              |
| Failing:      0              |
| Pending:      0              |
| Skipped:      0              |
| Screenshots:  0              |
| Video:        true           |
| Duration:     3 seconds      |
| Spec Ran:example_spec.js|
└──────────────────────────────┘
```

This type of report is useful for immediate feedback while writing or debugging tests.

Cypress and reporting

Cypress comes with built-in support for test reporting. By default, it provides a live and interactive report in the Test Runner during development. For CI/CD environments, it can generate static reports in various formats, including JSON and JUnit XML.

In addition, Cypress can be integrated with third-party reporting tools and plugins to provide more advanced reporting features, such as historical trends, parallel test reporting, and more.

Finally, Cypress provides APIs and hooks that can be used to generate custom reports tailored to the specific needs of your project.

Built-in Cypress reporting

Cypress offers excellent built-in reporting capabilities, allowing real-time feedback during test execution. It offers an interactive Test Runner that provides a visual display of your tests' progress and outcomes alongside detailed error messages when tests fail. This chapter will delve into the built-in reporting capabilities of Cypress, outlining how you can utilize them effectively in your testing workflow.

Cypress Test Runner

The Cypress Test Runner is the main feature of Cypress's built-in reporting. It provides a unique interactive UI where tests are executed in real-time. During test execution, you can see each step of your test cases unfold, which includes page loads, user interactions, assertions, and network requests.

The left-hand side of the Test Runner lists all your test suites and test cases, providing a snapshot of which tests have passed, failed, or are currently running. On the right-hand side, an interactive iframe displays your application, allowing you to see your tests run in the context of your application.

Here's a simple test suite displayed in the Cypress Test Runner:

```
describe('Button' in Storybook, function() {
    it('loads Button in storybook', function() {
       cy.visit('/iframe.html?id=example-button--primary')
       cy.contains('Button');
       cy.get('[data-cy="button"]')
         .should('be.visible')
         .invoke('css', 'background')
         .should('include', 'rgb(30, 167, 254)') // here it should fail
    });
});
```

When running this test suite, the Cypress Test Runner displays each test case, showing each command as it executes and providing immediate feedback if a test case passes or fails.

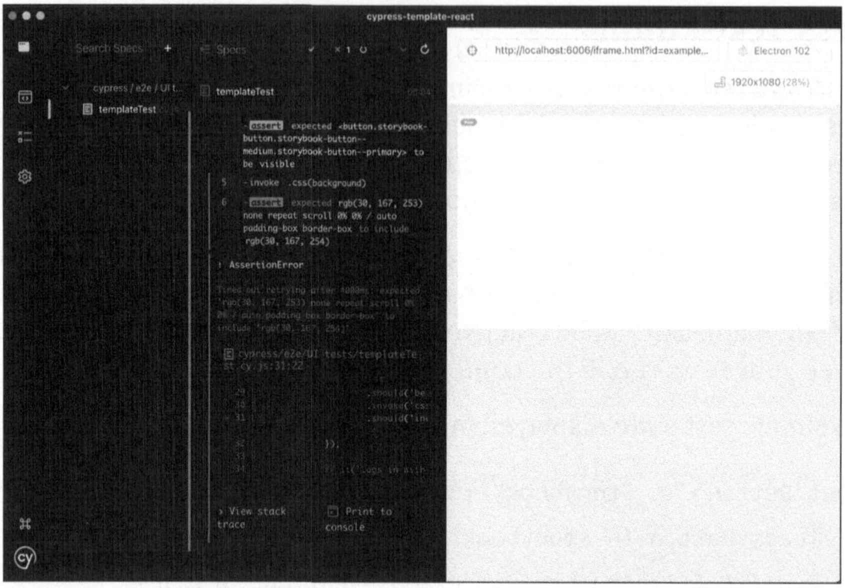

***Figure 12.2**: Cypress Test Runner example*

Test status and command log

When a test runs, the Test Runner updates the test status in real-time. Successful tests are marked in green, and failed tests are marked in red. If a test is currently running, it is highlighted in white.

The Command Log on the right shows each command as it executes, along with its outcome. If a command is successful, it is marked in green. If it fails, it is marked in red, and an error message is displayed to help you understand the cause of the failure.

For each command, you can hover over the command in the Command Log to see the state of the DOM at the point when that command is executed. This is extremely helpful for understanding the state of your application at different stages of your test.

Screenshots and videos

Cypress also has built-in support for capturing screenshots and recording videos of your test runs. This is particularly useful when running tests in a continuous integration environment, where you don't have the visual feedback the Test Runner provides.

By default, when a test fails, Cypress automatically takes a screenshot of the failure. These screenshots are stored in the `cypress/screenshots` directory.

```
it('logs in with valid credentials', function() {
    cy.get('#username').type('user');
    cy.get('#password').type('wrong-password');
    cy.get('#login-button').click();
    cy.contains('Welcome, user!');
});
```

In the preceding example, since the login will fail, Cypress will automatically capture a screenshot at the point of failure.

Cypress can also record a video of the entire test run. To enable video recording, you need to set the video configuration option to true in your `cypress.config.js` file:

```
{
  "video": true
}
```

When video recording is enabled, Cypress records a video for each spec file run and stores the videos in the `cypress/videos` directory.

Test results in CI

When running tests in a CI environment, the Test Runner isn't available to provide visual feedback. However, Cypress still provides detailed test results in the console. The output includes the total number of tests, the number of passing and failing tests, and detailed information about any failures.

Moreover, if you've enabled screenshots and video recordings, you can access these artifacts in your CI server to understand the state of your application at the time of test failures.

Cypress's built-in reporting capabilities offer immediate, detailed feedback during test development and execution. These features help developers understand the behavior of their applications, diagnose failures, and maintain high-quality, robust tests.

Third-party reporting tools and plugins

Although Cypress has a rich set of built-in reporting tools, sometimes these are not enough, especially when dealing with complex projects or teams with specific needs. This is where third-party reporting tools and plugins come into play, adding additional capabilities and customization options to your Cypress reporting toolkit. This section will discuss some of the popular third-party reporting tools and plugins you can use with Cypress.

Mocha reporters

Cypress uses Mocha's test runner internally, and therefore, it can leverage a variety of third-party Mocha reporters for enhancing test reporting. Mocha reporters can add several features, such as customizable report formats, additional output types (like JSON, CSV, and so on), and better visualizations.

Mochawesome

Mochawesome is a popular choice for Cypress projects. It generates a full-fledged HTML/CSS report that visualizes your test run. It also creates a JSON output that you can use to process the results further.

First, install Mochawesome and its merge and report generator:

```
npm install --save-dev cypress mochawesome mochawesome-merge
mochawesome-report-generator
```

Configure Cypress to use Mochawesome in your `cypress.config.js`:

```
{
  "reporter": "mochawesome",
  "reporterOptions": {
    "reportDir": "cypress/results",
    "quiet": true,
    "overwrite": false,
    "html": false,
    "json": true
  }
}
```

In the preceding configuration:

- `reportDir` specifies the directory where the reports will be saved.
- `overwrite` set to false ensures that each new test run is saved in a new file rather than overwriting the previous reports.
- `html` and `json` set to true ensure that reports are generated in both HTML and JSON formats.

Mochawesome generates a separate report for each spec file. If you have multiple test suites and you want a consolidated report, you can use `mochawesome-merge` to merge all JSON files into one. Then, you can generate a single HTML report using `mochawesome-report-generator`.

```
npx mochawesome-merge cypress/reports/mochawesome-report/*.json >
mochawesome.json

npx marge mochawesome.json
```

This will merge all JSON files in the `cypress/reports/mochawesome-report` directory and generate a consolidated `mochawesome.json` file. And `marge` is the command-line tool to generate the HTML report from this JSON file.

By default, Mochawesome overwrites the report files with each test run. To prevent this, and save reports from each run uniquely, you can add timestamps to your report filenames.

You can specify the `reportFilename` in `reporterOptions` in the `cypress.config.js` configuration file:

```
{
  "reporter": "mochawesome",
  "reporterOptions": {
    "reportDir": "cypress/reports",
    "reportFilename": "report-" + new Date().toISOString(),
    "overwrite": false,
    "html": true,
    "json": true,
"timestamp" : "mm_dd_yyyy_HH_MM_ss"
  }
}
```

In this example, the reporter will generate a new report with a unique name, like `mochawesome_mm_dd_yyyy_HH_MM_SS.json`.

Incorporating scripts within the `package.json` file is critical for test execution and report generation when using Mochawesome. The following are some examples of scripts you might include:

```
"scripts": {
  "test": "cypress run --reporter mochawesome",
  "posttest": "npx mochawesome-merge cypress/reports/mochawesome
-report/*.json > mochawesome.json && npx marge mochawesome.json"
}
```

In this example:

- The `"test"` script runs the Cypress tests using Mochawesome as the reporter. This script generates JSON and HTML reports in the directory specified in the Cypress configuration (`cypress/reports/mochawesome-report` in the previous examples).
- The `"posttest"` script is a convenient way to automatically merge the reports and generate a consolidated HTML report after running the tests. The `posttest` script is run automatically by npm after the test script.

With these scripts in place, you can run your tests and generate the reports by simply executing `npm test` in the command line.

Cypress-multi-reporters

`Cypress-multi-reporters` is a great tool when you need to generate multiple reports in different formats. This tool combines multiple Mocha reporters, allowing you to get the best of multiple worlds.

First, install the required packages:

```
npm install --save-dev cypress-multi-reporters mochawesome
mocha-junit-reporter
```

Then, update the `cypress.config.js` configuration:

```
{
  "reporter": "cypress-multi-reporters",
  "reporterOptions": {
```

```
    "configFile": "reporterOpts.json"
  }
}
```

Create a `reporterOpts.json` with your preferred reporters:

```
{
  "reporterEnabled": "mochawesome, mocha-junit-reporter",
  "mochawesomeReporterOptions": {
    "reportDir": "cypress/results",
    "quiet": true,
    "overwrite": false,
    "html": false,
    "json": true
  },
  "mochaJunitReporterReporterOptions": {
    "mochaFile": "cypress/results/junit/test_results[hash].xml",
    "toConsole": false
  }
}
```

This setup will generate both Mochawesome and JUnit reports.

cypress-mochawesome-reporter

The `cypress-mochawesome-reporter` is a custom Mocha reporter tailored specifically for Cypress, extending the capabilities of Mochawesome to suit Cypress's functionalities and output structure better. It is designed to generate Mochawesome JSON reports after every spec file, which is particularly useful for handling parallel runs in Cypress.

Firstly, install `cypress-mochawesome-reporter` as a dev dependency:

```
npm install --save-dev cypress-mochawesome-reporter
```

Next, adjust your Cypress configuration file (typically `cypress.config.js`):

```
const { defineConfig } = require('cypress');
```

```
module.exports = defineConfig({
  reporter: 'cypress-mochawesome-reporter',
  e2e: {
    setupNodeEvents(on, config) {
      require('cypress-mochawesome-reporter/plugin')(on);
    },
  },
});
```

If you're planning to override `before:run` or `after:run` hooks, use this configuration instead:

```
const { defineConfig } = require('cypress');
const { beforeRunHook, afterRunHook } = require('cypress-mochawesome
-reporter/lib');

module.exports = defineConfig({
  reporter: 'cypress-mochawesome-reporter',
  e2e: {
    setupNodeEvents(on, config) {
      on('before:run', async (details) => {
        console.log('override before:run');
        await beforeRunHook(details);
      });

      on('after:run', async () => {
        console.log('override after:run');
        await afterRunHook();
      });
    },
  },
});
```

Add the following import line to `cypress/support/e2e.js`:

```
import 'cypress-mochawesome-reporter/register';
```

Then you can run your Cypress tests as usual.

To further customize your HTML reports with `mochawesome-report-generator` flags, you can add the desired flags to `reporterOptions`:

```
const { defineConfig } = require('cypress');


module.exports = defineConfig({
  reporter: 'cypress-mochawesome-reporter',
  reporterOptions: {
    charts: true,
    reportPageTitle: 'custom-title',
    embeddedScreenshots: true,
    inlineAssets: true,
    saveAllAttempts: false,
  },
  e2e: {
    setupNodeEvents(on, config) {
      require('cypress-mochawesome-reporter/plugin')(on);
    },
  },
});
```

If you need to append extra information to the report, `cypress-mochawesome-reporter` provides a handy function `cy.addTestContext()`. This function allows you to add additional context to your report manually. Here's an illustrative example:

```
describe('Test 2', () => {
  it('todo exists', () => {
    cy.visit('site/index.html');


    cy.get('#todo-list').should('be.visible');
```

```
  });

  it('add context to mochawesome report', () => {
    cy.visit('site/index.html');

    cy.get('#todo-list > li').then(($liElements) => {
      cy.addTestContext(`There were ${$liElements.length.toString()}
items found in the todo-list`);
    });
  });

  it.skip('skipped test', () => {
    cy.visit('site/index.html');
  });
});
```

In this example, the second test `'add context to mochawesome report,'` adds custom context to the report. It does this by getting the length of the list elements under the `'#todo-list'` id, and then using `cy.addTestContext()` to add a string to the report that states the number of items found in the 'todo-list'. This additional context will appear in the Mochawesome report, giving you more granular information about your tests.

Third-party reporting tools and plugins, as explored in this chapter, extend the reporting capabilities of Cypress to better cater to specific project requirements or team preferences. They can significantly improve the visibility and traceability of test results, thereby improving the overall quality and reliability of your application.

Generating custom reports with Cypress

Generating custom reports is a crucial component of effective test automation. They offer unique insights into the functionality and reliability of the application under test, enabling teams to make quick, data-driven decisions. While the default reporting capabilities of Cypress and other third-party plugins may cater to most use cases, there could be instances when a more customized report would serve better. In this chapter, we'll explore how to generate custom reports with Cypress.

Customizing Mochawesome reports

Mochawesome, as discussed earlier, is an excellent choice for creating JSON and HTML reports. The default report is quite detailed and interactive. But there are situations where you may want to adjust the content or layout to fit specific requirements.

Let's take the example of adding custom styles to the Mochawesome report. We already know Mochawesome produces an HTML report that can be styled using CSS. We can leverage this feature to customize the look and feel of our reports.

Let's say we have a CSS file, `custom.css`, with the following content:

```
body {
    font-family: Arial, sans-serif;
}

.mochawesome {
    background-color: #f5f5f5;
}

.test.pass .duration {
    color: #5cb85c;
}

.test.fail .duration {
    color: #d9534f;
}
```

This CSS file changes the font of the report, alters the background color, and sets different colors for a pass and fail test durations.

To apply this custom style to your Mochawesome report, you need to refer to this file in the `reporterOptions` section of the `cypress.config.js` file:

```
{
  "reporter": "mochawesome",
  "reporterOptions": {
```

```
    "reportDir": "cypress/reports/mochawesome-report",
    "overwrite": false,
    "html": true,
    "json": true,
    "css": "path/to/custom.css"
  }
}
```

Generating reports with custom data

Another common requirement is to generate reports with custom data. For instance, you might want to include the execution environment details (for example, OS and browser, Cypress version) in your reports. Cypress doesn't have this data by default, but we can add it using hooks and the capabilities of our reporter.

First, we need to gather this data. We can use the `Cypress` object and Node.js `'os'` module to get the details we need:

```
const os = require('os');


before(() => {
  cy.log(`Platform: ${os.platform()}`);
  cy.log(`Cypress Version: ${Cypress.version}`);
});
```

This will log the platform and Cypress version at the start of your test run.

Next, we want to include these details in our Mochawesome report. We can use the `cy.addTestContext()` function, which we discussed in the previous section. The `cy.addTestContext()` function allows you to add extra information to your tests that will appear in the final report.

Let's update our before hook to add these details to the report:

```
before(() => {
  const platform = os.platform();
  const cypressVersion = Cypress.version;
```

```
  cy.addTestContext('Platform', platform);
  cy.addTestContext('Cypress Version', cypressVersion);
});
```

Creating custom reports

In addition to customizing existing reports, you can create entirely custom reports using various Node.js libraries. This process involves parsing the JSON reports generated by Mochawesome (or any other reporter), extracting the relevant data, and generating a new report.

As an example, we can use the `json2html` (should be installed with `npm install json2html`) and `fs` libraries to generate a simple HTML report:

```
//generate-report.js
const json2html = require('json2html');
const fs = require('fs');

// Read the JSON report
const report = JSON.parse(fs.readFileSync('mochawesome.json'));

// Define the HTML structure
const htmlReport = json2html.transform(report, {
  '<>': 'div',
  'html': [
    {
      '<>': 'h1',
      'html': '${stats.suites} Suites - ${stats.tests} Tests - ${stats.
passes} Passes - ${stats.failures} Failures'
    },
    {
      '<>': 'ul',
      'html': function() {
        return json2html.transform(this.results, {
          '<>': 'li',
```

```
          'html': '${title} - ${state}'
        });
      }
    }
  ]
});


// Write the HTML report
fs.writeFileSync('custom-report.html', htmlReport);
```

This script reads the `mochawesome.json` report, transforms it into a simple HTML report with suite and test results, and writes it to `custom-report.html`. You can run the script using Node.js from the command line as follows:

```
node generate-report.js
```

This command tells Node.js to execute the script contained in `generate-report.js`. Please make sure that the `mochawesome.json` report file exists in the same directory where you're running the script from.

In conclusion, creating custom reports with Cypress is relatively straightforward and flexible. You can customize existing reports, add custom data, or even generate entirely new reports to meet your specific needs. Always remember that a good report is one that provides valuable insights, aids quick decision-making, and, ultimately, contributes to the quality of the application.

Analyzing test results for insights and improvements

Once test reports are generated, the next critical step is to analyze these reports for insights and improvements. Analyzing the test results can provide a wealth of information about the application's quality, uncover potential issues, and guide the next steps in the testing process. This chapter will cover how to analyze Cypress test results effectively.

Before delving into the methodologies, it's vital to understand why we analyze. Analysis:

- Uncovers patterns of failures.

- Offers actionable insights for codebase improvements.
- Informs decision-making processes in the SDLC.
- Aids in optimizing the testing process itself.

Basic analytical techniques

Result filtering: Begin by segregating tests based on their result statuses: `Passed`, `Failed`, `Skipped`. Using these filters helps focus on areas needing immediate attention, typically the 'Failed' tests.

```
const results = require('./path-to-report.json');


const passedTests = results.filter(test => test.status === 'passed');
const failedTests = results.filter(test => test.status === 'failed');
const skippedTests = results.filter(test => test.status === 'skipped');
```

Error categorization: Group failures based on error types or messages. This aids in recognizing recurring issues or common patterns.

```
const errorCategories = failedTests.reduce((acc, test) => {
    const errorMsg = test.error.message;
    if (!acc[errorMsg]) acc[errorMsg] = [];
    acc[errorMsg].push(test);
    return acc;
}, {});
```

Advanced analytical techniques

Trend analysis: This involves observing test results over time. Patterns like recurring failures can be indicative of deeper systemic issues.

Root cause analysis (RCA): When a test fails, instead of just fixing the symptom, delve deeper to identify the underlying cause. This might involve:

- Reviewing associated code changes.
- Analyzing application logs.
- Reproducing the issue in a controlled environment.

Heat maps: Visualize where the most failures occur. A heat map can quickly highlight problematic areas in your application. Tools like cypress-dashboard provide heat map capabilities.

Actioning insights

Once the analysis is complete, it's time to act. Some common action points are:

- **Bug logging:** Ensure that clear, reproducible bugs are logged for genuine issues.
- **Test optimization:** Some failures might be due to flaky tests. This could be an opportunity to enhance the test itself.
- **Feedback loop:** Ensure developers are informed promptly about the issues. The quicker the feedback loop, the faster the resolution.

Measuring test effectiveness

It's crucial to gauge the effectiveness of our tests. Key metrics to consider:

Metric	Description	Why it's important
Test Pass Rate	Percentage of tests that passed.	Indicates the stability of the build.
Coverage	Amount of application code exercised by the tests.	Helps identify untested parts of the application.
Mean Time to Detect (MTTD)	Average time taken to identify an issue.	Lower MTTD indicates faster feedback loops.
Mean Time to Repair (MTTR)	Average time taken to fix an identified issue.	Lower MTTR indicates efficient resolution processes.

Table 12.1: *Analyzing key metrics*

It's worth noting that no single metric can provide a comprehensive view. Instead, consider these metrics together to gauge overall test effectiveness.

Understanding the test report

Before we delve into analyzing the test reports, it's essential to understand the components of a typical Cypress test report. Here's a quick breakdown of what you can expect to see in a Mochawesome test report, for instance:

- **General statistics:** This includes the total number of suites, tests, passes, failures, pending tests, and the percentage of passed tests.
- **Duration:** The total time it took to run the test suite.
- **Suites:** A breakdown of each suite and its corresponding tests, including the status (pass or fail), duration, and error messages (if any).

Analyzing test failures

Analyzing failures is arguably the most critical part of test result analysis. A test failure indicates a potential issue with the application under test, so understanding the cause of the failure is critical to improving the application's quality.

Cypress provides detailed information about test failures, including the exact failed step, the expected and actual results, and a complete stack trace. Here's an example of a failed test:

```
{
  "title": "should display the correct page title",
  "fullTitle": "Homepage should display the correct page title",
  "timedOut": false,
  "duration": 32,
  "state": "failed",
  "speed": "fast",
  "pass": false,
  "fail": true,
  "pending": false,
  "context": null,
  "code": "expect(title).to.eq('Expected Title')",
  "err": {
    "message": "expected 'Actual Title' to equal 'Expected Title'",
    "stack": "AssertionError: expected 'Actual Title' to equal 'Expected
Title'..."
  },
  "uuid": "d88302c8-9d16-4b83-9b39-dc8019f4a0b4",
```

```
  "parentUUID": "1740a918-1d3a-4b8b-8e08-4f1e365a767a",
  "isHook": false,
  "skipped": false
}
```

In this case, the test `"should display the correct page title"` failed because the expected title did not match the actual title. The stack trace will show you exactly where in your test code this assertion failed, which can help you identify whether this is a bug in the application or a mistake in the test case.

Analyzing test duration

Analyzing the duration of your tests can provide insights into the performance of your application and your tests.

If specific tests take longer than expected, it might indicate performance issues in your application. On the other hand, it could also signify that your test cases are not optimized. Perhaps they need to do more than the necessary work or wait for certain conditions that take too long to fulfill.

Here's how you can analyze test duration using the Mochawesome report:

```
{
  "title": "should load the homepage quickly",
  "fullTitle": "Performance Tests should load the homepage quickly",
  "timedOut": false,
  "duration": 5000,
  "state": "passed",
  "speed": "slow",
  "pass": true,
  "fail": false,
  "pending": false,
  ...
}
```

In this case, the test `"should load the homepage quickly"` took 5000 milliseconds to run, which was flagged as `"slow"` by Mochawesome. This could indicate a performance issue with the homepage loading time that needs to be addressed.

Identifying patterns

Another critical aspect of test result analysis is identifying patterns. If the same test fails consistently, it strongly indicates a persistent issue with the application. If a group of tests that interact with the same part of the application fail, it likely means a broader issue with that particular feature or module.

You should go beyond the standard test report and use additional data visualization or analysis tools to identify these patterns. For instance, you could import your test data into a spreadsheet or a database and use its built-in analysis features. Alternatively, you could use a data visualization library, like `D3.js`, to create custom graphs and charts.

Summary

Analyzing test results effectively requires a deep understanding of the application under test and a keen eye for detail. By thoroughly examining each failure, keeping track of test durations, and identifying patterns among test results, you can gain valuable insights into the quality of your application and identify areas for improvement.

Ultimately, analyzing test results aims to use these insights to improve both the application and the tests themselves. Whether it's fixing a bug, optimizing a slow-running test, or updating a test case to reflect the application's expected behavior better, each improvement contributes to your application's overall quality and reliability.

Conclusion

We explored various reporting techniques and tools available for Cypress test automation. The chapter begins with an overview of reporting, highlighting its importance in presenting test results effectively. Readers will learn about the built-in Cypress reporting capabilities, which provide essential information on test runs and failures within the Cypress Test Runner. Additionally, the chapter delves into third-party reporting tools and plugins, offering readers options to enhance reporting features and visualization. Readers will also discover how to generate custom reports tailored to their specific project requirements, enabling them to present test results in a more personalized and informative manner. Lastly, the chapter covers the significance of analyzing test results to gain insights and identify areas for improvement in the test automation process. By the end of this chapter, readers will have a comprehensive understanding of various reporting options and techniques to communicate and analyze their test results effectively.

The upcoming chapter serves as a conclusion to the book, summarizing the key concepts and topics covered throughout the chapters. It provides a comprehensive recap of critical concepts related to Cypress, ensuring readers understand the test automation tool. The chapter also discusses best practices for effectively using Cypress in web automation testing, offering practical tips and recommendations to enhance the testing process. Additionally, readers will gain insights into various resources and communities that can aid in further learning and staying up-to-date with the latest developments in Cypress and web automation testing. By the end of this chapter, readers will feel confident in their Cypress skills and be equipped to apply these techniques to their projects successfully.

Further reading

To expand readers' knowledge on the topics discussed in this chapter, I suggest exploring these additional resources:

- **Mochawesome reporter plugin:** The Mochawesome Reporter plugin for Cypress (https://github.com/LironEr/cypress-mochawesome-reporter) allows you to generate attractive and customizable HTML reports for your Cypress tests. This plugin integrates seamlessly with Cypress and provides additional visualization options for your test results.
- **Cypress plugins - reporting:** The Cypress Plugins documentation (https://docs.cypress.io/plugins/directory#reporting) provides a curated list of plugins specifically designed for reporting in Cypress. Readers can explore various reporting plugins to find the one best suits their reporting requirements.
- **Mochawesome reporters:** This blog post by Gleb Bahmutov (https://glebbahmutov.com/blog/the-awesome-battle/) explains how to generate better Mochawesome reports, including videos and screenshots.

These resources will give you a broader understanding and practical examples of the concepts you've learned in this chapter.

CHAPTER 13
Conclusion

Introduction

The final chapter summarizes key concepts covered throughout the book, discusses best practices for Cypress, and provides guidance for further research. Readers will gain a solid understanding of Cypress and its capabilities and feel confident applying these skills to their projects. It will also conclude with a list of resources and communities to help readers continue their journey with Cypress and stay abreast of the latest developments in web automation testing.

Structure

In this chapter, we will discuss the following topics:

- Recap of critical concepts
- Best practices for using Cypress
- Resources for further learning

Recap of critical concepts

The journey through the realm of Cypress has been extensive. As we near the conclusion of this resourceful guide, let's retrace our steps, re-emphasizing the pivotal concepts, techniques, and integrations we've explored.

Introduction to Cypress

Cypress is a cutting-edge JavaScript-based end-to-end testing solution. It provides a comprehensive platform for writing, executing, and monitoring web application tests, ensuring that web applications function as intended across diverse scenarios.

Benefits of using Cypress for automation testing:

Real-time reloading: See test outcomes instantly as you write.

Time-travel: Step back through your tests to see the exact point of failure.

Consistency: Fewer flaky tests compared to many other frameworks.

Single language: Tests are written in JavaScript, like most modern web apps.

Difference between Cypress and Selenium

While Selenium interacts with browsers through the WebDriver protocol, Cypress operates directly within the browser. This distinction allows Cypress to offer more consistent results and better error handling.

Feature	Cypress	Selenium
Environment	Runs directly in the browser	Requires WebDriver to communicate with the browser
Language	JavaScript/TypeScript	Supports multiple languages (Java, Python, C#, and so on)
Execution Speed	Generally faster due to direct browser execution	Can be slower due to intermediate WebDriver
Architecture	All-in-one (bundled with Mocha, Chai, and other utilities)	Modular, needing separate setups

Table 13.1: *Cypress vs. Selenium*

Setting up and starting with Cypress

Installing Node.js: As the foundation for many modern web tools, Node.js is pivotal for Cypress. Installation is straightforward and supports multiple platforms. Once set up, it acts as the backbone for Cypress operations. Visit the Node.js official website (https://nodejs.org/en/) and download the Node.js installer.

Installing Cypress: Via npm (Node.js package manager), installing Cypress is a breeze. You can have the entire testing framework at your disposal with a simple command.

```
npm install cypress --save-dev
```

Configuring Cypress: Cypress's configuration is adaptive, catering to different testing environments or scenarios. Whether adjusting timeouts or setting base URLs, Cypress ensures a tailored testing environment. Learn how to set base URLs, default timeouts, and other important settings in `cypress.config.js`.

Creating your first Cypress project: Initiate a new project, open the test runner, and explore the default example tests provided by Cypress.

```
npx cypress open
```

Writing tests in Cypress

Cypress test runner: A powerful tool that visualizes your tests, showing real-time reloads, status, and detailed error messages. This interactive UI is the cockpit for your tests. Here, you can watch tests execute in real-time, delve into the specifics of each test step, and even rewind actions to understand test behaviors.

Basic test structure: A starter test could be as simple as verifying a webpage's title or checking the visibility of an element.

```
describe('Test Suite', () => {
    it('Test Case', () => {
        // Your testing commands here
    });
});
```

Cypress commands and assertions: Commands drive actions, while assertions validate outcomes. Commands are the building blocks of Cypress tests. With many built-in commands, tasks like DOM manipulation, network requests, or custom commands are seamless.

```
cy.get('.element').should('be.visible');
```

Understanding hooks and aliases: Use hooks like `before()`, `after()`, `beforeEach()`, and `afterEach()` to set preconditions or clean up after tests. Aliases can simplify the reuse of previous command results.

```
describe('My Test Suite', () => {
  before(() => {
```

```
    // Runs before the first test in the suite
  });

  after(() => {
    // Runs after the last test in the suite
  });

  it('My Test Case', () => {
    // Test steps go here
  });
});
```

End-to-End (E2E) testing with Cypress

End-to-end (E2E) testing is a thorough methodology that validates an application's performance across all integrated systems and components. It aims to ensure that the entire application functions harmoniously, delivering a smooth and efficient user experience. These tests mimic real-world user interactions, evaluating the whole sequence of actions from initiation to conclusion. E2E testing, an indispensable component of software development, can be effortlessly crafted, managed, and debugged using Cypress, enhancing applications' overall functionality and user satisfaction.

Here's an example of a simple E2E test in Cypress:

```
describe('My First Test', () => {
  it('Visits the Kitchen Sink', () => {
    cy.visit('https://example.cypress.io')
    cy.contains('type').click()

    // Should be on a new URL which includes '/commands/actions'
    cy.url().should('include', '/commands/actions')

   // Get an input, type into it and verify that the value has been
updated
    cy.get('.action-email')
      .type('fake@email.com')
```

```
      .should('have.value', 'fake@email.com')
  })
})
```

Testing User Interactions: Interactions like button clicks, form submissions, and hover actions can be emulated and tested with precision.

```
cy.get('button').click();
```

Handling Timeouts and Retries: Cypress's in-built intelligence waits for commands and assertions, eliminating the flaky behavior seen in other tools. Retries further ensure that transient issues don't lead to test failures. Managing timeouts and retries efficiently is crucial for a robust end-to-end test suite, as it fortifies tests against brief delays and sporadic problems. This capability is especially beneficial in real-world situations like network delays or slow-loading elements.

```
cy.request({
  url: '/slow-api',
  timeout: 20000
});
```

Component testing

Cypress Component Testing focuses on individual components, using the same test runner, commands, and API familiar from End-to-End testing. It differs from end-to-end testing in the environment setup, where components are built using a development server instead of the entire website context. This results in faster tests with fewer dependencies on the broader infrastructure. Cypress's user-centric API is approachable and intuitive, and setting up component testing is straightforward, as Cypress automatically guides you through the process.

```
import React from 'react'
import MyComponent from './MyComponent'


it('works', () => {
  cy.mount(<MyComponent />)
  cy.contains('Hello Cypress!')
})
```

API testing

Cypress is renowned for its end-to-end UI testing capabilities, but it also offers robust features for efficient API testing that can be seamlessly integrated into your testing workflow. Its intuitive API allows you to easily write tests for HTTP endpoints, validating the behavior, performance, and reliability of both RESTful and GraphQL APIs. Making HTTP requests and asserting the responses are crucial for ensuring your API's contract is maintained and functions as expected.

```
describe('API Test', () => {
  it('Validate the header', () => {
    cy.request('https://jsonplaceholder.typicode.com/posts/1')
      .its('headers')
      .its('content-type')
      .should('include', 'application/json; charset=utf-8');
  });
});
```

Data-driven testing

Data-driven testing is a crucial part of modern testing methodologies that facilitates the creation of flexible, reusable, and scalable test cases. This approach enhances test scenario coverage by allowing the same functionality to be tested with various input data. It typically involves setting up a collection of test data outside of the test scripts, which can be stored in formats such as databases, CSV files, Excel files, or JSON files. Cypress can easily read JSON files or data from databases to facilitate this.

```
const users = require('../fixtures/users.json')


users.forEach((user) => {
  it(`should process the order for ${user.name}`, () => {
    // Test steps using user data
  })
})
```

Advanced techniques

Here, we ventured into the deeper waters of Cypress. We examined techniques to bolster test potency, from crafting custom commands and employing videos for debugging to using plugins.

Example of a custom command:

```
Cypress.Commands.add('login', (username, password) => {
  cy.request('POST', '/login', {
    username: username,
    password: password
  })
})
```

Debugging using screenshots or videos: You can capture a screenshot of a specific element, the entire screen, or even a specific position and size:

```
cy.get('#username').screenshot() // captures screenshot of username
input
```

Cypress plugins: Working with them can significantly enhance your testing capabilities, allowing you to alter, enhance, or extend Cypress's internal behavior. While your test code, application, and Cypress commands typically execute in the browser, plugins enable you to tap into the Node process running Cypress and execute custom code at different stages of its lifecycle. In this section, we will explore how to create and use plugins. Here's an example of a simple plugin to log messages to the console. In the plugins file, we create a logging task within the exported function that prints any received message to the console. The "return null" statement is included because Cypress expects the task function to return a value.

```
const { defineConfig } = require('cypress')


module.exports = defineConfig({
    e2e: {
     setupNodeEvents(on, config) => {
       on('task', {
         log(message) {
```

```
          console.log(message)
            return null
        },
      })
    }
  },
})
```

Cypress cloud and advanced features

Cypress cloud provides test recording, analytics, and insights. Its features, like Smart Orchestration, ensure efficient test runs.

Integration with VCS and BDD

In modern software development, using version control systems is not a matter of choice but a necessity. GitHub and GitLab are two of the most popular version control platforms today. We explored how you can integrate Cypress with these platforms to enhance your test automation processes.

We discovered tools like `husky` to trigger Cypress tests before commits or pushes.

```
// package.json
"scripts": {
  "pre-commit": "cypress run"
}
```

Furthermore, we touched on the union of Cypress with Cucumber for Behaviour-Driven Development.

```
// Feature: User Login

Scenario: Successful Login
    Given I am on the login page
    When I enter valid credentials
    Then I should be redirected to the dashboard
```

Continuous integration and deployment

Incorporating Cypress into CI/CD pipelines, like with Docker and Jenkins, ensures testing remains a continuous, automated part of the deployment process.

Reporting

Effective reporting is a crucial aspect of software testing as it offers insights into the software's functionality, quality, and performance, enabling informed decision-making by stakeholders. In Cypress, various reporting techniques are available, ranging from built-in reports to third-party tools and custom reports. This book overviews these reporting techniques to help you choose the most appropriate one for your project. Reporting in testing focuses on presenting clear and comprehensible reports on the test results. It is not sufficient to run the tests; the results must be effectively communicated to all relevant stakeholders through these reports, summarizing the testing activities and their outcomes.

Best practices for using Cypress

To make the most out of Cypress, adopting a series of best practices ensures the creation of reliable, efficient, and maintainable test suites. This chapter delves into these practices, supported by code examples and comparisons, helping you sharpen your Cypress skills.

Structure your tests

Cypress tests should be organized into logical suites with the 'describe' function. Each test case within the suite should be written using the 'it' function. Make sure to use descriptive titles to enhance the readability of the test results.

```
describe('Login Page Tests', () => {
  it('should login successfully with valid credentials', () => {
    // Test code here
  });

  it('should show an error on invalid credentials', () => {
    // Test code here
```

```
  });
});
```

Waiting strategies

Limit the use of timeouts: Cypress automatically waits for elements to become available. Avoid using explicit waits unless necessary, as this introduces unpredictability. Instead, adjust the default maximum wait time if needed.

```
// Not recommended
cy.get('button', { timeout: 10000 }).click();

// Recommended
cy.get('button').click();
```

Avoid hard-coded waits: Using `cy.wait(1000)` can be unreliable and make tests slower. Instead, they always prefer waits that rely on actual conditions.

```
// Bad Practice
cy.wait(1000);

// Good Practice
cy.get('.notification').should('be.visible');
```

Use assertions to wait for elements: Cypress automatically waits for elements to appear in the DOM, become visible, not be covered, etc. Ensure you're making full use of these assertions.

Using Page Object Model (POM)

POM organizes elements and functionalities of a page into a class, enhancing maintainability.

```
class LoginPage {
  visit() {
    cy.visit('/login');
  }
```

```
  getUsernameField() {
    return cy.get('input[name=username]');
  }

  getPasswordField() {
    return cy.get('input[name=password]');
  }

  getSubmitButton() {
    return cy.get('button[type=submit]');
  }

  login(username, password) {
    this.getUsernameField().type(username);
    this.getPasswordField().type(password);
    this.getSubmitButton().click();
  }
}

const loginPage = new LoginPage();
loginPage.visit();
loginPage.login('alice', 'password123');
```

Handling dynamic data

Intercepting and waiting on network requests allows for reliable tests, ensuring responses before assertions.

```
cy.intercept('POST', '/login').as('loginRequest');
cy.get('button[type=submit]').click();
cy.wait('@loginRequest').its('response.statusCode').should('eq', 200);
```

Stub or intercept network requests: Instead of relying on real backend data which can change, use `cy.intercept()` to control the response.

```
cy.intercept('GET', '/api/profile', { fixture: 'profile.json' }).as
('getProfile');
```

Use fixtures for test data: This ensures consistent data for each test run.

Avoid dependent tests

Each test should be independent. Avoid writing tests that depend on the output of another.

Efficient selectors

Avoid using brittle selectors: Use data-specific attributes instead of relying on complex CSS or Xpath selectors that might change.

```
// Bad Practice

cy.get('div.content > div.header > div.title');


// Good Practice

cy.get('[data-cy=profile-title]');
```

Strategy	Pros	Cons
CSS	Familiar syntax	Can be brittle
Xpath	Powerful, can traverse the DOM	Complex, verbose
Data attributes (such as data-cy)	Stable, not affected by style or structure changes	Requires modification of production code

***Table 13.2**: Selector strategies comparison*

Regularly update Cypress

Staying updated ensures you're leveraging the latest features and security patches.

```
npm install cypress@latest
```

Implement continuous integration

Incorporate Cypress tests into your CI/CD pipeline, ensuring tests are run with every code change.

```
pipeline {
  agent any

  stages {
    stage('Install') {
      steps {
        sh 'npm install'
      }
    }
    stage('Run Tests') {
      steps {
        sh 'npx cypress run'
      }
    }
  }
}
```

Run Cypress in Headless Mode for CI: This speeds up the run time.

```
npx cypress run --headless
```

Reusable functions

While custom commands can dry up repeated code, overusing them can make tests harder to read. If there are actions you find repeating across tests, like login or populating a form, create custom commands.

```
// cypress/support/commands.js
Cypress.Commands.add('login', (username, password) => {
  cy.visit('/login');
  cy.get('input[name=username]').type(username);
  cy.get('input[name=password]').type(password);
```

```
  cy.get('button[type=submit]').click();
});

// In your test
cy.login('alice', 'password123');
```

Adopt data-driven testing

Enhance your test coverage by running the same test with different datasets.

```
const users = [
  { username: 'alice', password: 'password123' },
  { username: 'bob', password: 'securepass456' },
];
users.forEach((user) => {
  it(`should log in with user ${user.username}`, () => {
    cy.visit('/login');
    cy.get('input[name=username]').type(user.username);
    cy.get('input[name=password]').type(user.password);
    cy.get('button[type=submit]').click();
    cy.contains('Logout').should('be.visible');
  });
});
```

Cross-browser testing

Cypress supports multiple browsers. Ensure you test on all the browsers your application supports.

Regularly run tests on all supported browsers: This ensures compatibility.

```
npx cypress run --browser firefox
```

Handle browser-specific logic: Sometimes, behaviors can differ slightly across browsers. Use the `Cypress.browser` property to handle these edge cases.

```
if (Cypress.browser.name === 'firefox') {
```

```
    // specific logic for firefox
}
```

Reviewing test failures

Utilize Cypress's automatic screenshots and videos: Cypress takes a screenshot and video by default when a test fails. This can be immensely helpful in understanding what went wrong.

These best practices act as a compass, directing you toward writing resilient, effective, and maintainable tests. Combining the knowledge acquired throughout this book with these practices will set you on the path to Cypress mastery.

Resources for further learning

As we come to the close of this book, you should feel proud of the expertise you've garnered in Cypress. But remember, the tech world is ever-evolving. Continuous learning is the hallmark of a competent developer. This section spotlight some top-tier resources, tools, and communities that can help you sustain your growth with Cypress and web automation testing.

Official documentation

No resource is more authoritative than Cypress's official documentation (https://docs.cypress.io/guides/overview/why-cypress). They consistently update it, ensuring the material remains aligned with the latest release. It's exhaustively detailed, laden with examples.

Cypress Real World App (RWA)

Cypress has developed a Real World App (https://github.com/cypress-io/cypress-realworld-app), a full-stack example application you can clone, deploy, and test. It's built with modern frameworks and integrates various testing strategies.

Code snippet (from RWA):

```
describe('Dashboard', function() {
  beforeEach(function() {
    cy.task('db:seed')
```

```
    cy.database('find', 'users').then((user) => {
      cy.login(user.username, 's3cret', true)
    })
  })

  it('logs out', function() {
    cy.getBySel('sidenav-signout').click()
    cy.url().should('eq', `${Cypress.config().baseUrl}/login`)
  })
})
```

Blogs and tutorials

Various experts in the field have authored blogs and tutorials which offer insights, tips, and tricks that aren't always covered in the official documentation. Notable among them is Gleb Bahmutov (https://glebbahmutov.com/blog/), ex-VP of Engineering at Cypress, and his extensive writings.

Udemy and other online courses

Platforms like Udemy (https://www.udemy.com/), Coursera (https://www.coursera.org/), and Pluralsight (https://www.pluralsight.com/) offer in-depth courses on Cypress, often spanning several hours of video content and interactive lessons.

Cypress plugins

The Cypress Plugins directory (https://docs.cypress.io/plugins) is a fantastic place to explore extensions that can augment Cypress's capabilities. From visual regression to network stubbing, the sky's the limit!

Cypress GitHub repository

Engage directly with the developers behind Cypress on their GitHub repository (https://github.com/cypress-io/cypress). Whether you're troubleshooting an issue, proposing a feature, or just keeping tabs on the latest updates, it's the hub of Cypress development.

Communities and forums

Communities like Cypress Gitter (https://app.gitter.im/#/room/#cypress-io_cypress:gitter.im), Cypress Spectrum (https://github.com/features/discussions), and sections of Stack Overflow (https://stackoverflow.com/) dedicated to Cypress are invaluable for getting peer support, learning from shared experiences, and networking with other testers.

Conferences and workshops

At tech conferences, Events like Cypress's official webcasts and workshops (https://docs.cypress.io/examples/media/webinars-media) often present the latest advancements, case studies, and best practices.

Continuous integration services

Delve into the world of CI with services like CircleCI (https://circleci.com/), Jenkins (https://www.jenkins.io/), or GitHub Actions (https://github.com/features/actions). Integrate Cypress tests for seamless development and deployment workflows.

Embarking on a continuous learning journey with Cypress can be as fulfilling as rewarding. While this book has provided a foundational grasp of Cypress and its best practices, the resources above will ensure you remain at the forefront of web automation testing advancements. Embrace them, and watch your proficiency grow exponentially.

Index

A

D

E

F

G

R

S

V

W

Y